Authentic African Christianity

American University Studies

Series VII
Theology and Religion

Vol. 210

PETER LANG
New York • Washington, D.C./Baltimore • Boston • Bern
Frankfurt am Main • Berlin • Brussels • Vienna • Canterbury

Peter Nlemadim DomNwachukwu

Authentic African Christianity

An Inculturation Model for the Igbo

PETER LANG
New York • Washington, D.C./Baltimore • Boston • Bern
Frankfurt am Main • Berlin • Brussels • Vienna • Canterbury

BR
1463
.N5
D66
2000

Library of Congress Cataloging-in-Publication Data

DomNwachukwu, Peter Nlemadim.
Authentic African Christianity: an
inculturation model for the Igbo / Peter Nlemadim DomNwachukwu.
p. cm. — (American university studies. Series VII,
Theology and religion; vol. 210)
Includes bibliographical references and index.
1. Christianity and cutlure—Nigeria—Imo State. 2. Igbo
(African people)—Religion. I. Title. II. Series.
BR1463.N5D65   276.69'4—dc21   98-54379
ISBN 0-8204-4450-2
ISSN 0740-0446

Die Deutsche Bibliothek-CIP-Einheitsaufnahme

DomNwachukwu, Peter Nlemadim:
Authentic African Christianity: an inculturation model
for the Igbo / Peter Nlemadim DomNwachukwu.
–New York; Washington, D.C./Baltimore; Boston; Bern;
Frankfurt am Main; Berlin; Brussels; Vienna; Canterbury: Lang.
(American university studies: Ser. 7,
Theology and religion; Vol. 210)
ISBN 0-8204-4450-2

The paper in this book meets the guidelines for permanence and durability
of the Committee on Production Guidelines for Book Longevity
of the Council of Library Resources.

© 2000 Peter Nlemadim DomNwachukwu

Printed in the United States of America

In Evergreen Memory of
My loving and dedicated
Father

Dominic Igbonekwu Nwachukwu

Table of Contents

Glossary

Agbara	carved image
Ala	land, land deity
Ala Mmadu	land of the living
Ala Mmuo	spirit world
Amadioha	Lightning deity
Anyanwu	sun
Chi	personal god, destiny
Chineke	Creator-God
Dibia	medicine man or woman
Dibia Afa	diviner
Ekwensu	Satan
Elu-igwe	the sky
Eze	king
Eze Mmuo	chief priest
Ezi Ndu	the good life
Ifejioku	the deity of farm work
Igwe	crowd
Ihe ojoo	evil
Ike	strength, power
Ikenga	the deity of adventure in hunting or business enterprise
Iwa-akwa	initiation to manhood
Madu	human being
Mbanta	an Igbo village in *Things Fall Apart*
Ndichie	ancestors
Ndi Okenye	elders
Ndu	life
Nwanyi	woman
Nwoke	man

Ofo	carved wooden stick which serves as a staff of office
Oji	kolanut
Okpara	first-born
Onwu	death
Oru Mbara	common farmland
Umunna	patrilineage, community
Uwa	the earth

Foreword

It is my pleasure and my privilege to introduce the readers to Peter DomNwachukwu's new book. Peter DomNwachukwu is a graduate of the Nigerian Baptist Theological Seminary and holds two masters and the doctorate in World Religions from The Southern Baptist Theological Seminary in the United States. He currently serves as pastor of the First Baptist Church in the Owerri Province of Nigeria. He has taught at the Ogbaru Boys High School in Ogbaru, Nigeria, held several posts with the Nigerian Baptist Convention, served as pastor of several churches in Nigeria, and served as minister of youth and education at a local Baptist church while pursuing his education in the United States. He has published articles in academic journals in Nigeria. This is his first book.

I first met Peter DomNwachukwu in 1992. I had the privilege to serve as his teacher and to direct his graduate study. This work is the culmination of his studies at Southern Seminary. I have continued to maintain contact with Peter DomNwachukwu and to profit from his insight into African Christianity in general, and Nigerian Baptists in particular. DomNwachukwu presents to his readers broad and accurate research, clear thinking, and straightforward prose. As a follower of Jesus, Peter DomNwachukwu is committed to the Christian Faith. As a Nigerian, he is deeply committed to his own cultural heritage, the complete liberation of Africa, and the powerful movement of inculturation of Christianity in Africa. These are the qualities he brings to this work.

Black Africa has suffered great loss of life, culture, and community values at the hands of Western imperialism. The dark shadows of Colonialism and racism still hang heavily over the continent. At the eve of a new millennium, Africa eagerly awaits a "second liberation." And any meaningful future must be grounded in Africa's own cultural, moral, and religious values. John Mary Waliggo is certainly correct when he states that "to do otherwise is nothing less than communal suicide." If the African Church is to play a meaningful role in the New Africa, she must be firmly rooted in the Black soil.

The synthesis of the African cultural heritage, including traditional religious practice and world view, with the Christian Faith brought by western missionaries is the most critical issue facing the African Church. While the history of the indigenous church movement reaches well back into nineteenth century Nigeria, the Western Missionary tradition, including those Nigerians who are inheritors of that tradition, have been more than reluctant to embrace such a synthesis.

DomNwachukwu's contribution comes at just this point. Though extensive research, the use of sociological analysis, and thoughtful interviews with significant persons, he has excavated the religious reality of a small but significant region of Southern Nigeria. He then offers a vision for rebuilding a Church whose foundation in Jesus Christ, but whose architecture and materials are Igbo of the Owerri Province.

It is my hope that Nigerian religious leaders will read and learn from this work. Scholars and students of African Christianity and the Mission of the Church should use this book to discover an African insight into what will surely be the most significant theological challenge to face world Christianity in the next century.

James D. Chancellor, Ph.D.
W. O. Carver Professor of World Religions
The Southern Baptist Theological Seminary of Louisville

Preface

This book was originally a doctoral dissertation submitted to the faculty of the Southern Baptist Theological Seminary, Louisville, Kentucky, USA. It is written to fulfill my long-time desire for a critical and realistic evaluation of Christianity in Igboland, with a view to suggesting a practical and enduring remedy for the inauthentic nature of much Igbo Christianity. The Primary focus is the examination of Christianity in Igboland and a proposal for dialogue as an effective inculturation model for authentic Igbo Christianity.

I believe that Christianity will become authentically Igbo only when the Igbo hear the Christian message in their own language and conceive Christian meanings in the symbols and metaphors which are native to them. With a combination of literary and field research, this book presents the current nature of Igbo Christianity, highlighting its inadequacies, and formulates practical steps to achieving authentic Igbo Christianity.

With a total of nine chapters, this book examines the general nature of African religions and places a special emphasis on Igbo religion. The introduction of Christianity in Igboland is discussed, and a brief history of each of the major mission and indigenous Churches is given. The book examines also the current condition of the church in Igboland, with a special focus on the Owerri Igbo. Discussing definitionally, seven theories of inculturation, and offering an explanation of dialogue and the dialogical method of evangelism, the book suggests that dialogue is at the core of the authentic appropriation of Christianity by the Igbo.

My gratitude goes to the following individuals and group of individuals who through their moral or financial contributions made it easier for me to come up with this book: Rev. and Mrs. James L. Snardon and members of Joshua Tabernacle Baptist Church, Louisville, Kentucky; Rev. and Mrs. M.D. Sledd; James and Annette Sledd, Steven and Bertha Jones,

Deacon and Mrs. John H. Young, Miss Emogene Harris and Dr. James D. Chancellor, who served faithfully as my adviser during the writing of the original manuscript and offered valuable suggestions. I also owe a great debt of gratitude to my wife Catherine, and my three daughters, Chibuzo, Chisom and Chidimma, for their prayers and encouragement without which, this book would not have become a reality. Finally and most importantly, I thank God, my heavenly father, for enabling me and providing me with all the spiritual and material resources necessary for the writing of this book.

Peter Nlemadim DomNwachukwu

Igbo Cultural Areas

Chapter 1

General Nature of Igbo Christianity

The purpose of this book is to examine the nature of Christianity in Igboland, with special reference to the Igbo of old Owerri Province of Eastern Nigeria, and suggest dialogue as an inculturation model for Christianity in Igboland. It is my contention that for the Igbo to understand Christianity and its demands, the Christian message must be delivered to the Igbo in their socio-cultural context.

The Christian faith should be presented to the Igbo in such a way that they will feel an indigenous sense of belonging to the faith. The Igbo are inherently religious, and "the Igbo cosmos, like that of other African peoples, has no partition that separates the sacred from the secular. All of life is one inseparable whole in which God is everywhere immanent."[1] In other words, Christian missionaries who came to Igboland during the mid-nineteenth century did not come to a virgin land of religious experience.

> Igbo religious life is an integral element of their total cultural life which aims at self-realization of some sort which consists in nothing other than living in harmony with the cosmic order. But in their practical day to day life, the overall aim is to secure balance with nature in favour of the human element—a pragmatic bias.[2]

Before the advent of Christianity in Igboland, the Igbo already had systems of clearly defined customs and practices in both the religious and secular arenas. In practice, there was no clear line drawn between secular and religious life.

The Igbo are highly democratic, functioning in autonomous communities. The concept of collective bargaining was, and still is, prominent in Igbo traditional society, thus giving room for dialogue and for the sharing of differences of opinion, which is one of the distinctive features of the Igbo among the African communities.

The Igbo have an adage which goes thus: *Igbo amaghi eze*, meaning "Igbos know no king." What this adage means in a practical sense is that no one person rules any Igbo community, especially in old Owerri Province. Each Igbo community, or the *Umunna*, which is the basic social unit, is governed by elders or *ndi okenye*. This committee of village administrators does not have absolute authority over the rest of the members of the village. The primary function of these elders is to serve as spokespersons for the entire community and to settle political, social and religious disputes among members of the community. This committee of elders is normally composed of first sons (*okpara*) of the different families in the village.

Unfortunately, early missionary endeavors by Euro-American mission groups took little or no cognizance of these important features of Igbo traditional society. Christian churches with Western cultural models were planted in Igboland and Christian practices with Western cultural biases were imposed on the Igbo. Igbo culture, customs, traditions, and institutions were treated as inferior to their Western counterparts by most missionaries. In some cases, missionaries arbitrarily replaced Igbo customs, traditions and institutions with Western ones. As a result, Christian converts were subjected to the agony of going through the very difficult process of becoming Western in an Igbo society, in the name of religion.

Today, the Igbo Christian community is still struggling to resolve the consequences of this cultural imposition. Some of the consequences include superficial Christian conversion, a craving for Western education and Western socio-economic development, and commercializing the gospel of Jesus Christ. In some cases, Igbo Christian groups and ministries eagerly desire and work for affiliation with Western Christian agencies or organizations in order to gain credibility and acceptance by the Igbo society. Indigenous churches are caricatured and discounted, especially by members of the orthodox churches, even when it is clear that these indigenous churches are making more converts and are helping these converts to appropriate the message of the gospel of Jesus Christ to themselves in their cultural, social, and economic milieu.

The problem here is not only Western missionaries or Western culture. After all, nobody lives in isolation and no culture is static. As people interact with one another both locally and internationally, cultural interchange takes place and changes take place and people change. But a healthy and beneficial interaction is one that is bilateral and not unilateral.

The major problem with the Christianization of Igboland is that the Igbo culture was not understood or given serious consideration by many of the missionaries. Consequently, many who came under the influence of the missionaries paid lip-service to the "foreign faith" and stayed superficially committed because of its development-oriented appeals. There were those who refused to accept the new faith because of its flagrant neglect of, and sometimes attack on, traditional customs and institutions.

This book will attempt to discover and analyze the problems created by the imposition of Western Christianity. We will suggest some solutions to them in hope that the average Igbo man or woman can clearly understand Christianity and its teachings and desire to embrace it with or without Western missionary influence. We will therefore suggest that for Christianity to become meaningful to the Igbo, the Igbo must be allowed to interpret the gospel message in Igbo conceptual metaphors and practice their faith within their cultural milieu, including those of their traditional systems and institutions which do not conflict with Biblical affirmations. "In inculturating gospel values . . . one must always turn to the center, to Jesus Christ, his life and message."[3] Pure Christianity does not exist; it always appears as a synthesis between the revelation of Jesus and a cultural context. Authentic Igbo Christianity seeks to minimize or eliminate the mediation of Western culture, seeking out a more authentic synthesis with Jesus.

The research for this book focuses on the old Owerri Province in the Imo State of Nigeria. The Igbo constitute one of the three largest ethnic groups in Nigeria. They are part of the Negro race in Africa. They speak Igbo, a language which belongs to the "Kwa group" of languages in West and Central Africa, and which has many local dialects.[4]

> According to the 1963 population census in Nigeria, the Igbo number about 8 million, but current estimates put their population at about 9 million. The territory cuts across the Equatorial Forest in the South and the Savanna in the North . . . Put in terms of longitude and latitude, one can say, Igboland is roughly circumscribed between 6° and 8½° East Longitude and 4½° and 7½° North Latitude.[5]

This work is the result of research and analysis on the religious life of Owerri Christians as it relates to their day-to-day living in their personal lives, their homes, their communities, the church, and the larger community. It is the intent of this study to employ this analysis to formulate a model for authentic Igbo Christianity

As an Igbo who has been a Christian for the past thirty-four years, and has been a minister of the gospel for thirty years, the author contends that much is still to be desired in the practice of Christianity in Igboland.

The Methodist bishop of Owerri, R. O. Uwadi, said, "When you come to sentimental consciousness, it is very high. When you come to the in-depth permeation of Christianity, I will have my reservation."[6] Christianity in Igboland lacks cultural depth.

On the surface, most Igbo Christians think, talk, sing, preach and behave like Westerners because this is what Christianity has required. This tradition has carried on from the mid-nineteenth century to the present. To behave differently is to be out of tune with the faith. These Christians retain many of their indigenous traditions, customs, and institutions. These factors influence their thought patterns and mode of behavior even in the church.

> The church in Nigeria must be "the church in Nigeria" and not a prefabricated structure designed especially from overseas to enable Europeans to carry on in Nigeria what Forsyth describes as a "Kingdom-of-God-industry." Apart from the fact that the damaging association, or even identification, of the church in Nigeria with a European cult has given the misleading impression that she has no profitable relevance for Nigerians, the European Structure of the Church has, to a large extent, made spiritual sterility in her life. And the reason for the sterility is that the Church is not really speaking to Nigerians in their spiritual needs. Rather, she speaks in strange idioms which make her language of evangelism and the speech of her devotion somewhat unintelligible to them. . . .[7]

We consider it traumatic for persons to practice their faith in an atmosphere of pretense and chameleon-like life-style. We are concerned that many Christian churches of Igboland in almost every denomination still slavishly follow the Euro-American forms of worship. They function this way for a set of reasons: perpetuating church traditions, ceremonies, and rituals; gaining acceptability by international Christian bodies and organizations; avoiding the stigma of syncreticism; and adhering to the "correct" belief, not minding its relevance and applicability to the society.

We are concerned that Christianity in Igboland does not adequately meet the people's socio-cultural and spiritual needs.

> For successful evangelism as well as the edification of the church, it is necessary for the preacher to put himself in the position of his hearers, "sit where they sit," and thus interpret God to them in terms which they will grasp.[8]

Most Nigerians regard the majority of the Igbo as Christians. Almost everyone in Igboland will claim to be a Christian. Christianity is popular in Igboland. What most Igbo men and women mean when they identify with Christianity is that they belong to one church or the other. However, not all Igbo people are Christians.

There are some Igbo who still worship the Supreme Being through carved images and local deities. These people constitute a minority. Fortune-tellers and medicine men and women, *ndi dibia*, abound everywhere in Igboland. Some *ndi dibia* claim to be Christians. In the past, most *dibias* had their own shrines where people visited for fortune-telling, and for the treatment of physical, emotional and spiritual problems. Now we see a replacement of some of those shrines with prayer houses. The same persons are still the consultants, dressed not in shabby and awe-evoking costumes, but in white robes, normal native attire, or Western-style dress. They do not divine with elements such as cowries, white chalk, pieces of stone, pieces of red cloth, and so on. Their main tool of divination and fortune-telling is the Bible. Almost everyone now wants to associate in one way or the other with the church. This situation is detrimental to the health of Christianity in Igboland.

Many go to church, not because they desire the salvation of their souls, but because they are physically and/or emotionally sick and they need healing and deliverance. Some go for economic reasons. Sometimes, well-known church men and women go to *ndi dibia* and fortune-tellers for answers to their problems. Though they claim to be Christians, they lack faith in the Christian God.

Other people regard the church as a mere social club. Though they attend the church regularly, they still consult with diviners and fortune-tellers when they encounter problems, especially spiritual ones. The role of the church, as they perceive her, is to provide avenues for fellowship and social interaction. Beyond these, the church has no real relevance for their daily existential problems. Many people still feel they are doing the leadership of the established churches a favor when they put their names in the church's register. The church becomes for them not only a social club, but a status-conferring agency. They do not really understand what Christianity means.

The *1992 Diary of Imo State* contains the following statement:

> There is freedom of worship in Imo State and religion occupies a central place in the lives of the people. The people are predominantly Christians of different denominations among which are the Roman Catholic, the Anglican, the Methodist, the Presbyterian and other churches. . . .[9]

In spite of this affirmation, the consensus amongst most Igbo, is that Igbo Christianity lacks cultural identity. This condition makes it difficult for the average Igbo to understand the true essence of Christianity and what it means for him or her existentially.

As a result of this lack of meaning and understanding of the nature of Christianity, many Igbo Christians turn to traditional religion when they are faced with very important life issues, such as sickness, death, barrenness, childlessness, business failures, and so on. For these people, the church is only good for the acquiring of Western education, for giving insights which may lead to the modernization of society and for socialization.

This understanding stems from their initial orientation to the Christian faith. From the beginning of the missionary endeavor in Igboland, a majority of the missionaries concerned themselves more with quantity than quality. Catholic and Protestant mission agencies scrambled for converts and did everything they could to outdo one another. Both the Protestant and Catholic mission agencies built schools and medical facilities as means of evangelization. Missionaries preached and taught Bible study sessions regularly for new "converts." One cannot overemphasize the sacrificial nature of the work of these early missionaries in Igboland. As an Igbo, I commend them for their good work.

These mission groups intended to convert the "heathen." However, in some cases, especially with missionaries of the two major mission groups in Igboland, the Catholic and the Anglican, it appears that interest lay more in the number of attendants to church services and to other activities of the church than in the salvation experience of the individual or the development of an authentic Igbo Christian tradition. The main reason for this situation was the home boards or bodies that sent those missionaries needed quantifiable statistical reports to back up their drives for funds. This scramble for "converts" gave rise to bigotry and disunity.

> Each denomination emphasized its own importance and spared no pains to prove that one denomination was better than the other. Consequently, right from the advent of Christianity in Nigeria, dissension and disunity were rampant among the Christian missions and, to the bewildered African, it was hard to believe that one white Christian mission would discredit another white Christian mission in a desperate attempt to win converts and send glowing reports back to the home mission.[10]

That seed of disunity took on a stronger root in Igboland than in any other part of Nigeria. In an interview with the recently-appointed Archbishop of Owerri Catholic Archdiocese, on the present state of the Catholic Church, A. J. V. Obinna said:

> People will look up to us in spite of the multiplicity of other church groups. They make a lot more noise through the megaphone than ourselves, but that does not mean they are the ones that shape society. We are the ones that shape it. And

many of these younger churches now like to invite me in order to get a bit of my own integrity.[11]

Continuing his affirmation of the superiority of the Catholic Church over other church groups, the Archbishop quoted Paul Tillich:

Professor Paul Tillich of the University of Chicago in the United States said, "When it comes to Christianity, the Catholic Church has retained all the substance of the Christian faith; what the Protestants have added is the protest element," which he says can also be found in the Catholic Church because the protest element has to do with criticizing a few things.[12]

We contend that understanding and mutual respect among Christian churches in Igboland are a necessary first step in developing the health of Christianity in Igboland.

Many articles, including scholarly ones, have been written on the advent of Christianity in Igboland. Books have been written on different issues concerning Christianity in Igboland. Few, if any, writings have been done on the present state of Christianity in Igboland, especially in the old Owerri Province, the heart of Igboland.

Before Nigeria gained independence from Great Britain in 1960, there was not much written about the religion of the Igbo by *ndi Igbo*. The few works that were done were by foreign writers. Since Nigerian independence, however, especially from the 1970s to the present, the Igbo have taken a new and vigorous stance towards their religious and cultural heritage."[13]

Some people have written from the historical point of view; some have written from social angles, some have written from the theological perspective; and others have merely done interpretive works. However, no one has written an analysis of the practice of Christianity in the Owerri Province of Eastern Nigeria. This is what this book attempts to do. It also suggests dialogue as an inculturation model for Christianity in Igboland

With the aid of literary and field research, including interviews, especially those which were conducted in the Owerri area, this study briefly presents Igbo philosophical and religious world views, mentioning some core traditional Igbo beliefs, and draws a comparison between them and some Bible-based Christian beliefs. The motive for the comparison is to highlight areas of agreement and areas of disagreement between Igbo religion and Christianity, with a view to helping Igbo Christians see things for themselves and make up their own minds about which faith to adopt.

The Igbo love to dialogue. They do not like to be preached at. They are very active people in their social, political and religious lives. They are not the type of people who sit down passively and listen to someone tell them what to do. They ask questions and desire to be heard.

It is probably in its humanist and civil libertarian traditions that Igbo culture stands head and shoulders above the cultures of most West African society. Its sources lie in the associated traditions of democratic government properly so-called or government by consensus—a more democratic system than any "democracy by representation" ever practiced in the Western world. [14]

In addition to drawing a comparison between the Bible and Igbo traditional beliefs, this study suggests points of contact between Christianity and Igbo traditional thought. The aim here is to construct a conceptual bridge for the Igbo to understand Christianity better. These points of contact involve, more than anything else, Igbo concepts, symbols and metaphors, and how they agree or disagree with Biblical ones. The idea here is not syncreticism, but better and clearer understanding of Christianity.

For an authentic Igbo Christianity, those who preach and teach Christianity in Igboland should use the Bible as their primary source and use Igbo concepts, symbols and metaphors as their communication vehicles. They should also become aware of the peculiarity of the Igbo among all other African communities, with reference to their sense of individualism, social autonomy and democratic process. The Igbo are very religious, but most of them need to understand what Christianity means for them as Igbo. Hence this book recommends dialogue as an effective method of leading the Igbo into this understanding.

Notes

1 Cyril C. Okorocha, *The Meaning of Religious Conversion in Africa: The Case of the Igbo of Nigeria* (Aldershot, England: Grower Publishing Company, 1987), 48.

2 T. Uzodinma Nwala, *Igbo Philosophy* (Ikeja, Lagos: Lantern Books, 1985), 137.

3 Peter Schineller, S. J., *A Handbook on Inculturation* (New York: Paulist Press, 1990), 59.

4 Nwala, *Igbo Philosophy,* 15.

5 Ibid.

6 R. O. Uwadi, Methodist Bishop of Owerri, interview by author, 9 January 1996, Owerri, Nigeria, tape recording.

7 E. Bolaji Idowu, *Towards An Indigenous Church* (London: Oxford University Press, 1965), 15.

8 Ibid., 18.

9 *1992 Diary of Imo State* (Owerri: Government Press, 1992), v.

10 A. Babs Fafunwa, *History of Education in Nigeria* (London: George Allen and Unwin, 1979), 84.

11 Kúúbra-Afiakóyó Uya, ed. in-chief, "120 Minutes With Archbishop Anthony Obinna," *Catholic Post* (Owerri, National Association of Catholic Corpers, Imo State, 1995), 11–12.

12 Ibid., 8.

13 Okorocha, *The Meaning of Religious Conversion in Africa,* 9.

14 Mark Chijioke Okoro, "Ugwumba—The Greatness of a People," *Ahiajoku Lecture* (Annual Igbo Traditional Lecture), (Owerri: The Government Printer, 1989), 9–10.

Chapter 2

The Nature of African Traditional Religions

The Igbo are a vital part of Africa. African peoples are inherently religious, and the Igbo approach their religious life with great seriousness. Judging from the cultural and social behavior of all African communities, it could be rightly said that to be an African is to be religious.

B. H. Kato suggests that religion is the heart of culture. He therefore maintains that any change in religion will necessitate a re-adjustment in culture.[1] This assertion is certainly true among African peoples. Kato mentions nine aspects of culture which he feels are functional and are also intertwined with religion. These are language, food-gathering, housing, clothing and art, law, magic, philosophy and funerals.[2]

> Traditionally, for the African, religion is not merely a matter of going to church or observing a set of principles; it is a way of life that permeates all spheres and levels of living. One seeks material well-being, like healing, as well as spiritual well-being, like forgiveness of sin, within the religious context.[3]

African traditional religion has been open to a wide range of Western and African scholars. It is appropriate at this juncture to examine some of the definitions.

Western scholars of varied academic disciplines, especially in the broad area of humanities, have advanced a number of distinct definitions.

Geoffery Parrinder, in his book, *African Traditional Religion*, examines the nature of traditional religion in Africa, especially sub-Saharan Africa. He recognizes the work of a British anthropologist, E. B. Tylor, who in 1871 coined the term "animism," or "the theory of souls," as the fundamental concept of religion.[4]

This term "animism" was first used by Tylor in an article he wrote in 1866, and which he "later developed into a major work, *Primitive Culture* (1871)."[5] For Tylor, animism, carries the idea of aliveness. It is both dynamic and functional.

> Animism is a word derived from the Latin *anima* which means breath, breath of life, and hence carries with it the idea of the soul or spirit . . . . for Tylor the basic definition of religion was the belief in spirit beings. He saw *anima* as a shadowy vaporous image animating the object it occupied.[6]

For most Western scholars, animism "has come to be widely used in describing traditional religions of Africa and other parts of the world."[7] For John Mbiti, animism has an evolutionary connotation. Mbiti contends that Western scholars who use this term to describe traditional African religion understand animism as the beginning point of religious consciousness, human religious consciousness, then to polytheism and ultimately, monotheism. The evolutionary scheme was popular in the nineteenth and early twentieth centuries. Now, most scholars have abandoned it.

> This type of argument and interpretation places African religions at the bottom of the supposed line of religious evolution. It tells us that Judaism, Christianity and Islam are at the top, since they are monotheistic.[8]

Mbiti rejects this theory, stating that "another theory equally argues that man's religious development began with monotheism and moved towards polytheism and animism."[9] Animism and its evolutionary implications are unacceptable to Parrinder. He argues that however suitable these evolutionary notions "may be in biology, it does not follow that they can be applied strictly in the very different sphere of religion."[10] Parrinder observes that current debate, especially on the nature of religious consciousness among peoples of the world, has begun to question the evolutionary argument on the issue of religion. He asserts that modern African religion does not need to be called a "primitive religion."

> For one thing, this consideration of African religion as essentially "Primitive" leaves out of account altogether the possibility of revelation of God to Africans and inspiration by him. Such a question, theological no doubt and neglected by sociologists, is vital to the religious man of any race.[11]

The term "animism," as originally used by Tylor and propagated by his disciples, suggests the superiority of one race to the other. Kato observes that Tylor "uses such phrases repeatedly: 'savages'. . .and civilized men."[12]

Kato argues that Tylor's use of the terms, "higher culture" and "lower culture" is a product of his own bias. "Culture may be defined as simply the way of life of a social group. The question of superior/inferior relationship does not arise."[13]

He asserts very strongly that "animism," as a definitional or a descriptive term for African traditional religion, is grossly inadequate. Adherents of the traditional religions of Africa believe in and communicate with spiritual beings. However, African traditional religion is far more complex than that in both belief and practice. The term "animism," with its evolutionary implications, is far too limiting, and is a misnomer.

Other terms which Western scholars have used to define or describe African Traditional Religion include: Idolatry, Paganism, Heathenism, Fetishism, Witchcraft, Juju, Magic and Primitive Religion.[14] Most African scholars have found these terms inadequate. E. Bolaji Idowu coins the term, *olodumareism* to describe African traditional religion.[15] Idowu developed this term from *Olodumare*, which is one of the Yoruba names for God.[16] "Olodumare connotes one who has the fullness or superlative greatness; the everlasting majesty upon whom man can depend."[17] In employing *olodumareism* for the definition of African traditional religion, Idowu attempts to highlight the monotheistic dimension of religion in Africa.

However, *Olodumare* and its monotheistic implications do not adequately capture the nature of African traditional religion, especially in the areas of theological presuppositions, worship and practice. Recognizing the inadequacy of Idowu's definition for the traditional religions of Africans, Osadolor Imasogie, another Nigerian theologian, suggests "bureaucratic monotheism."

Using Nigerian culture as his frame of reference, Imasogie argues that the Western term monotheism should be retained but *Olodumare* be discarded. He writes:

> In order to retain monotheism and yet preserve its peculiar expression in the Nigerian Traditional Religion, this writer would suggest the phrase "bureaucratic monotheism." This has the advantage of pointing to the socio-political conditions which greatly influence the Nigerian religious expression of the intrinsic monotheism which undergirds its religious experience.[18]

He highlights the fact that the traditional "Nigerian society is hierarchical in nature,"[19] placing the king at the top of the hierarchy and the king's appointed ministers down the ladder, depending on their ranks and functions. Imasogie sees a direct correlation between the Nigerian socio-political structures and the African traditional conceptualization of the Divine Presence.

> In such a bureaucratic context where the king is seldom seen or talked to, the ministers who see to the day to day activities of the realm appear to be more prominent and independent. Whereas in actual fact the ministers derive their power from the king, yet the ordinary citizen looks up to the ministers rather than the king except when the ministers fail him. This is reflected in the Nigerian Traditional Religion. The ultimate source of life and power is the Supreme Being. The Supreme Being created the divinities and appointed each of them to take charge of specific departments of nature to be governed in accordance with his order and to receive sacrifices on his behalf.[20]

It is not possible to present a comprehensive definition of African traditional religion. In reality there is no such thing as African Traditional Religion. Rather there are a vast number of African religions. Every African community is different. Oliver Alozie Onwubiko, an Igbo scholar and theologian, recognizes the problem of so-called African traditional religion. He asserts, "African religion has grossly been misrepresented and misconceived. In a sense it is better to talk of African traditional religions."[21] He does not attempt to present a definition of African traditional religions. Instead, he outlines five common socio-cultural elements of all African communities, which affect religious understanding and religious behavior. These are:

(i)   The concept of and an indigenous name for the Supreme Being—Invisible, Sovereign and Benevolent;

(ii) A moral sense of justice and truth, and knowledge that there exists good and evil;

(iii) The belief in the existence of the human soul and the belief that this soul does not die with the death of man;

(iv) The existence of spirits—good and bad—and the belief that communion with the Supreme Being is possible through the intermediation of these spirits and of the ancestors who are believed to be interested in the well being of their living descendants;

(v)   The existence of myths as rational and philosophic explanations to justify the continuance of some religious practices, the order they follow, and the use of specific symbolic objects as concrete means of strengthening the relationship between man and the transcendental realm of existence, the celebration of all these in feasts and festivals for the purpose of their continuity and culture transmission.[22]

In another work, interestingly titled *African Traditional Religion: A Definition,* Idowu outlines the history of the study of African traditional religion and then devotes two chapters to describing African "traditional" religion, its nature and structure. He asserts there is "a common Africanness about the total culture and religious beliefs and practices of Africa,"[23] and this common factor may be a result of "diffusion" from Africans' common origins, especially in the areas of race, customs, and religious practices.[24] He goes on to speak of the concept of God as the central factor which is responsible for the cohesiveness in the religiosity of African peoples.[25]

Idowu contends that the term "African traditional religion" is tentative.[26] There cannot be a comprehensive or conclusive definition for the religions of Africa. He discusses the word "traditional," stating that words such as "native" and "indigenous" have been used to define it. "Traditional," suggests the idea of a phenomenon which is aboriginal or foundational. "Tradition," conveys the notion of continuity in both belief and practice. The term is inadequate to the extent that it limits the dynamics of African traditional religion.[27]

Idowu asserts that the "concept 'traditional religion' is a contradiction in terms."[28] For Idowu, a person is not religious because he or she is only traditional. To be religious goes beyond adhering to tradition. Religion is existential. It stems from a person's need for something or someone higher than a human being, "something beyond history."[29]

The point most African scholars of religion make, and which Idowu emphasizes here, is that there is no such thing as traditional religion in the sense that all African peoples have a common religion. Idowu contends that any thorough and academically grounded study of the traditional religions of the African people must be done on a regional basis.[30] The scope of study should be limited geographically in order to be profitable to the academic community.

Notes

1   Byang H. Kato, *African Cultural Revolution and the Christian Faith* (Jos, Nigeria: Challenge Publications, 1976), 11.

2   Ibid.

3   Justin S. Ukpong, *African Theologies Now* (Eldoret, Kenya: Gaba Publications, AMECEA Pastoral Institute, 1984), 11.

4   Geoffery Parrinder, *African Traditional Religion,* 3d ed. (London: Sheldon Press, 1974), 20.

5   John S. Mbiti, *African Religions and Philosophy* (London: Heinemann Educational Books, 1969), 7.

6   Ibid.

7   Ibid.

8   Ibid.

9   Ibid.

10   Parrinder, *African Traditional Religion,* 18.

11   Ibid.

12   Byang H. Kato, *Theological Pitfalls in Africa* (Kisumu, Kenya: Evangel Publishing House, 1975), 19.

13   Ibid., 20.

14   Ibid., 20–23.

15   E. Bolaji Idowu, *Olodumare: God in Yoruba Belief* (London: Longmans, 1962), 204.

16   The Yorubas are found in the southwestern part of Nigeria. They make up one of the three major ethnic groups in Nigeria. They speak Yoruba language.

17   J. Omosade Awolalu, *Yoruba Beliefs and Sacrificial Rites* (London: Longman Group, 1979), 11.

18   Osadolor Imasogie, *African Traditional Religion* (Ibadan: University Press, 1982), 28.

19   Ibid.

20   Ibid., 29.

21 Oliver A. Onwubiko, *African Thought, Religion and Culture* (Enugu, Nigeria: SNAAP Press, 1991), 59.

22 Ibid., 9–60.

23 E. Bolaji Idowu, *African Traditional Religion: A Definition* (Maryknoll, NY: Orbis Books, 1973), 103.

24 Ibid.

25 Ibid., 104.

26 Ibid., 105.

27 Ibid., 104.

28 Ibid., 105.

29 Ibid.

30 Ibid., 106.

Chapter 3

Igbo Religion

There is no singular African traditional religion. What exists are religions of Africa. The concept of the person of the Supreme Being is common to almost all African communities. Virtually all Africans worship the Supreme Being, but the form or mode of worship and the set of meanings imbedded in that worship vary from place to place.

Idowu's *olodumareism* as the definition of African traditional religion is not only inadequate; it is parochial. *Olodumare* is one of the many Yoruba names for God. The Yorubas are only one cultural entity among the many cultural entities of Africa. Therefore, it is not representative enough to use *olodumareism* as the definition for the many and multifaceted religions of Africa. This same argument applies to definitions such as animism, paganism, fetishism, idolatry, magic, primitive religion, heathenism, juju, bureaucratic monotheism and so on. Bureaucratic monotheism, which Imasogie espouses, has little or no relevance in Igboland because *Igbo amaghi eze* (the Igbo know no king). In Igboland, except for Onitsha and a few other parts of the Northern Igbo, functional kingship is nonexistent. In recent times, some Igbo autonomous communities have begun the practice of the installation of kings, but power and authority still belong to the *Umunna*, the communities and not to one individual. In most communities in Igboland, *Okparas* (first sons of different families) and the *ozos* (titled men) play important roles such as giving advice and settling disputes; they carry the functional authority within the *umunna*.[1]

Another distinctive feature of the socio-political life of the Igbo is that even in places where kings (*ndi eze*) are recognized, the kings rule their autonomous communities through the first sons, who are heads of their families, lineages and clans.[2] The kings may be powerful, but they do not rule their subjects through their own appointed staff.

There were no Ezes whose authority extended to very wide areas and so the Ibo
did not in the past organize empires and kingdoms. Rather marriages, and common interests like defence against any warrior intruders, united many communes
into voluntary confederations.[3]

Considering these political structures in Igboland, Imasogie's "bureaucratic monotheism" cannot adequately define Igbo traditional religion,
much less African traditional religions.

Therefore, attention should be devoted to describing and understanding of the religious life of the African. This can be done through disci-
plined and systematic study, with participant observation, as a cornerstone of method. In this list, the scholar who attempts to understand
traditional Africans and their religions is not setting out "to glorify the
dead past of Africa . . . but to discover what Africans actually know,
actually believe, and actually think about Deity and the supersensible
world."[4] Igbo religion is one of the many religions of Africa. The Igbo, as
an ethnic and cultural group live in the southeastern part of Nigeria. The
Igbo are a religious people.

Among Ndi Igbo, religion is integrated with the political, social and economic
lives of the people so that religious beliefs have control over many aspects of the
people's lives.[5]

In the past, Igbo society was composed predominantly of peasants,
most of whom depended on agriculture for their living.[6] Agriculture, in
addition to hunting, was important to the traditional Igbo. These two
areas of the Igbo life had very deep connections with their religious life.
Alexander Obietoka Animalu, in his 1990 Ahiajoku Lecture, quotes Bishop
Ajayi Crowther:

We learn from the foregoing narrative that the material or economic order of the
Igbo people in 1857 was based on the cultivation of yam, corn and cotton. . . .[7]

The importance of agriculture in the life of the Igbo cannot be over-
emphasized. Later on in this book, the yam festival will be discussed.
Land is essential to agriculture, hence the Igbo attach great religious significance to land. For example, in the sub-village of Umuobom, Umuafor,
Amaimo of the old Owerri province, there is a large expanse of land
known as Oru Mbara. This farm land is commonly owned by the adult
males of the village, who have gone through the rite of passage called iwa
akwa. The iwa akwa is a ceremony of initiation in which every male child
of the village is introduced to the society of adult males. This ceremony is

both social and religious in nature. Following this initiation rite, a male child becomes formally an adult in Umuobom. He will then be entitled to all the rights and privileges which are assigned to adult males in the community.

One of the major privileges which an initiated male derives is the allocation of a portion of the common farm land (*Oru Mbara*). *Oru Mbara* is allocated to Umuobom males every four or five years, depending on the number of years it takes the land to be fertile. This socio-economic structure carries deep religious significance and is evidence of the extent religion plays in the everyday life of the Igbo.

> For the Igbo attachment to land is, if not unique in the Nigerian setting, fundamental to the understanding of his world view and his relation to the universe.[8]

Nwala observes that the traditional Igbo people are deeply religious.[9] To buttress his assertion, he quotes Arthur Leonard, a renowned Western observer of Igbo religious life.

> Arthur Leonard . . . says that they (Igbo) are . . . a truly religious people of whom it can be said as it has been said of the Hindus, that they eat religiously, drink religiously, bathe religiously, dress religiously, sin religiously . . . Religion of these natives is their existence and their existence is their religion.[10]

Nwala recognizes five elements of Igbo religion: (1) Belief in a Supreme Being, who is called *Chukwu, Chineke* or *Osebuluwa*; (2) Numerous local deities with specific but overlapping functions. These deities are called *Agbara* or *Arusi*; (3) the divinity of the ancestors, known as *Ndichie* (4) oracles and systems of divination, and (5) numerous abstract forces which are personified and religiously manipulated through sacrifices, prayers, medicine and charms in order to achieve certain objectives.[11]

It is necessary to re-emphasize that there is no recognizable separation between the sacred and the profane in the Igbo worldview or in practical behavior in society. In the mid twentieth century, an ethnographic survey of Africa was conducted under the auspices of the International African Institute, Oxford University. In the compilation of the results of their survey, Part 3 of the publication dealt with the Igbo and Ibibio-speaking peoples of southeastern Nigeria. At the time of this survey (1945–50).[12] Southeastern Nigeria was divided into six provinces. They were: Onitsha, Owerri, Rivers, Ogoja, Benin and Warri.[13] Among their many findings was a very important and characteristic value of the Igbo—their democracy and autonomy.

> The Ibo are generally held to be tolerant, ultra-democratic and highly individualis-
> tic. They dislike and suspect any form of external government and authority.
> They have a strongly developed commercial sense and a practical unromantic
> approach to life.[14]

These features of the Igbo carry strong implication for their religious life. Cyril C. Okorocha, another Igbo scholar, analyzes the soteriology of traditional Igbo religion. He understands the primary goal of religion for the Igbo as salvation.[15] Okorocha suggests two reasons for his choice of salvation as the focal point of Igbo religion. The first is "my conviction that the search for salvation is the goal of man's religiousness."[16] Secondly, since salvation is the goal of religion everywhere in the world, the concept of salvation is a universal phenomenon and therefore "becomes a most versatile common denominator."[17] He writes:

> People search for God because they are in need of salvation. They meet Him as
> they search for salvation and in meeting him, they know that they have encoun-
> tered the "joy of man's desiring"—the sum of his religious strivings and ideals—
> that is salvation.[18]

Okorocha's definition of salvation for the Igbo is *Ezi Ndu* (the good life). He argues that the Igbo are anthropocentric in their religious existence, hence they strive to ward off anything, both physical and spiritual, that poses a threat to their existence. They do this through power encounters. He mentions two main contributions of the Igbo to the understanding of "man's religiousness."[19]

First, the Igbo emphasize the need to not distinguish the sacred from the secular. They view the whole of life as one indivisible, though unconfused, sacrosanct whole, which is altogether sacred because it is created and inhabited by *Chineke* and his innumerable spirit agents.[20]

The second Igbo contribution is that religion is created by people and for their service. Okorocha states:

> Religion is for man, for his own benefit, and not man for religion. This means that
> to claim to be religious and at the same time refuse to be human, to respond
> humanly, to the pressing practical needs of one's fellow human beings is, to the
> Igbo mind, a contradiction in terms. Igbo Primal Religion is more of a lived reli-
> gion than a mere theoretical exercise in fantasy, dogmatism or philosophy which
> is devoid of, or insensitive to "Life" and to man as "man."[21]

Put in the present day Christian missiological context, what Okorocha is saying is that while Igbo religion has both "eternal salvation" and "social gospel" elements, it places greater emphasis on "social gospel" as validation for "eternal salvation." Igbo religion is indeed a practical religion. According to Cyprain Ogazi Chiagoro, a juju priest in Ulakwo, Owerri, "Igbo religion is authentic; worshippers practice what the religion says. They do not pretend."[22]

In the Igbo mind, people's religious affirmations must be important to them because this person's whole existence is bound up in his or her wholistic behavior. For the Igbo, the religious life-style has no limitations; it informs all of life. It must be lived both in secret and in public. While Okorocha should be commended for his thorough study of Igbo religion, it should be observed that salvation for the Igbo goes beyond the physical. It is also spiritual. *Ala Mmuo* (land of the spirits) is another important concept in Igbo religious thought. The type of life a person will live in *ala mmuo* will depend on the type of life that individual lives *nime uwa* (on earth).

While the good life or *ezi ndu* is the concern of the Igbo here on earth, it is also their concern in the spirit world. Hence, they place strong emphasis on good burial so that the dead will not be stranded at the crossroads in the other world.[23] Okorocha's definition of salvation in Igbo religious experience is inadequate. He limits his definition to power encounters in the physical realm. The traditional Igbo believe fully in life after physical existence in this world. This writer finds it difficult to agree with Okorocha that the Igbo are only anthropocentric in their religious existence. The Igbo believe in existence in this world, and in existence after this physical world. They attempt to conduct themselves well in this world, so that when they die, they will live well with the gods and their ancestors in the spirit world.

Nwala recognizes the Igbo concept of life after death. He agrees that for the Igbo, the good life, *Ndu* or *Ndu oma* is the *Sumum bonum* or of highest value.[24] Nwala suggests that the common case of the name, *Ndubuisi*, meaning life is of supreme value, confirms the assertion that the Igbo place supreme importance on life.[25] He mentions other names which depict life as the greatest quest for the Igbo: *Nduamaka* (life is good) and *Nduka* (life is greater).[26] *Ndu di uto* (life is sweet) is another Igbo name. Nwala recognizes that for the Igbo life goes beyond the physical or material realm. It is also spiritual. He writes,

In such institutions as mortuary and marriage, one sees the supreme importance attached to Ndu. To them Ndu is a never-ending process and its perpetuation is the goal of all activity and aspirations. Ndu, in their conception, is the dynamic quality of material and human existence. Ndu is also existence itself and existence could take various forms either material/spiritual or pure spirit. Death in this world is seen as the dissolution of the flesh during when the spirit enters a separate existence maintaining the Ndu of the individual in another sphere or form of existence.[27]

Continuing in this line of argument, Nwala highlights the great regard which the Igbo conceive for Ndu in the spirit world and states that for the Igbo "death of the spirit is the greatest tragedy for any individual."[28] He asserts, "To say to an Igbo man *Nwua onwu na nmuo,* (may you die in the spirit world) is the greatest unforgivable curse to him."[29]

Scope and Practices

Generally, Igbo religion is practised everywhere in Igboland. According to Forde and Jones in their survey of the Igbo and Ibibio-speaking peoples of Southern Nigeria, the Igbo-speaking geographical area was made up of five main divisions.[30] These divisions were Northern or Onitsha Ibo; Southern or Owerri Ibo; Western Ibo; Eastern or cross River Ibo and North-Eastern Ibo[31] (please see appendix 2).

The Igbo religion was and is still practised in all these areas. There may be local variations in the mode of worship, but the basic tenets of the religion are conventional to the Igbo of these five geographical divisions.

Oracles and religious cults are prominent features of Igbo socio-religious life. These are numerous, but the four prominent ones are:

1. The Ibini Okpabi or the long Juju at Aro-Chukwu
2. Igweka-Ala of Umunneoha
3. Agbala of Awka
4. The Nri priestly cult[32]

Practitioners of Igbo religion include juju priests (*ndi eze agbara*), diviners (*ndi ogo mmuo* or *ndi ohu uzo*), messengers (*ndi oga ozi agbara*) and mere worshippers (*ndi na-efe agbara*). Let us now look at each of these four groups of practitioners.

Priests

The Igbo have a strong belief in the priesthood of the heads of households, lineages and clans.[33] In some sections of Igboland, especially the northern section, *ozo* title holders, all of whom are supposed to be men, may serve the priestly function. They may "offer sacrifices and perform ritual functions including praying to *Chukwu* and to the ancestors."[34] Ilogu mentions two classes of priests in the traditional Igbo society. The first group is made up of the *osu*[35] caste. The second group is made up of men who by appointment become priests. The appointment referred to here is done by ancestral spirits.[36]

It is pertinent to note that the *osu* caste system was abolished by the former government of Eastern Nigeria on May 10, 1956, during Nnamdi Azikiwe's tenure as Premier of Eastern Nigeria.[37] Before this abolition, an *osu* was always chosen among many *osus* to be the special priest of a god, and he (the *osu*) was required to live near that god's shrine.[38] This practice has ceased.

Juju priests are perceived to possess powers because of their "appointment" by the ancestral spirits. This appointment follows the condition of special spirit-possession of the appointee, known as *agwu*. This possessed individual behaves abnormally, until the god or the ancestral spirit requiring his service is appeased. Then there is a ceremony of initiation which is normally conducted by *ndi dibia* (medicine men). For example, priests of *Ala* (earth goddess) are specially appointed, and they enjoy an enhanced status among the priests of the other deities. *Ala* is the most prominent deity in Igboland. She is highly regarded by all traditional Igbos. She is the queen of the underworld and the owner of all people, both the dead and the living. "The cult of ancestors is closely associated with *Ala*."[39] We shall say more about this goddess later on.

"Appointment," means that juju priests are selected by divination.[40] Divination is a magical process by which lots fall on prospective juju priests. In most communities in Igboland, priests come from designated lineages. However they do not enjoy automatic prestige by virtue of their lineage. Prestige depends on personality, character and effectiveness.[41] Thus the status of priests varies from community to community.[42]

Priests primarily function as mediators between their people and the gods. Nwala states that the most important personality in the religious life of the Igbo is the priest.[43] He calls the priest, *Eze Muo* which literally means, "chief spirit." This term for the juju priest has a confusing connotation because it tends to consign this human personality to the domain of the spirit world. However, Nwala quickly corrects himself with his subsequent description of the priest. He states that the nearest definition of the priest "is the elder of the family who is himself a mini-priest, for he performs priestly function.[44]

As has been already stated, "every deity has a priest who ministers to him."[45] Juju priests function as keepers and maintainers of the public shrines and temples. They receive objects of sacrifice from the worshippers on behalf of the gods, and they perform necessary rituals which are connected with those sacrifices. They also organize ceremonies and feasts to honor the deity they serve. On a daily basis, they celebrate prayers and sacrifices of their own as a form of their own worship and that of all who worship the same deity.[46]

In *Arrow of God*, Chinua Achebe provides a description of Ezeulu, a juju priest, and also describes the Shrine of the Oracle, Agbala:

> He wore smoked raffia which descended from his waist to his knee. The left half of his body—from forehead to toes—was painted with white chalk. Around his head was a leather band from which an eagle's feather pointed backwards. On his right hand he carried *Nne ofo*, the mother of all staffs of authority in Umuarro, and in his left he held a long iron staff which kept up a quivering rattle whenever he struck its pointed end into the earth.[47]
>
> The way into the shrine was a round hole at the side of a hill, just a little bigger than round opening into a hen house. Worshippers and those who came to seek knowledge from the god crawled on their belly through the hole and found themselves in a dark, endless space in the presence of Agbala. No one had ever beheld Agbala, except his priestess.[48]

In Igbo religion, the priesthood is not exclusively male. Females also serve as priests. They perform the same functions as their male counterparts,[49] except *igo ofo*.[50] The ofo stick is very important in traditional Igbo religion. An ofo stick is not taken from just any tree, but from a special tree, "the Detarium Senegalense tree."[51] Nobody deliberately cuts the ofo tree, because among the traditional Igbo worshippers, it is believed that the Supreme Being created the ofo tree purposely to be sacred and for its branches to fall off unbroken.[52] The unbroken branch that falls off of the main branch is used to carve ofos of various sizes.

> The ofo made out of these branches is the abode of the spirit of dead ancestors, hence the authority and the sacredness of the ofo, as well as the special place given to it as the emblem of unity, truth and indestructibility for the individual or the group possessing the ofo.[53]

The ofo stick functions in some ways like the Bible among Christians. Priesthood in traditional Igbo religion is a noble calling. It is not taken lightly by those who are called. "Occasionally a person succeeds his father as a priest to a deity, but in majority of cases the deity selects his priest himself."[54]

Cyprain Duru Ogazi Chiagoro, of Umuovum, Ulakwo, speaking about his role as a juju priest, confirmed all that has already been said about traditional priesthood in Igboland, and, then talked specifically about his own roles.

I am priest of Amadioha.[55] I have my own altar, which is dedicated to Amadioha. I have *Ihu chi* in my altar (symbol of personal god). People come to me when they are in need of consulting their personal gods about the problems they are facing or perplexing situations in their lives. They also come to offer sacrifices to their *chi* (personal god) when something good happens to them. Items of sacrifice may include yams, chickens, especially cock, goat, kola nuts, money and so on. They bring these items to their *chi* in order to show appreciation to him for the blessing they have received. When they come, I act as a mediator between them and their *chi*."[56]

Chiagoro understands his priestly role in the community to include that of a peace-maker. In Igbo traditional life, priests serve as custodians of peace and unity in the community. They regularly consult the oracles to make sure that nothing evil will happen to the community. If the gods become annoyed with the people for any reason, the priests have the responsibility of making suitable sacrifices to appease the gods. They also stay in touch regularly with the community's ancestors.

The saying that "charity begins at home" holds true for Ndi Igbo. Strong Igbo families make up strong Igbo communities. The role of family elders as priests of their families cannot be over-emphasized. Nwala gives particular attention to the priestly roles which elders play in their families. He writes:

The elders serve as on-the-spot priests for their respective families. They control the family ancestral shrine and conduct all immediate priestly services for their families. An elder offers prayers daily and especially early in the morning on his behalf and that of his family. He pours libation of wine to ask Chukwu; the local deities and the ancestors to bless each day's undertaking; he prays for children, wealth, health and protection for himself and his family.[57]

The priest in Igbo traditional religion serves as a connector between the natural and the supernatural worlds. He plays a major role in making sure that there is harmony between these two worlds. By virtue of his "appointment," the deities endow the priest with special powers to play this role effectively. The community which he or she serves must also sanction these functions. The priest has a responsibility to demonstrate that "he is in harmony with his environment. He must exhibit an understanding of Igbo thought."[58]

Diviners

In many parts of Igboland, a diviner is called *Dibia Afa*. The diviner in the Igbo traditional religion is a person who works with charms and manipulates the spirits so that he/she can "foretell the future and give directions for procedure in the matter of sacrifice."[59] Sometimes, the same person who serves as a deity's priest can also act as a diviner. G. T. Basden notes that in Igboland, a priest could be called *Onye-Nagba-Aja* or *Onye-Igba-Aja* (one who offers sacrifices). The same person may also be called *dibia* (medicine man or a diviner).[60]

The diviner's role in Igbo religion centers around fortune-telling. He/she consults with the deities and the ancestral spirits and makes predictions that are ontological or existential in nature. In many cases, diviners operate independently of the priests and the community's shrine. They build their own divination altars in their homes and engage in their practice much like business. People who face perplexing problems, such as infertility, childlessness, acute sickness and theft of their belongings, go to the diviners to seek solutions. Sometimes, cases involving land disputes among individuals and communities are taken to the diviners for resolution through divination.

Some students who are preparing for examinations go to diviners seeking fore-knowledge of examination questions. Some civil servants and business people, seeking for promotions and business breakthroughs, consult diviners. Their role is somewhat similar to that of the psychics in the present Western world.

When visited by a person who desires information that is beyond his or her powers,

> The diviner commences operations by placing an inverted tortoise shell on the ground which contains the *afa*, the medium of divination, commonly called charms.[61]

This diviner, who is called *Agbasoaka* (able adviser) or *Okwuruka-Ojere* (one who is able to explain by divination), will then set up his elements of divination. Elements include, *Nkwu Agwu, Ikenga, Ofo, Udele-Agwu, Udu miri,* and *Ugene.*[62] It should be noted that elements of divination may vary from place to place and even from diviner to diviner. Some include more elements than have been mentioned, but the ones mentioned are basic.

At the beginning of his divination, the diviner will call upon the petitioner to greet *Ogwugwu.*[63] Basden states that one of the reasons the petitioner is asked to call on *Ogwugwu* is to beg this deity not to allow any harm to come to him or to his family.[64] After this has been done, the diviner will request the petitioner to raise his/her hands to the sky in order to receive long life.[65] The petitioner will then be told to keep his or her feet firmly on the ground and repeat these words, "I have recovered my life in this world."⁶⁶ The diviner will at this time spread his charm around the room and tell the petitioner what sacrifice should be made to *Ngwu*, a deity represented by a sacred tree.⁶⁷

Through the medium of diviners or *dibia afa*, people learn from their ancestors and the spirits about things that happened in the past, understand the present, and foreknow the future.⁶⁸ People do not just claim to be diviners. Diviners are initiated, and "being initiated into the Dibia Afa Society is one thing: living in the Afa Spirit as a genuine convert to its religious genius is another."⁶⁹

Messengers

In most locations in Igboland, messengers act as "altar boys" during worship. They are called *Ndi oga-ozi agbara* (those who deliver messages for the deity.) Up until the mid twentieth century, most messengers of local deities were made up of the *osus* (outcasts) and the down-trodden of the society. It was a common practice then, especially in Amaino, Ikeduru, in old Owerri Province, to call a person *Oga-ozi agbara* if that individual behaved sluggishly or abnormally.

In another sense, deities serve as messengers of the Supreme Being. In Owerri Province, *Amadi oha*, the god of thunder and lightening, serves as God's messenger to punish evil doers with lightning.⁷⁰ Other deity-messengers in Igbo traditional religion include *Anyanwu* (the sun god), *Igwe* (the sky god) and *Ala* (the earth goddess).⁷¹ *Ala*, is a prominent Goddess in Igboland. She is perceived by the Igbo as the most important deity in Igboland.

> She is the guardian of morality, the controller of the minor gods of fortune and economic life. . . . It is she who works in conjunction with the spirits of dead ancestors to order the prohibitions and the ritual avoidances. Many social offences become *aru* or pollution or abominations because they infringe the laws of the earth goddess. Because of her importance in ensuring health, agricultural fortune and hunting successes, she is well known all over Iboland. Most public worship of various communities is offered to the earth goddess as well as seasonal celebrations which relate to the various seasons of the year. Her shrine is found in most homes and public squares of any village.⁷²

Ilogu mentions other gods, which he refers to as "minor deities." They include *Ifejioku* (the god of farm work); *Agwu Isi* (the god of divination and herbal medicine); *Ndebunze* or *Ndichie* (the deified spirit of dead ancestors); and *Ikenga* (the god of adventure in hunting or business enterprise).⁷³ All these deities serve as messengers of the Supreme Being.

Worshippers

The worshipping community in the Igbo traditional society is made up of most of those who do not accept Christianity and Eastern religions, such as Hinduism, Buddhism, and Islam. There are a few nonconformists. Presently, adherents of Igbo religion are in the minority.

There are two main types of worship: private and public. According to Ilogu, private worship has two parts to it, the routine and the occasional. The routine includes the daily offerings which every household head makes to the ancestors at the *Ndubunze* shrine.[74] He usually makes use of Kola-nuts and white chalk for drawing necessary lines appropriate for that kind of worship. Prayer is also a big part of this routine worship. The leader asks the Supreme Being "for protection, prosperity and well-being of the family, while holding up the ofo stick."[75]

Once a year the *Igo ofo* worship is performed. This is a ceremonial cleansing of the ofo with the blood of a chicken, sacrificed to the ancestors during the worship experience.[106] Occasionally, private worship could be performed following the order of a diviner in order for the family concerned to ward off some impending catastrophe. It could also be performed in order to appease a deity. In this case, after the diviner's prescription, the person concerned goes to the priest of that deity and does everything the priest tells him or her to do.

The priest's special intention for performing this act of private worship for the individual is usually one or more of such needs as:

(1) To seek favor from the ancestral spirits.
(2) To seek protection from evil spirits, witches or evil-minded persons.
(3) To seek healing from an illness or cleansing from defilement in eating forbidden animal, or entry into "bad bush," or contact with menstruating women.
(4) To propitiate neglected ancestral spirits or angered gods.
(5) To seek the gift of children.[77]

Public worship has two types: the family and the lineage worship, and the clan or village worship.[78] They are each celebrated annually or biannually. Public worship provides forums for bringing traditional worshippers together for the enactment of the various aspects of family, lineage or clan history. However, the more important reason for public worship is the celebration of "aspects of natural and agricultural manifestations of the local and family gods."[79] Forms and elements of worship have local variations throughout Igboland.

Theological Presuppositions

The average Igbo man or woman is inherently religious. Elders, both living and dead, play significant roles in the religious life of the Igbo. Like
their counterparts in other African communities, especially in Nigeria,
the Igbo politico-social and socio-cultural lives are intertwined with their
religious life. Nowhere else is this truth more prominent than in their
theological presuppositions.

Their views concerning the Supreme Being, anthropology and the
universe are ontological. With this in mind, we will consider some of the
major theological presuppositions in Igbo traditional religion. We will discuss five of them, namely, the Supreme Being, deities, anthropology, the
ancestors and the universe.

The Supreme Being

The Igbo believe in a Supreme Being, called *Chineke* (Creator) or *Chukwu*
(Highest Being). This Being is not created. The Supreme Being's origin is
unknown, but this being, who is not normally conceived in terms of male
or female, is responsible for the creation of the universe and all that is in
it. Evolutionary theory has no place in Igbo religion. *Chineke* or *Chukwu*
created and is responsible for the maintenance and sustenance of the
universe and all the things in it. It is a common belief among the Igbo that
knowledge of the Supreme Being comes from the ancestors, who bring
this revelation to the living through the priests and the diviners. For the
Igbo, "the Supreme Being is a personification of the absolute in human
life and thought."[80] As *Chineke*, the Supreme Being functions as Creator.
As *Chukwu*, the Supreme Being functions as the highest spiritual personality. *Chukwu* is the source of human life, and therefore is the bestower
of human destiny. The Igbo believe in destiny. Nwala refers to this idea of
destiny as *chi* or *uwa*,[81] while Ilogu calls it *chi*.[82]

Chi or uwa (nature or destiny) is given to a person at birth by *Chineke*.
This is the reason why a person behaves in a certain way. The Igbo will
often say, "This is his or her nature" (*obu otu uwa ya na chi ya di*).[83]
Ilogu observes that the Supreme Being "gives to each man at the time of
his birth that man's particular portion of the divine being called *chi*."[84]
This divine presence in each person serves as a personal god.

The Igbo have various descriptive names for the Supreme Being which
relate to His roles and functions. It is in this regard that most adherents of
Igbo religion begin to look at the Supreme Being as possessing male
characteristics. For example, in Amaimo, Ikeduru and the surrounding
towns in the old Owerri Province, people use this male phrase for *Chukwu*,

"*Nwoke no n'elu igwe ogodo ya na-awu n'ala,*" meaning, "the man who stays in the sky but his loin-cloth keeps flowing down the earth." This phrase, when used for the Supreme Being, describes his male status and his all-powerfulness. The Supreme Being is also referred to as *eze elu igwe* (king of the sky); *onye nwe uwa* (owner of the universe); *obasi di n'igwe* (the king who lives above); *chukwu-okike* (Creator God); *onye kere elu-igwe na uwa* (the one who created heaven and earth).

The Supreme Being's moral attributes include love, justice, fair play, honesty, righteousness, forthrightness and impartiality. His two major functions are creation and sustenance of the universe and everything in it. He alone creates, but shares his sustenance role with other deities. Each deity is appointed to oversee a specific department of nature, and to carry out the Supreme Being's purpose regarding that department.[85] The deities serve as his ministers and as "liaison officers between God and men."[86]

Deities

Deities are very prominent in Igbo religion. They are perceived as helpers or ministers who have been appointed by the Supreme Being to carry out his bidding and report back to him. Deities are not confused with the Supreme Being; they are not objects of worship. Individuals worship the Supreme Being through their local deities and their ancestors. The presence of numerous local deities in Igbo religion does not define the religion as polytheism. The Supreme Being is one divine person, and He is the only one who is worshipped. The deities function as His messengers or ministers.

Nwala does see religion in Igboland as polytheism.[87] He argues that in every community there is a major deity in the pantheon of the gods of that community, to which worship is ascribed. Close observation of Igbo traditional worship does not sustain this position. The argument about the rank of deities has nothing to do with worship, though it may have something to do with power of operation. People in some quarters of Igboland talk about their community's god or gods possessing more power than the gods of their neighboring communities. But there is no concept that any of these local gods challenge the singular place of *Chukwu.*

In *Things Fall Apart,* Achebe highlights *Agadinwayi,* the dreaded Oracle of the Hills and the Caves in Umuofia.[88] This goddess was feared by all the other villages around Umulfia because of her unmatchable power at war, not because she was Umuofia's object of worship.

Chukwuma J. Iroezi claims that the four major deities in Igboland were created by God and given to man to worship. Again this position is not sustained when one takes seriously the Igbo as interpreters of their own experience. On the surface, it could seem like worshipping the deities, when Igbo religionists worship the Supreme Being. In reality, worshippers go to the Supreme Being through the deities. Cyprain Ogazi Chiagoro makes this very clear: "*n'ezi-okwu, n'ezi-okwu, anyi ana-ghi-efe agbara; ihe anyi na-efe wu Chukwu*" (Truly, truly, we do not worship gods; we worship the Supreme Being [God]).[89]

Ilogu recognizes four major deities in the pantheon of Igbo gods. They are *Anyanwu* (the sun god); *Igwe* (the sky god); *Amadi-Oha* (the god of thunder and lightening) and *Ala* (the earth goddess).[90] He looks at these gods as objects of worship. This is another unsustainable position.

Anthropology

William A. Haviland, of the University of Vermont, defines anthropology as

> The study of humankind, which seeks to produce useful generalizations about people and their behavior and arrive at the fullest possible understanding of human diversity.[91]

Among the Igbo, there is no clear demarcation between secular and religious lives. These two are fused together. In Igbo cosmogony, humankind came into being as a result of the creative act of *Chineke*. Since Igbo religion is not a "religion of the book," there are no available written documents to throw more light on the traditional Igbo stories of creation. The stories are passed down orally from generation to generation, and they remain in the domain of myths.

According to one creation story, *Ifenta* (Junior light) was the name of the first man whom the Supreme Being created. The name of the first created woman was *obo-omananya* (this name connotes the beauty of women). The Supreme Being created the universe and everything in it.[92] *Ifenta* or *Ihenta* signifies that humans are next to *Chukwu* in the order of created beings in the visible order.[93]

In another version of the Igbo creation story:

> . . . the first word man learnt from the Supreme Deity (Chukwu) is *mma-nma* (which, to say, is an expression used as greetings among the Igbo). The Supreme Deity told the first parents: 'This is your home. Everything here is for your good and they are so intended. At the beginning man and every creature lived like

brother and kinsmen, spirits, animals, tiger, snakes, birds, and even earth and sky were all together. Men joked and wrestled with spirits and animals.[94]

The Igbo love community. Though they cherish independence and individual freedom, they also love to move in communities. *Umunna* (literally, children of the same father) is the basic social unit of Igbo society. The *Umunna* is made up of the patrilineal descendants of "a founder ancestor by whose name the lineage is sometimes called." The size of *Umunna* (lineage) varies. Since the *Umunna* is patrilineal, its size will depend on the number of males. A small *Umunna* may comprise twenty families, while a large one may have more. Sometimes, a large *Umunna* can be segmented into major and minor sublineages. "Very often members of *Umunna* occupy a single hamlet of scattered homestead."[95]

The concept of collective bargaining, along the *Umunna* line, is prominent in Igbo traditional society. While individuals retain their independence and freedom, every member of the *Umunna* is expected to be loyal to the community's laws and mores. Nobody will dare function alone, because among the Igbo, *Umunna bu ike* (community is strength).

Ancestors

The ancestors are the living-dead. In Igboland, ancestors are looked upon for protection by those who are living in the visible world. Ancestors stand before the gods as intercessors for their living relatives. They intervene for the good of their living relatives, especially in a case where a deity seeks to inflict harm on the living.

In all of Africa, the cult of the ancestors is a significant dimension of indigenous life.

> The group that takes part in ancestor worship usually consists of persons related to one another by descent in one line from the same ancestor or ancestress. The rites in which the group participates have reference to their own ancestors to whom they make offerings of food and drink. A cult group may consist of a lineage, or a clan, or a large chiefdom, as among the Akan peoples of Ghana, or the Lovedu of the Transvaal.[96]

Among the Ga of Ghana, the ancestors "live" with their living relatives. These relatives include their ancestors in all they do, including eating food.[97] The Bantu of South Africa regard their ancestors as their "most intimate gods," while in Zambia, "the family divinities are the ghosts of one's grandfathers, grandmothers, father and mother, uncles and aunts, brothers and sisters."[98] The Igbo of Nigeria believe that life is profoundly influenced by their ancestors. Hence, in their daily prayers, they request the ancestors to mediate between them and the Supreme Being.

Ancestral shrines are common in most Igbo communities. Names such as *Ndichie* (elders), *Ihu-Ndichie* (face of the elders) and *Mgwu* (mud pyramid) are used for ancestral shrines. In Mbaise, Imo State, "ancestors are referred to as *Ndi-nwe-ala*—owners of the land."[99] The ancestors play important roles in the life of their living relatives. In addition to their roles of intercession, and protection, they can also punish those who misbehave. Blessings in form of wealth and child-bearing could be denied the erring members of the community.[100] In Arochukwu of Abia State,

> ancestral cults are the most important religious body next to the Supreme Deity. The ancestors, with the Earth Deity, control traditional morality and ensure social order and the welfare of the members of their respective communities.[101]

In Igboland, ancestors are respected and sometimes deified, but not worshipped. The fact that most Western anthropologists and even theologians, as well as some African ones, talk about ancestral worship does not mean that Africans, especially the Igbo, worship their ancestors. Mbiti is more accurate when he observes that:

> . . . the departed, whether parents, brothers, sisters or children, form part of the family, and must therefore be kept in touch with their surviving relatives. Libation and giving of food to the departed are tokens of fellowship, hospitality and respect; the drink and food so given are symbols of family continuity and contact. "Worship" is the wrong word to apply in this situation; and Africans themselves know very well that they are not "worshipping" the departed members of their family.[102]

The Universe

The Igbo universe is created by *Chineke*. It has two structures, the sky (*Eluigwe*) and the earth (*Elu-uwa* or *Ala*). These two divisions are equal in size. There is also a duality of the universe in terms of the natural and the supernatural. There is *Ala Madu* (the world of human) and *Ala Mmuo* (the spirit world or the land of supernatural order).

Ala Madu or *Elu-uwa* refers to the sphere of human existence, with all the natural resources in it, including bushes, forests, animals, birds, rivers, minerals and so on. The earth "is the scene of most mythologies where gods and men interact. Some spirits 'visit' the earth, while some live on it."[103] Many deities live on earth, though their proper place of abode is *Ala Mmuo* (the spirit world).

Elu Igwe (the sky) is the home for all the celestial bodies. These include, *kpakpaudo* (stars), *onwa* (the moon), *anyauwu* (the sun), *irukpu* (the cloud), *mmiri* (rain) and others.[104] It is believed that the sky is the home of some deities, especially *Anyanwu* (the sun god) and *Amadioha* (the god of thunder). *Chineke* (the creator-God) or *Chukwu* (the Supreme Being) also resides in the sky.

Humans and spirits co-exist in the two levels of existence

> The spirits are involved in the day to day affairs of men. . . . There are human beings called *Ndi o gala nmuo*—those who visit the land of the spirits. These are believed to be able to visit the spirit world and communicate with them.[105]

Some Igbo believe that from time to time, certain deities take on human form and visit the living. Most Igbos believe that spirits inhabit certain natural objects, such as large and unusual trees, rivers, mountains, caves, seas and forests. The Igbo understand that all material things, including humans, will eventually return to their source, *Ala* (the earth). There are two schools of thought about the location of *Ala Mmuo* (spirit world) in Igbo cosmography. The first school locates it beneath the earth, while the second school locates it above the earth.[106]

Rites of Passage

Life (*Ndu*) is a very significant value in Igbo religious thought. They do everything within their power, and the powers of the ancestors, to protect life. Life is nurtured and preserved. Life is preserved through rituals and cultural celebrations. Rites of passage play a very important role in this process of life preservation. Charles Ok Onuh defines Rites of Passage:

> "Rites of Passage" is a category of rituals that mark and accompany the passage of an individual through the successive transitional and crisis moments in one's life cycle, from one stage to another over time, from one role or social position to another.[107]

Onu observes that rituals integrate the biological facts of life, such as birth, growth, reproduction and death, "with the human and cultural experiences."[108] I do not know of any other culture in which this observation is more true than the Igbo culture.

> Rites of Passage try to concretise the fact that humans are not only naturally born as men and women, nor merely procreate and die, but they are culturally made

what they are through ceremonies and rituals. Even though by birth one is male or female, yet through the rites of passage a society culturally defines and makes them man or woman, adult, husband or wife etc.[109]

Ordinarily, there are four major biological rites of passage in Igboland, associated with the four major transitional stages in an Igbo man's or woman's life. These stages are birth, puberty, marriage, and death.

To the Igbo, *Chukwu na-enye nwa* (God gives a child). No other person has the power to give children. The arrival of a child in any Igbo family is a thing of joy. It is more so when the child who is born is a male. The Igbo value children very much, whether they are males or females, but they value males more than females because of the principle of *Ahamefula* (may my family name not fizzle out). *Ahamefula* embodies the principle of inheritance. Women do not inherit their fathers' land or landed property. Every Igbo man desires and prays for a male child so that *ama ya agaghi echi* (his family lineage will not close).

When a child is born to an Igbo family, both the immediate family and the *Umunna* celebrate the birth. The celebration, (*omugwo*), takes different forms in different communities. *Okwa mba na-ebe n'olu n'olu* (geese cry differently depending on where they live). However, certain practices are common. These are circumcision, especially of males after twenty-four days. In the communities where females are circumcised, the rite comes a little later. "In a few isolated Igbo areas like Aboh on the southwest banks of the Niger, girls are circumcised about the time of their puberty with greater religious and social celebrations."[110]

The newborn is presented to the ancestors for protection and the cleansing of the mother from birth pollutions.[111] These two activities involve elaborate rituals. *Igu Aha* (naming ceremony) is another ritual that is associated with birth all through Igboland.

Puberty (*itozu n'mmadu*) is a transitional stage in the life of every Igbo boy or girl. It "is the passing from boyhood or girlhood into adult life."[112] At this stage, a young person is ready to assume a responsible position in the Igbo society. Sex roles are clearly marked. For example, boys tend domestic animals (goats, sheep, cows and so on) while girls sweep living rooms and the compounds. They also help their mothers in the preparation of food for the family. Boys and girls dress differently.

Communities have their different age requirements for puberty rites. However, most communities have different age requirements for boys and girls, about fifteen years for boys, sixteen for girls. Various religious and social ceremonies accompany the puberty stage.[113]

Marriage is another rite of passage all over Igboland. Following the ritual celebration of puberty, the adult is expected to marry and start his or her own home. "Celibacy finds no favour whatsoever with the Igbo; men and women who remain unmarried are mocked."[114] Marriage in Igboland involves all kinds of ritual ceremonies, and the form they take varies from one locality to another.

It is believed that it is the man who marries. He is expected to pay some agreed-upon sum of money (bride price) to the parents of his bride, as a token of appreciation to them for bringing up his would-be wife to adulthood. Up until the mid twentieth century, most marriages were arranged, but today many young people make the choices themselves.

The third major rite of passage is death. Death is never prayed for; it is regarded as a calamity. The Igbo treasure life, and will do anything they can to protect it. But this notwithstanding, death still strikes. When a person dies, the belief among most people will be *onwughi okporo* (he or she did not die without a cause). In Igboland, every death has a cause. In most cases, a person's enemies will be accused. An angry deity could also cause the death of an individual. A wicked dead relative of an individual could come out of *ala mmuo* (spirit world) and attack an individual, causing that person's death.

In each case, funerals involve rituals and ceremonies which correspond with age and social status. Funeral rites and ceremonies involve the whole community because *otu onye adighi eli ozu* (one person does not bury the dead).

> The death of young people and children do not call for religious ceremonies of any magnitude. Such deaths are regarded as great calamities and the gods do not merit much consideration on such occasions. The death of elder women and *ozo* titled men on the other hand entails very expensive and colourful rituals.[115]

In the traditional Igbo mind, physical death does not terminate one's existence, not even existence on earth. Reincarnation explains the reason for this belief. The Igbo believe that life is a continuous process. It has no end, except in the case of the wicked who may die finally in the spirit world.[116]

In Igboland, the death of old people is not as painful as that of young people. Old people, when they die, are capable of coming back to life on earth through the process of reincarnation. When a person dies, he or she can come back to life by being born in another person, or in some cases in more than one person.[117] Therefore, everything possible is done to give the dead a befitting burial so that this individual will enjoy easy passage into the spirit world, and eventually return to earth without any hindrance, either by the ancestors or by the gods.

Rituals

Rituals are very important parts of almost all aspects of Igbo life. Among the numerous rituals in Igboland, we will briefly discuss the three which are most significant to the religious life. These are New Yam festival, the breaking of Kola-nut and *Igba Ndu* (covenant-making).

New Yam Festival

The New Yam Festival carries different names across Igboland. Some communities call it *Ufiejoku, Ifejioku, Njokuji, Ihinjoku, Ahiajoku,* or *Ahajoku.* Others call it *Fijioku, Ajoku, Njoku,* or *Ajaamaja.*[118] It is a fertility rite.

In Igboland, yam is at the top of the list of food items. Yam enjoys a prestigious place in Igbo culture, and those who have an abundance of it are highly respected. They are called *Ndi eze ji* (kings of yam). New Yam festival is also celebrated in some other parts of West Africa. We are yet to know when and where this festival began in West Africa.[119] "The New Yam Festivals usually represent the major event in the annual calendar of socio-religious functions."[120] New Yam Festival is an annual traditional event in most Igbo communities. The rituals which are observed during this occasion, which may last a day or several days, mainly accord recognition and honor to *Ala,* the goddess of fertility, for blessing the people's farm crops and acting on behalf of *Chukwu* to bless families with children.

The Breaking of the Kolanut

The Igbo name for kolanut is *oji.*[121] Kolanut is an important object in Igboland. Certain rituals go with the breaking of the kolanut, especially publicly. Kolanut does not normally have a pleasant taste, but it is treasured by the Igbo of Nigeria. The Igbo have a saying which is associated with the giving, breaking, and eating of the kolanut. They say, "*Onye wetara oji wetara ndu*" (whosoever brings kola, brings life).

For the Igbo, the giving of kolanut to one's house guest signifies acceptance of that guest. Kola is a sign of friendship and goodwill. It signifies love and good neighborliness. It is shared among friends both in Igbo homes and in public social gatherings. "It is shared among friends, as a token of goodwill and is offered to a visitor as a sign of appreciation for his coming."[122]

Kolanuts play important roles in marriage transactions and ceremonies. It is also an important object for sacrifices of all kinds, especially those that are made to ancestors and the gods.

When the kolanut is brought, the ceremony is performed by the oldest person present and he carries out what is called *igo oji*[123] this may consist in blessing the kola, as well as the person who provided it; in giving thanks to their ancestors, and wishing those present good fortune. After this, the person performing the *igo oji* splits the nut, and it is shared among all those present.[124]

It is important at this point to say that *igo oji* is one of the rituals women are not allowed to perform throughout Igboland.

Covenant-Making (*Igba Ndu*)

Covenants are a prominent feature of the Igbo traditional life. Ordinarily, covenant means agreement made between two parties or oath-taking, *igba ndu*. *Ofo na ogu* (moral rectitude) is a principal ethical principle connected with covenant-taking. With *ofo no ogu*, people engage in business transactions freely, without fear of being duped by either party. With *ofo na ogu* marriages are contracted, money-lenders lend money, and pure moral relationships are entered into and maintained. *Ofo na ogu* establishes the traditional ethical code or *omenala*[125] in Igboland.

The traditional ethical code or *omenala* defines moral ethics in terms of the good and the bad. Good behavior is rewarded and approved by the traditional Igbo society, while bad behavior is frowned upon, condemned and punished.

Some things are regarded as abominations (*nso ala* or *ihe ala so nso*). Ilogu has two categories of these abnormalities. The major ones are:

— Stealing yams either from the barn or from the farm
— Homicide
— Incest
— A freeman having sexual relationship with *osu* (outcast or slave of a shrine) or spending the night especially with the *osu* in her house
— Suicide especially by hanging
— Poisoning someone else to take his life secretly
— Theft of domestic fowls especially a hen in her hatching pot where it can easily be taken away with the eggs.
— A woman climbing palm tree or a kolanut tree especially if in addition she attempts doing so with the special palm tree climbing rope
— Theft of any kind by an *ozo* titled man

The minor prohibitions or abnormalities are:

— Adultery by the wife
— A wife throwing the husband off the ground during a fight
— Killing or eating any *totem* animal on purpose. If accidentally (which will be committing an abomination all the same) the guilt of the offender is viewed a little more lightly
— Anyone deliberately cutting the tendrils of young growing yams in somebody's farm
— Anyone altering land boundaries in secret especially in the night
— Burning another person's thatch house maliciously
— Disclosing the identity of the masquerade in public especially by a woman
— A woman in her menstrual period cooking and serving her husband such food especially if the husband is *ozo* titled person
— A widow having sexual relationship while still "wearing" for her late husband mourning clothes. She is considered to be in ritual danger until she had performed the "cleansing rite" normally after one year; such sex relation is regarded as spreading pollution
— Someone dying a "bad death" (deaths resulting from leprosy, small pox, etc.) or after swearing an oath and then dying from the enlargement of the stomach
— A husband deliberately breaking or throwing away the wife's earthenware cooking pot [126]

In addition to the twenty listed above, Ilogu lists four other abominations which relate to unnatural occurrences. These are:

— A cock crowing in the night (from about 8 p.m. to 3 a.m.)
— A woman giving birth to twins
— A baby coming out of the womb with the feet instead of the head
— A growing child cutting the upper tooth first[127]

Each of the above-mentioned abominations offends the gods and the ancestors and incurs their wrath against the offender or offenders. In order to appease the gods and save the offender from death, certain rituals and sacrifices must be done. Each offense has its own specified rituals and sacrifices. Of course, the gods have the discretion to accept or reject the rituals and sacrifices.

Every member of the *Umunna* is required to abide by these moral codes to the letter, in order to be in good standing with the community.

The ethical codes adopted by the community rule and guide that community's moral and ethical behavior. They bind the community together in covenant.

The Role of Women

Igbo women are active participants in the religion. They lead in every aspect of worship except *igo oji* (blessing and breaking the kolanut) and *igo ofo* (using the ofo stick ritually or ceremoniously). Igboland is a male-dominated culture, much like all the other cultural areas of Nigeria. There are many cultural norms which delimit women's societal life, but in the arena of religion, Igbo women enjoy enormous freedom. They serve as priestesses, diviners, messengers and worshippers. The most important deity in Igboland, *Ala* (earth goddess) is female. Her chief minister is always a woman. As the deity in charge of the domains of fertility and agriculture, she is very popular among the Igbo.

Women do not keep *Ikenga*[128] The power of *Ikenga* is inherent in every male, and resides in his right hand. *Ikenga's* symbolic representation is a ram-headed image. "*Ikenga* is the force behind male aggression which, like a ram, is fearless and undaunted."[129] Certain cultural prohibitions affect females more than they do males. For example, when a married woman commits adultery with a married man, only the woman will be condemned. A woman cannot climb a palm tree (the tree which produces palm-wine), especially in the presence of a man. Women who die young, and leave no children behind, do not become ancestors.

Igbo women, especially in Owerri, are held responsible for the moral education of their children. They pay more attention to their daughters. Virginity is a treasured thing in Igboland. For this reason, polygamy is not a serious issue in Owerri area. It is not common in this area. There are three reasons for this:

(1) Endogamy is the usual practice. No father is willing to allow his daughter to become a second, subordinate wife within the community. To become a second wife suggests that the woman was neither a virgin nor good-mannered, and her parents simply wanted to get rid of her. Second wives are often looked upon with contempt.
(2) Bride-prices in Owerri area are very high.
(3) Owerri women have always been great believers in female liberation.[130]

Generally, Igbo women are economically self-reliant, socially influential, politically powerful, and religiously involved. However, the average Igbo woman is subject to a man, preferably her husband or father. If she is single, she enjoys more freedom, rights and privileges.

The Igbo traditional world is still a man's world. Women, especially widows, do not own much property. "There are instances of women becoming rich, but they are the kind who prefer an independent life and are able to dominate the situation."[131] Traditional Igbo women do not live in the same room with their husbands, especially if the husband is a priest. However, Igbo women function actively in the religious life of their communities. This is the substance of Igbo religious life, before the advent of Christianity.

The next chapter will introduce us to the beginnings of Christianity in Igboland. We will briefly examine four major groups of Christians. These are: the mainline churches, the Pentecostals, the indigenous churches and the Scripture Union of Nigeria.

Notes

1   Edmund Ilogu, *Christianity and Igbo Culture* (Leiden: E.J. Brill, 1974), 14–15.

2   Ibid., 16.

3   Ibid.

4   Idowu, *African Traditional Religion: A Definition*, 106–107.

5   L. E. Amadi, *Igbo Heritage: Curriculum Materials for Social and Literary Studies* (Owerri, Nigeria: Imo Onyeukwu Press, 1987), 42.

6   T. Uzodimma Nwala, *Igbo Philosophy* (Ikeja, Lagos: Lantern Books, 1985), 15.

7   Alexander O. E. Animalu, "Ucheakonam: A Way of Life in the Modern Scientific Age," *1990 Ahiajoku Lecture* (Owerri, Nigeria: Ministry of Information and Culture, 1990), 27.

8   Pius N. C. Okigbo, "Towards a Reconstruction of the Political Economy of Igbo Civilization," *1986 Ahiajoku Lecture* (Owerri, Nigeria: Ministry of Information and Culture, 1986), 14.

9   Nwala, *Igbo Philosophy*, 113.

10   Ibid., 114.

11   Ibid., 115.

12   Daryll Forde and G. I. Jones, eds., *The Ibo and Ibibio-Speaking Peoples of South-eastern Nigeria* (London: Oxford University Press for The International African Institute, 1950), 5.

13   Ibid., 9.

14   Ibid., 24.

15   Cyril C. Okorocha, *The Meaning of Religious Conversion in Africa: The Case of the Igbo of Nigeria* (Aldershot, England: Grower Publishing Co, 1987), 51.

16   Ibid., 49.

17   Ibid., 49–50.

18   Ibid., 50.

19   Ibid., 78.

20   Ibid.

21   Ibid.

22 Cyprain O. Chiagoro, Juju Priest in Ulakwo, Owerri, interview by author, 9 January 1996, Ulakwo, Owerri, Nigeria, tape recording.

23 Ibid.

24 Nwala, *Igbo Philosophy*, 144.

25 Ibid.

26 Ibid.

27 Ibid.

28 Ibid.

29 Ibid.

30 Forde and Jones, *The Ibo and Ibibio-speaking Peoples of South-eastern Nigeria*, 10.

31 Ibid.

32 Nwala, *Igbo Philosophy*, 120.

33 Ilogu, *Christianity and Ibo Culture*, 52.

34 Ibid.

35 *Osu* is the name given to a living human sacrifice, a person owned by an idol, a slave in a double sense. When a person was kidnapped and dedicated to any local deity, he became an *osu*. A slave kept as the property of the gods (or a god) was known as an *osu* (J. Carnochan and Belonwu Iwuchnkwu, *An Igbo Revision Course* [London: Oxford University Press, 1963; reprint 1976], 90–91).

36 Ibid., 53.

37 J. O. L. Ezeala, *Can the Igboman Be a Christian in View of the Osu Caste System?* (Orlu, Nigeria: B.I. Nnaji and Sons Press (Nig), n.d.), 32.

38 Ilogu, *Christianity and Ibo Culture,* 53.

39 Ibid.

40 Ibid.

41 Ibid.

42 Ibid.

43 Nwala, *Igbo Philosophy*, 122.

44 Ibid., 123.

45 Ibid.

46 Ibid.

47   Chinua Achebe, *Arrow of God* (New York: Doubleday and Co., 1969), 80, quoted by Anthonia C. Ogbonnaya, "Chinua Achebe and the Igbo World View" (Ph.D. diss., University of Wisconsin-Madison, 1984), 16.

48   Chinua Achebe, *Things Fall Apart* (London: Heinemann Educational Books, 1985), 12.

49   The case of Agbala's priestess was a good example. According to Achebe, Agbala's "Priestess stood by the sacred fire which she built in the heart of the cave and proclaimed the will of the god." *Things Fall Apart,* 12.

50   Ofo is a wooden stick specially carved to serve as a staff of office.

51   Ilogu, *Christianity and Igbo Culture,* 18.

52   Ibid.

53   Ibid.

54   Nwala, *Igbo Philosophy,* 123.

55   Amadioha is the name for the Igbo god of thunder. This is the deity who is in charge of the domain of Power, involving thunder and lightening.

56   Chiagoro, interview.

57   Nwala, *Igbo Philosophy,* 125.

58   Ogbonnaya, "Chinua Achebe and the Igbo World View," 85.

59   G. T. Basden, *Niger Ibos* (London: Seeley Service and Co., n.d.), 55.

60   Ibid.

61   Ibid., 51.

62   Ibid.

63   Ogwugwu is an idol which is capable of imparting life.

64   Ibid.

65   Ibid., 52.

66   Ibid.

67   Ibid.

68   Okorocha, *The Meaning of Religious Conversion in Africa,* 18.

69   Ibid.

70   Ilogu, *Christianity and Igbo Culture,* 35.

71   Ibid., 34.

72   Ibid.

73 Ibid., 35–36.

74 Ibid., 49.

75 Ibid.

76 Ibid.

77 Ibid.

78 Ibid.

79 Ibid., 50.

80 Ibid., 115.

81 Ibid., 116.

82 Ilogu, 34.

83 Nwala, 116.

84 Ilogu, 34.

85 Imasogie, *African Traditional Religion*, 38.

86 Ibid., 39.

87 Nwala, *Igbo Philosophy*, 117.

88 Achebe, *Things Fall Apart*, 9.

89 Chiagoro, interview.

90 Ilogu, *Christianity and Igbo Culture*, 34.

91 William A. Haviland, *Cultural Anthropology*, 5th ed. (New York: Holt, Rinehart and Winston, 1987), 7.

92 Nwala, *Igbo Philosophy*, 28.

93 Ibid.

94 Ibid., 29.

95 Ibid., 11.

96 K. A. Busia, "Ancestor Worship, Libation, Stools, Festival," in *Christianity and African Culture* (Accra, Ghana: Christian Council of the Gold Coast, 1955), 19.

97 Parrinder, *African Traditional Religion*, 57.

98 Ibid.

99 Nwala, *Igbo Philosophy*, 119.

100 Ibid., 120.

101 Ibid.

102 Mbiti, *African Religion and Philosophy,* 9.

103 Nwala, *Igbo Philosophy,* 31.

104 Ibid., 30.

105 Ibid., 31.

106 Ibid., 33.

107 Charles Ok Onuh, *Christianity and the Igbo Rites of Passage: The Prospects of Inculturation* (Frankfurt am Main: Peter Lang, 1992), 58.

108 Ibid.

109 Ibid.

110 Ilogu, *Christianity and Igbo Culture,* 44.

111 Ibid.

112 Ibid., 46.

113 Ibid.

114 J. Carnochan and Belonwu Iwuchukwu, *An Igbo Revision Course* (London: Oxford University Press, 1963; reprint, 1976), 93.

115 Ilogu, *Christianity and Ibo Culture,* 47.

116 Nwala, 44.

117 Ibid.

118 Obiefoka E. Animalu, "Ucheakonam—A Way of Life in Modern Scientific Age," *1990 Ahiajoku Lecture* (Owerri, Nigeria: Ministry of Information and Culture, 1990), 2.

119 Bede N. Okigbo, "Plants and Food in Igbo Culture," *1980 Ahiajoku Lecture* (Owerri, Nigeria: Ministry of Information, Culture, 1980), 20.

120 Ibid.

121 Kolanut is the innermost seed of kola fruit. Kola trees, which grow mostly in the tropical West Africa, produce them. Kolanuts taste bitter and sour.

122 Carnochan and Iwuchukwu, *An Igbo Revision Course,* 83.

123 *Igo oji* means to pronounce blessing on the *oji* and its giver, and to present it to the ancestors and the gods for purification and consecration.

124 Ibid., 83–84.

125 Okorocha, *The Meaning of Religious Conversion in Africa,* 101.

126 Illogu, *Christianity and Ibo Culture,* 125–126.

127 Ibid.

128 Okorocha, *The Meaning of Religious Conversion in Africa,* 192–193. Ikenga is
     the most important of all Igbo "power cults." It is the right hand with which a
     person works out successful living in this difficult world. Ikenga is primarily a cult
     of achievement and has to do with the possession of *ike* (Power) which gives one
     the *nga* (drive or push) towards success and achievement.

129 Ibid.

130 Ibid., 183.

131 Ibid., 171.

Chapter 4

Introduction of Christianity in Igboland

During the mid-nineteenth century, Western Christian denominations began sending missionaries to Nigeria. Earlier, in 1485, Portuguese merchants had made contact with the Oba (king) of Benin, in the midwestern Region of Nigeria. Benin is now the capital city of Edo State. That contact opened the door for

> spasmodic missionary activities which started in Benin in 1551 when some Catholic missionaries set up a school in the Oba's Palace for his sons, and the sons of his chiefs who were converted to Christianity.[1]

This missionary endeavor did not endure long. The slave trade which ravaged West Africa dimmed the Catholic influence here. Also the Oba who was receptive to missionaries died about 1516. A less receptive Oba came into power. Consequently, the missionaries withdrew.[2] This was the first missionary effort in Nigeria.

The second missionary endeavor, which produced lasting results, began about 1842. This missionary enterprise involved the "big four," according to Babs Fafunwa. The "big four" missions in the Nigerian Christian world were: the Methodists, the Church Missionary Society (Anglicans), the Baptists, and the Catholics. Other groups which came to Nigeria were the Church of Scotland Mission (United Presbyterian); the Qua Ibo of Northern Ireland; the Primitive Methodist Missionary Society, and the Basel Mission, which had its first base in the Cameroons.[3] We will now examine the denominations and their work in Igboland.

Church Missionary Society

The first mission group to establish work in Igboland was the Church Missionary Society (CMS). The first efforts began in 1857 in Onitsha, through the leadership of Samuel Ajayi Crowther.[4] Crowther worked with Simon Jonas, Augustus Radillo, and J. C. Taylor, who were liberated Igbo men.[5] These men came from Sierra Leone, where they had settled following their liberation from slavery in Britain. The growth of the work was slow. However, these liberated Igbo men from Sierra Leone worked tirelessly under the supervision of Ajayi Crowther to make sure that the work did not die. These three men provided the leadership for the work of the Church Missionary Society (CMS) in Igboland for the first thirty years.

> The story of these first three decades was characterized by slow physical and numerical expansion. The mission founded eleven out-stations (including the Niger Delta stations) and could count on less than five hundred adherents in Onitsha which had an estimated population of between 10,000 to 25,000. These were also years of fighting for survival against adherents of traditional religion and against mercenary traders.[6]

Kalu observes that at this time, the relationship between the mission and adherents of Igbo indigenous religion "was ambiguous."[7]

> The royal court appreciated the political and economic benefits of the missionary presence. It was hard put to ensure that missionary propaganda did not disrupt local institutions and mores. Consequently, the traditionalists, acting in frustration, sometimes resorted to open hostility against the missionaries, even attempting to sack the mission headquarters.[8]

It took the CMS almost fifty years to come down to Owerri after they had established work in Onitsha in 1857. Thomas John Dennis began mission work in Owerri area in April 1905. Dennis (a British white missionary) and Alphonso Chukwuma Onyeabo (an Igbo catechist from Onitsha area) arrived in Owerri through Oguta. [9]

Before the CMS missionaries came, the colonial British government had established an administrative base in Owerri. The first District Commissioner was Harold M. Douglas (nicknamed "Udonglashi" by most illiterate Igbo). The Acting British High Commissioner in charge of Southern Nigeria was Leslie Probyn. Probyn, an Anglican, was the one who initiated the expansion of the CMS work from the Onitsha area to the Owerri area. Incidentally, most colonial administrators were members of the Church of England, which was the main denomination supporting the CMS work in Nigeria.

> In 1904, Mr. Probyn suggested to Bishop Tugwell of the Church Missionary Society (CMS) that Owerri might prove a possible centre of mission work. Coinciden-

tally, this came at a time the CMS missionaries at Onitsha were anxious to find a better place than Onitsha itself for the study of the Igbo language, and had also been desirous of producing a Union Version of the Igbo Bible which would be used all over Igboland. Probyn added in his report about Owerri that "the Purest Igbo was probably spoken in Owerri area."[10]

The people of Owerri received Dennis and Chukwuma Onyeabo warmly. Dennis took some time to visit Owerri township and the villages around it. He was impressed by what he saw, particularly the good network of roads, and the close location of the villages. He was also impressed by the people's friendliness, evidenced in the warm reception and hospitality which they received. Consequently, Dennis recommended Owerri to the London headquarters of the Church Missionary Society very highly. This first visit lasted six nights;[11] then he returned to England.

In November of the same year, Dennis, Tugwell, Onyeabo, and some others came back to Owerri to continue the evangelization of the Owerri area. Douglas received them warmly into Owerri. He had received Dennis and Onyeabo during their first visit.

Egbu, a village located about two miles south of Owerri township, was chosen as "the ideal place for the new CMS centre of operation"[12] in the Owerri area. On September 27, 1906, Dennis, T. D. Anyaegbuna (a translator) and A. C. Onyeabo (the catechist who later became bishop), arrived at Egbu, and began what was then called "The Owerri Project."[13] They took up residence in the palace of Chief Egbukole, the Eze (king) of Egbu. They stayed there for some time (their length of stay here is not documented) and then moved to "Ogodo," a place where Eze Egbukole gave them land to build and settle. It is pertinent at this time to state that the Eze's palace was their first place of worship in Egbu. Worship services were conducted here as long as the missionaries stayed in the palace. Egbu was also the place for the first translation of the Igbo Bible.

In Egbu, by the 30th of December, 1906, Archdeacon T. J. Dennis, assisted by Mr. T. D. Anyaegbunam, A. C. Onyeabo, C. Green, David Eze, Moses Ofodueme and others, started the translation of the union Igbo Bible, and in 1919, two years after Dennis' death, the Union Igbo Bible came out in print.[14]

As a tribute to Dennis, Archdeacon Dennis Junior Seminary was opened in 1979 at the spot where Dennis and his colleagues translated the Igbo Bible in 1913. J. C. Otu was the first principal of the school.[15] The school has since moved to Obazu in Mbieri Parish of the Diocese.

Dennis and his fellow missionaries, both foreign and indigenous, made Egbu their base of operation for the "Owerri Project." From Egbu, they traveled to the neighbouring villages, and presented the gospel. "Such travels within the district were made possible by the new roads which radiated from Egbu. Hence Dennis regarded Egbu as "an ideal centre for a vigorous itinerating work."[16]

In 1907, the first Anglican Church in Owerri area was built at Egbu through local labor and CMS financial assistance. The attendance at one of the early services in this temporary building was about four hundred.[17]

> This large crowd was a source of hope and encouragement for the missionaries. Even at these early times, the missionaries appreciated the behavior of the congregation, which they described as "a model in itself." Dennis reports to the CMS authorities in London: "I have never seen such reverence amongst heathens elsewhere as manifested here."[18]

In addition to building a house of worship, the CMS missionaries started primary school classes in Egbu in 1906.[19] The classes grew and CMS Central School, Egbu, was formally inaugurated in 1912. In 1919, the school became a standard—six primary school. Its first headmaster was S. Oranye from Onitsha.[20]

According to Ahumibe and Orisakwe, the production of future Igbo leaders in all spheres of life was one of the primary reasons for the establishment of the CMS Central School in Egbu. These leaders would support the cause of Christianity in Igboland. In 1905, the British colonial government established a primary school in Owerri. The school began with an enrollment of about ninety boys. These boys were mainly sons of chiefs and other important leaders of Igbo communities. The school authorities did not provide any curriculum for religious education. This development gave Tugwell great concern. He decided to establish a school where future Igbo leaders would receive not only secular training, but religious instructions also. This was the principal motive behind the founding of CMS Central School in Egbu. Two factors

> helped to influence the vigorous educational drive of the CMS in Egbu and environs. First, and most important, was the responsive nature of the people, particularly the boys, and second was the emergence of the Government Primary School in Owerri. Furthermore, there was the fact that government or mission posts such as those of clerks, interpreters and teachers were held only by Bonny[21] and Onitsha indigenes. This helped to spur the Igbos in Owerri District to pursue education vigorously.[22]

The CMS Central School Egbu grew and became the school for the entire Owerri Province. Pupils came to the school both from Egbu and other places in Owerri District. As a result, the school authorities provided boarding facilities for those who came from distant places. Those who could not get accommodation in the school dormitories stayed in private homes. Later on, the missionaries started a school for girls, the Women Training Centre in Egbu. The school's site is the present site for Egbu Girls' School. Miss Dennis[23] became the first head of the school. The main purpose for this school was to give "young women training in how to run Christian homes."[24]

The Church Missionary Society, during its early days of mission work in Igboland, had a vision and love for the training of future leaders for church and society. The indigenous leaders of the Anglican Diocese of Owerri have continued in that tradition. Theological training through Theological Education by Extension equips church teachers and some lay persons for local church ministries. The Owerri Diocesan Bible College is in charge of this training arrangement. The school's Board of Governors meets every year to approve seminars, seminar leaders, and seminar centers. Archdeacons and Parish priests serve as the seminar leaders.[25]

The work of the Church Missionary Society in the Owerri area of Igboland has grown so much that a number of dioceses have been carved out of the former Owerri Diocese. They include Orlu, Mbaise and Egbu. Egbu diocese was inaugurated on February 15, 1996.

Roman Catholic Mission

The Roman Catholic Mission followed the Church Missionary Society into Igboland. Onitsha was also the first port of entry for the Roman Catholic Mission (RCM). The Mission established its work on December 5, 1885. Father Lutz (C.S.Sp) was the first missionary. He said the first mass on December 25, 1885.[26] He had been a missionary to Sierra Leone. Joseph Shanahan was the first Catholic bishop in Igboland. He arrived in Onitsha in 1902 from Ireland.[27]

There is no available record concerning the exact date of the coming of Catholic missionaries to Owerri. However, by the second decade of the twentieth century, Shanahan and "his assistants were visiting places never before reached by Europeans in Owerri Province to the south, and Ogoja Province to the east."[28] The first mass in the Diocese of Owerri was said in Ulakwo (a village about three miles south of Owerri) before 1912. Again, there is no record of the exact date, or the person who conducted the mass. Owerri's first bishop was Joseph B. Welan (CSSP, 1949–1970).[29]

After making his tour of the hinterland, Shanahan decided in 1906 that a village school would be the key to Catholic expansion in Igboland.

He had studied the Igbo, and discovered their love for education, enlightenment and modernity. He also wanted to establish major centers of Catholic activity in certain strategic places. Owerri was one of his choices. Shanahan planned a central or standard six school for each of the centers, including Owerri.[30] The first Catholic primary school was founded in 1935 in Owerri township, The St. Paul's Primary School. It is now called Central School Owerri. Holy Ghost College Owerri, the diocese's first secondary school, was founded in 1949. Its first principal was Patrick MacMahon, an Irish priest. A school for girls was later established in 1965, Holy Rosary College Owerri. It is now called Owerri Girls' Secondary School. The change of name occurred in 1970.

Hilary C. Achunike lists I R A Ozigboh's categorization of the four-method approach to evangelization, which the Catholic Mission adopted in the nineteenth century.

1 The provision of medical services
2 The redemption and rehabilitation of slaves, social outcasts and the helpless
3 Education in literacy and vocational training
4 The deliberate play on the psychological and aesthetic susceptibilities of the evangelized[31]

The Catholics used all four approaches in Owerri area.

The Catholic Mission established its first hospital in the Owerri area at Emekuku, a village about five miles away from Owerri. The name of this hospital is Mount Carmel Hospital Emekuku. It was established in 1935. Mount Carmel Hospital is a center for the training of nurses and midwives. Since the establishment of this hospital, the mission has established other fine hospitals in parts of Imo State (former Owerri Diocese). The Mission has also established maternity homes, orphanages and other similar medical and social service institutions.

The Catholic Diocese of Owerri grew so fast that five other Dioceses in and around the former Owerri Province have come out of it. These are: Aba, Umuahia, Orlu, Okigwe and Ahiara.[32] The mother Diocese, which is now Archdiocese of Owerri, has 50 parishes and 148 priests. Of this number, there are only two foreign priests. Catholics constitute 507,658 out of a total population of 1,258,799. The Archdiocese has 113 Nigerian Sisters, 2 missionary Sisters, and 12 Nigerian Brothers. There are 152 major seminarians, and 9 Sisters in Formation in the Archdiocese. Anthony J.V. Obinna is the Archbishop.[33]

Baptist Mission

The Baptist work in Nigeria started with the arrival of Thomas Jefferson Bowen in Badagry on August 5, 1850. The Southern Baptist Convention, USA, sent Bowen.[34] For the next forty-eight years Southern Baptist missionaries did their work mainly in the Western part of Nigeria (Yorubaland). In 1890, William Hughes, a Baptist missionary from Wales, arrived in Buguma in the river area of eastern Nigeria. He found a small group of Christians and gathered them together for worship. Thus, he began his evangelistic work. He also opened a school. Hughes was not a Southern Baptist missionary.

Hughes did not stay long in Buguma before "he was forced" to return to Wales. We do not have any records of the reason(s) for his departure.

Before his departure he made contact with Mojola Agbebi[35] of Ebenezer Baptist Church in Lagos and encouraged Agbebi to oversee the work that Hughes was leaving. Hughes and Agbebi had been working together for four years on a plan to evangelize Africa. . . . Hughes knew of Agbebi's work in unevangelized areas.[36]

Immediately following the departure of Hughes from Buguma, Agbebi visited Buguma and organized the Christians there into a church. The church grew. Soon, the members of Buguma Baptist Church began to spread the gospel of Jesus Christ where ever they went. As a result, churches started springing up throughout the Niger Delta region of eastern Nigeria. Until he died in 1917, Agbebi aided and directed those Baptists who were spreading the Good News. Today many non-Baptists, who knew or heard about Agbebi's work in Buguma, still refer to the Buguma Baptist Church as Agbebi Church. Agbebi was a powerful preacher, a tireless evangelist, and a good administrator. He founded and organized churches in Buguma, Abalamo Okirika, Joinkrama, Rumodogo, Rumuji, Obogo, Abua, Okolobiama, Kunusa, Egbeama, Rumuche, Rumuakunde, Ibaa, Oduohan and Amegi before his death in 1917.[37]

The first place where surviving Baptist work started in the heart of Igboland was Ihiagwa, a village about one and a half miles southwest of Owerri main town. The year was 1917, and the work began through the instrumentality of J. T. Princewill. He later became the Amanyanabo (king) of Kalabari. Princewill was a member of Buguma Baptist church, and a trader in Ihiagwa. About 1913, a Baptist preaching station and school were started at Umunkugo, a village two miles from Imerienwe. This work was started by Atata George, a trader at Umunkugo, and a member of Buguma Baptist church. Mr. Orutari was the first teacher and pastor in that station. Unfortunately, the work there did not survive. There is no available written record about the cause for the extinction of the work. However, an oral source said that the two men who started the work here were demanding pay from the people of Umunkugo for the teachings they were receiving. Since the people could not pay, the work closed.[38] Agbebi died in 1917. Before he died, he obtained the consent of the elders of Buguma Baptist Church in 1916 to appoint Wariboko Animiyeomu George Amakiri, "the traveling agent for all the Baptist Churches and Schools in Buguma, Engenni, Abua, and Ikwerre area."[39]

In 1917, Amakiri attended the Baptist Theological Seminary in Shaki to be trained for ordination into the full gospel ministry. He finished at the end of the same year, and was ordained in 1918. He became the superintending pastor and manager of all the Baptist Churches and schools on the Niger Delta. Amakiri succeeded Agbebi as leader of the Baptist mission enterprise in eastern Nigeria, including Igboland. In 1918, he visited Ihiagwa and organized the church there. Commenting on this incident, Amakiri said, "Then I founded Baptist churches at Umuanunu (Obinze) and Ezeobo and in 1919 and in 1920 both churches were organized."[40]

Foundation members of Ihiagwa church were Messrs. Alfred Ekenwa and Peter Udokporo while those of Umuanunu and Ezeobo were Messrs. Nathaniel Achobuo and Ezekiel Nwosu respectively.[41]

At the beginning, the church at Ihiagwa experienced persecution from both the adherents of indigenous religion and members of some of the Christian churches already established there. The situation became so bad that a telegram was sent by the Baptist people of Ihiagwa to Agbebi in Lagos. Agbebi received this telegram on his deathbed. Since he could not go to Ihiagwa, he dictated telegrams and petitions to the Colonial Secretary in Lagos and the District Officer in Owerri Province, "requesting protection for the Baptist people in that area."[42] We do not have any records of the action of the two colonial officers whom Agbegbi petitioned.

From Ihiagwa, Eziobodo, and Obinze the Baptist work spread to other parts of Igboland. The work in Imerienwe began in 1947; Amaimo, 1947; First Baptist Church, Uwani, Enugu, 1950; Uvuru, 1952; Onitsha First, 1953; Ezumoha, 1956.[43] Other churches and preaching stations followed.

The first contact between the American Baptist Mission and the work in Eastern Nigeria began when Messrs. W. A. Amakiri and K. J. John Bull were sent from Buguma Church for training at Shaki. According to information, Dr. George Green was the first American missionary to visit Eastern Nigeria when he led the two ordained ministers (Amakiri and John Bull) to Buguma towards the end of 1917.[44]

R. L. Lock became the first resident Southern Baptist missionary in the Owerri area of Igboland. He arrived in Owerri in 1959, and started Owerri Baptist Church in his temporary residence. Earlier (about 1943) W. H. Carsons had visited Obinze to meet with the people of Obinze on the issue of the Baptist Day School.[45]

Those who brought the Baptist work to Igboland, came with the church and the school side by side. The first pastor of Ihiagwa church was also the teacher of Ihiagwa school. The same was true of Obinze and Eziobodo. "Before 1943, the Baptist school was a one-teacher school. The teachers who came were in charge of the schools and the churches."[46]

The Baptist Day School at Ihiagwa was the first Baptist primary school in Igboland. The Baptist Day School at Obinze followed it, and became a standard six primary school in 1946. The school grew rapidly; its growth influenced the growth of the church in Obinze. The church experienced tremendous numerical growth. Most students and teachers who made up the population of the school became attendants and members of the church. Later, the Baptist Preliminary Teachers' Center (PTC) was founded in Obinze, and was located close to the church site. This situation also helped to swell the population of the church.

The Baptist Preliminary Teachers Center (PTC) was founded in 1956. Its first principal was Mr. Ateh. He was a non-Igbo from Bonny in the Rivers. C. O. Osuamkpe succeeded him. Osuamkpe was also a Rivers man from Joinkrama. He was a diligent and dedicated Baptist teacher and manager of schools. The PTC was later promoted to Elementary Teachers' College (ETC) and then to Baptist Teachers' College (BTC). As Baptist Teachers' College, it was approved by the National Ministry of Education in charge of teacher education to award Grade Two Teachers Certificate. This college closed down in 1966 as a result of the Nigerian/ Biafran war. After the war, the Nigerian government took over all mission schools, but the Baptist Teachers' College was not re-opened. Obinze Girls' Secondary School is now occupying its site.

Education and Medical Services
The Baptist Mission moved slowly in Igboland, especially in the areas of education and medical services. Before the Nigerian civil war, there were only five primary schools in Igboland, all of them located in villages of the old Owerri Province. The schools were each known as Baptist Day School. They were Ihiagwa, Obinze, Eziobodo, Imerienwe and Uvuru. Baptist

Girls' Secondary School Enugu, was the only post-primary school in Igboland. It started in 1967, shortly before the outbreak of the Nigerian/ Biafran war. It lasted less than one year because of the capture of the city of Enugu by the Federal troops. The school never re-opened as a Baptist School. The Baptist Bible College, now at Obinze, began in Owerri in 1960. We shall say more about this school later on.

The only medical work in Igboland is the Baptist Dental Centre, which Dr. and Mrs. Wayne Logan started in Enugu in 1959. The center began with the Logans (SBC missionaries) and four Igbo men.[47]

The Formation of Animo Baptist Conference

Animo[48] Baptist Conference is the name of the organization which covers the Baptist Churches and Associations of Igboland. This name was chosen by Igbo delegates to the 1977 session of the former Eastern Baptist Conference which took place at Rumakunde Baptist Church in Ikwerre Association. The author was one of the delegates to this conference, and was also among those who chose this acronym for the new Baptist Conference.

Before this time, the churches in Igboland had met several times under the name, Igbo Area Baptist Union.

> Before the meeting at Rumakunde, we were feeling that our brothers from the Rivers were not giving us positions in the Eastern Conference, so at Rumakunde, we decided to form our own organization. We were already meeting as Igbo Area Baptist Union. But Dr. Ayorinde and Dr. Dahunsi who were the subsequent General Secretaries of the Nigerian Baptist convention, felt that Igbo Area Baptist Union was political. They wanted me to change this name. Then we chose ANIMO for our new Conference, and they accepted it.[49]

The Igbo delegates to the 1977 Session of Eastern Conference went home and reported to their churches what had happened at Rumakunde. The churches rejoiced, and an adhoc committee was called by I. B. Nwaosu for the planning of the first session of the new Conference.

With the theme "The harvest is plentiful" (Matthew 9:37–38), the first annual session of Animo Baptist Conference met at the First Baptist Church, Uwani, Enugu. The date was December 11–14, 1978. I. B. Nwaosu served as the Executive Secretary, while R. U. Nwakuna was the first chairman for the Conference. Gody Orjinta became the Recording Secretary. Dr. and Mrs. Emmanuel Ajayi Dahunsi (the then General Secretary of the Nigerian Baptist Convention) attended the conference. Others from Ibadan, headquarters of the Baptist Convention, who attended were: S. Ola Olaniyan, Mary Fox and K. Walker.[50] There were 142 registered messengers from the churches of the Conference, and four visitors.[51]

Since the inception in 1978 of the Animo Baptist Conference, four pastors have served as its Secretaries. They are I. B. Nwaosu (first Executive Secretary, and later called Conference Secretary), H. C. Igwe, (Dr.) C. A. Amadi and J. C. Onyenwe. Joel O. Akubuiro served as an interim Secretary during 1994/1995 administrative year. The Animo Baptist Conference is composed of 12 Associations, 137 churches, and 77 Pastors.[52]

Methodist Mission

There are different strands of Methodism in Igboland, especially in Owerri area. In this section, I will focus on two of them: the Primitive Methodists and the Wesleyan Methodists. The Primitive were the first group of Methodists to enter Igboland. They penetrated Igboland in 1910, and established a church in Bende. By 1913, when the construction of Port-Harcourt-Enugu railroad started, the Primitive Methodists took a decision to found a chain of churches along the railroad. They established churches in Uzuakoli, Umuahia, Ihubi, Ovim, and Udi area. In 1917 and 1925, they founded churches in Aba and Port-Harcourt respectively. Villages on both sides of the railroad desired the Primitive Methodists' work.[53]

Isichei states:

In 1923, they established an important training college and secondary school at Uzuakoli, but in the main they stressed evangelization rather than education, an emphasis inherent in the church's own history and origins.[54]

The work of this group remained in the Aba/Umuahia and Okigwe/Enugu areas for a long time. Records of its first entry into the Owerri area are not available and up until today its work in this area is minimal.

Thomas Birch Freeman, son of a Negro father and an English mother, was the first Wesleyan Methodist missionary to Nigeria. He arrived in Badagry on 24 September, 1842.[55] He was accompanied by William de Craft, one of the earliest educated Ghanians.[56] For more than fifty years, the Wesleyan Methodist Mission remained in the Western part of Nigeria. The work of this group is new in Igboland, especially in Owerri. However, some mergers took place between Primitive Methodists and Wesleyan Methodists. As a result, it is now difficult to identify one from the other.

Another factor which has compounded this problem of identity is the division that has become almost a way of life for Methodists in Nigeria, since the exit of their foreign missionaries. For example, there are two groups of Methodists in Owerri. Each of these two groups has a cathedral and a resident bishop in Owerri. Though these two have a common tie to the world of Wesleyan Methodism, they have two different names: the Methodist Church Nigeria and the Wesley Methodist Church.

Methodist Church Nigeria, Owerri Diocese, was founded on November 1, 1975. Ten people (six men, three women and one child) attended its first meeting. The church met first at Township Primary School, Owerri. It now has a permanent place of meeting at Aladimma Housing Estate, Owerri. Isaac O. Ugbaja was the first minister.

Wesley Methodist Church, Owerri was founded in 1976. Its founding pastor was N. N. Nkemakolam. He became the bishop of the Owerri Diocese of Wesley Methodist Church in 1985. The diocese has fifteen churches and twelve pastors. Its cathedral and bishop court are located on the same ground at Aladimma, Owerri.

The Presbyterian Mission

The United Presbyterian Mission (UPM) arrived in Calabar, Nigeria, in 1846.[57] Calabar is one of Nigeria's seaport cities in the southeastern section. Hope Masterton Wadell was the first Presbyterian missionary to Nigeria. Since its arrival, this Mission, now Presbyterian Church of Nigeria,

has had its main base of strength in Calabar and the Ibibio area. Its impact in Igboland has been highly localized to a number of centres in Ohafia, Abiriba, Arochukwu and the northeast, but within these areas its impact has been great, both in education and in the sphere of medical missions.[58]

The Presbyterian's pioneer missionary to Arochukwu was Mary Slessor, otherwise known as "the Lady with the Lamp."

The Presbyterian Church of Nigeria stayed in these areas of Igboland a long time, with no further penetration into other parts of Igboland. The primary reason for this was the agreement between the major Protestant missions in Igboland, following their 1909 and 1911 conferences on "missionary boundaries," because of scramble for converts.

The Church Missionary Society was to carry out its missionary work within Onitsha, Awka, Enugu and Owerri areas; Presbyterian Church to work within the present Cross River State, Akwa Ibom State, Arochukwu, Ohafia, Abiriba (Bende Division), Afikpo Division, Ikwon and Ezza; Methodist Church to work within Oron, Ikot Ekpene, Aba, Port Harcourt, Ndoro, Umuahia, Uzuakoli, Ovim, Ihube and Agbani. The Qua Iboe Church was to work within Qua Iboe River area. Despite this agreement most denominations intruded into districts and areas assigned to other denominations . . . , the Presbyterian Church still maintained the original agreement. This is why Presbyterian Church is seen as a later-comer, in the areas it is now opening churches.[59]

"Missionary boundaries" came up as a result of unhealthy rivalries between the C.M.S., the Catholics, the Methodists, the Presbyterians and the Qua Iboe. Each of these groups was vying for mission space, acceptance and converts among the Igbo. These missionary groups used schools and hospitals to lure the Igbo to their individual denominations. The Baptist Mission was not prominently involved in this scramble.

At a certain time the Qua Iboe mission protested to the Divisional Commissioner that the entire territory of the Qua Iboe River should be left to them uncontested by any other mission since they had started missionary work there 20 years before anybody else. Government replied them (sic) that a "policy prescribing separate spheres of influence to different missionary societies" had been adopted. When this policy could not stop complaints about encroachments, the different missionary societies met in 1909 to negotiate for missionary boundaries. . . . The missionaries realising the undignifying and non-biblical dimensions of the competition, made several efforts to delimit areas of operation for each denomination.[60]

The Presbyterian Church of Nigeria kept this agreement until late 1960s and early 1970s. About 1970, the denomination had established churches in port-Harcourt, Aba, Abakiliki, Omoba, Mbawsi, Umuahia, Enugu and Ehamufu. There was no Presbyterian Church in Owerri at this time, so Presbyterian members who were living in Owerri worshipped in other Protestant churches.[61]

On Sunday, January 25, 1976, the first church service in Owerri conducted in the Presbyterian order of worship was held in No. 50 Zander Street, the residence of Elder Agwu Ikwecheghe. He conducted the service and preached the sermon. Lessons were read from Joshua 1:1–9, and Matthew 4:12–25, while the text for the day came from Psalms 118:23, "This is the Lord's doing; it is marvelous in our eyes."[62]

Thus, the Presbyterian Church of Nigeria began its work in the Owerri area of Igboland. Thirty people (sixteen adults and fourteen children) attended that worship service. The church experienced growth from its inception, especially under the leadership of James Udogu Ukaegbu. "By the end of September 1977, the average Sunday Church service attendance rose from 30 to 130."[63] On Easter Sunday, April 6, 1980, the church moved to its permanent building in Aladimna, Owerri, after four years of worship inside one of the buildings of Township School Owerri. The Owerri Church became a Parish on October 19, 1980. During the inauguration of the new Parish, Rev. Ukaegbu was formally inducted the first minister of the Parish.[64] Today, there are six Presbyterian churches in their Owerri Parish: Presbyterian Church Aladimma, Owerri, Ogberuru, Orji, Amakohia, Owerri, Orlu and Atta.[65]

Pentecostal Churches

There are many Pentecostal churches in Owerri, both mission and indigenous ones. We will present a brief history of one of them, the Assemblies of God Mission.

Assemblies of God Mission (AGM)

The history of the Assemblies of God Mission in Nigeria goes back to the years between 1931 and 1935 when a group of young men and young women in Old Umuahia, Abia State, Nigeria, read various religious periodicals about the Baptism in the Holy Spirit in other parts of the world.

> They became convinced that the Pentecostal experience was for them too. Within a short while many of them were blessed with the Baptism in the Holy Spirit. They established a number of churches, calling themselves "The Church of Jesus Christ." At that time they were not affiliated with any overseas Mission. After much prayer they requested the American Assemblies of God to send them a resident missionary. In June, 1939, Rev. and Mrs. William Lloyd Shirer, a missionary in what was then called Gold Coast (Ghana) was sent to meet the few pastors and young men of "The Church of Jesus Christ." They worked out an agreement of affiliation with the Assemblies of God in Springfield, Missouri, USA and the "Church of Jesus Christ" was officially renamed "Assemblies of God". . . . Late in August, 1939, the affiliation agreement was officially sanctioned.[66]

Everest L. Philips, the mission's first designated missionary, arrived in Nigeria in February 1940. Then came other missionaries. They, together with local pastors, began preaching the gospel and planting churches in and around Old Umuahia in Igboland.[67] In addition to evangelism and church planting, they established a Bible School in Old Umuahia for the training of pastors. They also established a printing press in Aba, Abia State, for the printing of needed church literature, both for the Assemblies of God and for the churches of other denominations. The Central Bible Institute is now called Assemblies of God Divinity School of Nigeria. This school was established in 1940.[68]

The work stayed in and around Old Umuahia area until the late 1950s[69] when the church had its first contact with people in old Owerri Province. This church met first at Uvuru, Mbaise. A church was founded there, and G.O. Alioha was its first pastor. From here, the gospel was taken to other places in Owerri area, including Owerri township. The Owerri District of the Assemblies of God, Nigeria, was created in 1980. This district was carved out of former Northern Igboland District. The late A. O. Asonye was its first Superintendent.

Indigenous Churches

There are many indigenous churches (churches founded by Nigerians) in Igboland. The motives for the founding of these churches are mixed. Speaking on the issue of the proliferation of churches in Igboland, Steve Gbazie said:

> Two things are responsible for this. Number one is name and money. Some people want to make money with the Bible, as they hide under the umbrella of God's call. Eighty percent of them are not called. On the other hand, there are those who are called, like myself.[70]

Indigenous churches are a common sight in every community in Igboland. Their names range from one word to almost one paragraph. We will examine one of the first indigenous church movements in Nigeria, from its beginning and entry into Owerri.

The Eternal Sacred Order of Cherubim and Seraphim

The Eternal Sacred Order of Cherubim and Seraphim is an independent African Church movement.[71] Its founder was Moses Orimolade Tunolase, an illiterate man. He came from a royal family in Ikare, in the former Western Nigeria. In about 1919, he began visiting towns and villages in Yorubaland, in the midwestern part of Nigeria, and in the provinces of Northern Nigeria.

> He preached the Christian Gospel in these places and helped to establish churches in a number of them. In every place he stunned his audience with his very accurate quotations from the Bible, even though he could neither read nor write. Whatever converts he won through his preaching, he directed to the existing churches, and where there was no church, he organized his converts into a small congregation and named it after the predominant Christian denomination in the area.[72]

His evangelistic travel took him to Lagos in July 1924. He lived with the sexton of Holy Trinity Anglican Church, Ebute-Ero. At this time, T. A. J.

Ogunbiyi was the vicar of this church. He stayed in this place for only two months. The reason for his expulsion from the parsonage is not known. However, "Cherubim and Seraphim members have held that he was expelled because he was becoming more popular than the Vicar of the church in consequence of his efficacious prayers and his healing powers."[73] In June 1925, a young lady, Christiana Abiodun Akinsowon began experiencing regular "angelic visitations, and reported that the angel had taken her to distant places, . . . usually in the firmament in her sleep."[74]

These spiritual experiences culminated into a climactic one on 18 June, 1925 during a Roman Catholic Church celebration of "Corpus Christi."[75] On this day, the angel appeared to Christiana again and followed her home. One week after this angelic appearance, Christiana went into "a prolonged trance during which time she claimed she went with her angel friend to the Celestial City where she had several spiritual experiences."[76] When she woke up, she had a problem regaining full consciousness. Her aunt, Comfort, sent for Moses Orimolade to come and pray for Christiana.

> He prayed and Abiodum recovered full consciousness and related her experience of the "Celestial City" to those who had gathered there. The incredible stories caused much sensation and more and more people poured into her Sabo Court residence to see her and hear her stories first hand. . . . Here, Orimolade himself suggested to those who regularly called to see the young lady, that the group should be constituted into a formal society. He was concerned to find something that would keep the group together after the excitement might have cooled off. Thus, the nucleus of what became known as the Cherubim and Seraphim was formed. . . . On September 9, 1925, the young society was named "Seraph" by the Reverend James C. Barber of the United native African Church. The twin name "Cherub" was added later in consequence of a vision in which the leaders were instructed that the two names should go together.[77]

The Cherubim and Seraphim, Owerri Province was founded in 1956. Its first place of meeting was 32 Wetheral Road, Owerri. From a founding membership of 30, the church has grown to about 10,000 members in all of its churches in the Owerri Province. Its first minister was Apostle General Ibegi.

The Cherubim and Seraphim movement experienced tremendous growth from 1926 through 1929 under the leadership of Moses Orimolade and Christiana Abiodum Akinsowon. However, a quarrel arose between Orimolade and Abiodun. The cause of the quarrel is not documented. Abiodun broke away to form her own group.

Since Orimolade's death in 1932 there has been continuous division, until now the Secretary of the Nigerian Christian Council estimates there are over 200 separate orders (denominations) of the Cherubim and Seraphim with a combined total of over 2,000 local congregations.[78]

Cherubim and Seraphim members are found all over Nigeria, and other parts of Africa. Their white garments make them easily recognizable. The organization is indigenous to the core.

Other Christian Groups

Many other Christian groups exist in Igboland. Some of them are mission churches; others are indigenous. Evangelical Churches of West Africa (ECWA)[79] and Qua Iboe Mission are among the prominent mission churches in Igboland. Other groups include Faith Tabernacle Congregations, Seventh Day Adventist Mission, and Episcopal Zion Methodist Churches, Churches of Christ and Four Square Gospel Church.

Apostolic Churches, African Church, Deeper Life Bible Church and various kinds of Pentecostal indigenous churches exist in Igboland. Accurate statistics regarding the number of this group of churches are not available. The problem of obtaining accurate number of these churches is compounded by the current trend whereby divisions occur in them almost every day. New groups emerge continually under different names.

Scripture Union, Nigeria

The Scripture Union began in 1867 in England. Its original intent was to minister to children evangelistically. Later, it became a Bible reading movement. A young lady, Annie Marston, added this dimension to the organization. She saw the need to "follow up converts by teaching them to read the Bible in a regular and systematic way."[80]

The Scripture Union (SU) began in Nigeria in 1958, when John Dean[81] visited the Qua Iboe Church Teachers' Training College at Afaha-Eket and opened the first Scripture Union group in Nigeria. He opened other groups in parts of the East and West. In Igboland, he opened two main groups, one at the Methodist College, Uzuakoli and the other at Dennis Memorial Grammar School, Onitsha[82] In its early beginnings the organization worked very closely with mainline Protestant and Evangelical Churches. Clergymen from these churches were elected presidents and vice-presidents. Most General Secretaries of the organization have come from the churches. They include its first General Secretary, late Moses

Olagundoye; Folu Soyannwo, Mike Oye, Muyiwa Olamijulo; Usip S. Usip and Ralph C. Okafor.[83]

Scripture Union, Nigeria, Owerri Area

The exact date for the beginning of the Scripture Union in Owerri area is not known. It started soon after the Nigerian civil war,[84] probably 1970. "By 1975, a group was already meeting at Christ Church, Owerri."[85] Before the civil war, Scripture Union was a movement in the secondary schools. Students volunteered and constituted themselves into groups of "Bible readers." Normally Christian teachers served as their leaders. The Bible was their primary source of teaching. However, they also used some Scripture Union literature, especially the *Daily Guide*. At the beginning of this movement in Owerri area, especially after the civil war, people came to it from most Protestant churches in Igboland. A few Catholics identified with the group also. The Bible was the primary textbook for Bible study.

No denominational dogma was propagated and the group did not duplicate local church programs, except Bible Study. Christians were encouraged to continue to attend their own churches, and new Christians who had no church affiliation were urged to identify with a church of their choice. The organization saw itself as a helper and not a rival to the local church. Of course, at this time, the movement had spilled over to the communities from the schools. Adults, including craftsmen and craftswomen, traders, civil servants, teachers, professionals, and people from almost every work of life were coming into the Scripture Union.

One of the main reasons for this influx was the experience of the civil war. People lost loved ones. Property damage was enormous, and much was irreplaceable. Food was scarce; there were very few hospitals and medical clinics to take care of people's enormous medical needs. The local gods could not help meet these needs. Medicine men and women were unable to help. The One who helped was the Christian God. He did this through Christian relief agencies, via local churches. The immediate result of this situation was a strong zeal for God. We will say more about the work of the relief agencies in the next chapter. The war opened the door of evangelism to some members of the Scripture Union. People became sober and receptive to the message of God because of the experiences they were going through. For example,

There was one Bill Roberts, an SU official, who was based at Uzuakoli and was organizing guest services at Umuahia. He had the habit of moving in and outside Biafra at that time. This man managed to influence the lives of many Igbo men and women. The origins of "Born Again" and "Are you saved?" in Igboland were traceable to him.[86] He won some converts whom he named "Born Again Christians." This team moved from place to place winning converts. . . . Fear of not surviving the civil war made many open up their hearts to the Lord. A good number accepted Jesus as their Lord.[87]

The Scripture Union in Owerri township grew stronger, especially as a result of the creation of Imo State from the former East Central State. Civil servants moved from Enugu to Owerri. Teachers and students did the same. The coming of these people from the Northern part of Igboland, and even from other parts of Nigeria, helped swell SU membership in Owerri township.

Soon, the movement ran into trouble with the Anglican authorities in Owerri. The cause of this problem is the issue of infant baptism. The Scripture Union was teaching against it. Since infant baptism was an accepted practice in the Anglican Church, the Anglican authorities asked members of the Scripture Union to vacate their church property (Christ Church Owerri). They left, but had no place to meet. Their leaders at this time, among whom were Joe Iyama, Awa, and Emmanuel Okwa approached the Baptist Church. They met the pastor of the church, Basil Ibejiuba Nwaosu, and talked with him. He allowed them to use the auditorium and premises of the Baptist Church. This incident took place about the late 1970. The Scripture Union, Owerri township still meets in the facilities of First Baptist church today.

Scripture Union, Nigeria, has an Area Office in Owerri. The office is located a block away from First Baptist church. This Area Office serves the entire Imo State Zones. There are twelve zones in Imo State.[88]

The message of Christ was a welcome message to the Igbo right from the beginning. Though the first permanent mission in Igboland began in Onitsha in 1857, the history of the Christianization of Igboland dates back to 1841, when Simon Jonas, an Igbo liberated slave, "spent three weeks at Aboh, and preached to the children who flocked around him."[89] Since then Igboland has become a "melting pot" for all kinds of Christian congregations. However, the extent of the penetration of Christian tenets into the hearts and minds of Igbo Church-goers is still a matter for debate. Many objective observers of Igbo Christianity contend that Christianity has not truly become an authentic Igbo religion. This writer shares the same view. To justify this view, we will now explore how Christianity finds expression in Igboland.

Notes

1   A. Babs Fafunwa, *History of Education in Nigeria* (London: George Allen and Unwin, 1974), 74.

2   Festus Kunleola Babalola, "The role of Nigerian Higher Education Institutions in Preparation of Christian Religious Studies Teachers" (Ed.D. diss. Southern Baptist Theological Seminary, 1993), 53.

3   Ibid., 81.

4   Samuel Ajayi Crowther was a liberated slave of Yoruba origin, who in 1864 became the first Anglican Bishop of the Niger Diocese in Igboland.

5   Ogbu Kalu, *Christianity in West Africa: The Nigerian Story* (Ibadan: Daystar Press, 1978), 309.

6   Ibid., 310.

7   Ibid.

8   Ibid.

9   Chukwuma Ahumibe and Austin Orisakwe, *The Anglican Enterprise in Egbu* (Owerri: Upthrust Design and Print Unlimited, 1996), 14.

10   Ibid.

11   Ibid.

12   Ibid., 15.

13   Ibid., 15–17.

14   Ibid., 17–18.

15   *Outreach Newsletter*, vol. I (February 1979): 5.

16   Ahumibe and Orisakwe, *The Anglican Enterprise in Egbu*, 18.

17   Ibid.

18   Ibid., 18–19.

19   Benjamin C. Nwankiti, *The Growth and Development of the Church in Nigeria* (Owerri: Ihem Davis Press, 1996), 38.

20   Ahumibe and Orisakwe, *The Anglican Enterprise in Egbu*, 19.

21   Bonny is located in the former River State of Nigeria. The indigenes of Bonny are non-Igbos. Bonny is about 100 miles away from Egbu.

22   Ahumibe and Orisakwe, *The Anglican Enterprise in Egbu*, 19.

23   Miss Dennis was the sister of Archdeacon T.J. Dennis. She was nicknamed *Nwatoro* because she was small in stature and beautiful. *Toro* was the Igbo name for a tiny three penny British coin which was in circulation at that time.

24   Ibid., 20.

25   Diocese of Owerri, "Diocesan Bible College," in *Synod Report* (Owerri: the Church of Nigeria [Anglican Communion], Diocese of Owerri, 1984), 63.

26   Catholic Church of Nigeria, "Archdiocese of Onitsha," *1995 Catholic Diary and Church Directory* (Lagos: Catholic Press, 1995), 158–159.

27   Nkeiruka M. Nwagbo, "Missionaries and Educational Development in Owerri LGA Before the Government Take Over of Schools from the Missionaries," BA Thesis, School of Education, Alvan Ikoku College of Education, Owerri, in Affiliation with the University of Nigeria, Nsukka, Nigeria, 1989, 15–16.

28   Ibid.

29   Catholic Church of Nigeria, "Owerri Diocese," in *1995 Catholic Diary,* 201.

30   Nwagbo, "Missionaries and Educational Development in Owerri LGA Before the Government Take Over of Schools from the Missionaries," 16.

31   Hilary C. Achunike, *Dreams of Heaven: A Modern Response to Christianity in NorthWestern Igboland, 1970-1990* (Enugu, Nigeria: Snaap Printing and Publishing, 1995), 46.

32   *1995 Catholic Diary,* 204–221.

33   Ibid., 200–201.

34   Travis Collins, *The Baptist Mission of Nigeria, 1850–1993: A History of the Southern Baptist Convention Missionary Work in Nigeria* (Ibadan, Nigeria: Associated Bookmakers Nigeria, 1993), 6.

35   Mojola Agbebi was an indigenous Baptist preacher of Yoruba origin. He was a product of the SBC, USA.

36   Ibid., 40–41.

37   J. A. Atanda, *Baptist Churches in Nigeria, 1850–1950: Accounts of Their Foundation and Growth* (Ibadan, Nigeria: University Press, 1988), 261–268.

38   Ibejiuba Basil Nwaosu, President and Founder, Basil Nwaosu Evangelistic Association, Owerri, interview by author, 10 March 1997, Owerri, Nigeria, tape recording.

39   Atanda, *Baptist Churches in Nigeria: 1850–1950,* 276.

40   Ibid., 277.

41   Ibid.

42   Ibid.

43   Nigerian Baptist Convention, "Animo Conference," in *1995 Directory of the Nigerian Baptist Convention* 29th ed, (Ibadan, Nigeria: Baptist Press, 1995),161, 196, 217, 224; Atanda, *Baptist Churches in Nigeria,* 283.

44   Atanda, *Baptist Churches in Nigeria, 1850–1950,* 280.

45   O. A. Onyeagocha, Community Leader in Obinze, interview by author, 10 March, 1997, Obinze, Owerri, Nigeria, tape recording.

46   Ibid.

47   Wayne Logan, Retired Southern Baptist Missionary to Nigeria, interview by author, 19 April 1997, Mineola, TX, by telephone.

48   ANIMO is the acronym for Anambra, Imo and Ogoja. Anambra and Imo were two Political States of the Federal Republic of Nigeria existing in Igboland at the time this name was chosen. Ogoja, though geographically located on southeast of Nigeria has always been a part of the Igbo.

49   Ibejiuba Basil Nwaosu, interview.

50   Animo Baptist Conference. "Proceedings of the First Animo Baptist Conference held at First Baptist Church, Uwani, Enugu" (Enugu, Nigeria: Animo Baptist Conference, 11–14 December 1978), 2–3.

51   Ibid., 3.

52   *1995 Directory of the Nigerian Baptist Convention,* 94–225.

53   Elizabeth Isichei, *A History of the Igbo People* (New York: St. Martin's Press, 1976), 179–180.

54   Ibid., 180.

55   Fafunwa, *History of Education in Nigeria,* 79.

56   Ibid.

57   Chukwu Ogbajie, *The Impact of Christianity on the Igbo Religion and Culture* (Umuahia, Nigeria: Ark Publishers, 1995), 46.

58   Isichei, *A History of Igbo People,* 177.

59   Oji U. Oji, and others. *Presbyterian Evangelism in Imo State* (Owerri, Nigeria: Presbyterian Church of Nigeria, Owerri Parish, 1996), 8–9.

60   Ibid.

61   Ibid., 13.

62   Ibid., 14.

63   Ibid., 17.

64   Ibid., 20–21.

65   Ibid., 26–27.

66   General Secretary of the Assemblies of God, *Assemblies of God, Nigeria, Current Facts, 1994* (Enugu, Nigeria: Assemblies of God, Nigeria, 1994), 6.

67   Ibid.

68   Ibid., 29.

69   Records of the exact date of this contact are not available.

70   Steve Gbazie, founder of Arm of the Lord Ministry, Owerri, interview by author, 11 January 1996, Owerri, Nigeria, tape recording.

71   See J. Akin Omojajowo, "The Cherubim and Seraphim Movement—A Study in Interaction," *Orita*: Ibadan Journal of Religions 4 [2 December, 1970]: 124.

72   Ibid., 127.

73   Ibid.

74   Ibid., 128.

75   Corpus Christi (body of Christ). This is a festival which honors the Eucharist (Lord's Supper) on the first Thursday after Trinity Sunday.

76   Ibid.

77   Ibid.

78   John B. Grimley and Gordon E. Robinson, *Church Growth in Central and Southern Nigeria* (Grand Rapids: William B. Eerdmans Publishing Co., 1966), 307.

79   ECWA was formally called Sudan Interior Mission (SIM).

80   Chris I. Okeke ed., "The Bible Reading Emphasis of S. U.," *Plumbline*, Journal of the Pilgrims Ministry, SU (Nigeria) vol. 921 (1992): 45.

81   John Dean was the first S.U. Traveling Secretary in Nigeria.

82   Okeke, "S.U.—Handmaid of the Church," *Plumbline*: 35.

83   Ibid.

84   The war between Nigeria and Biafra lasted three years (1967–1970). This was a civil war between former eastern Nigeria, which was predominantly Igbo, and the rest of Nigeria.

85   Daniel Onwukwe, Senior Lecturer, Alvan Ikoku College of Education, Owerri, interview by author, 14 March 1997, Owerri, Nigeria, tape recording.

86   The author of this dissertation is a Baptist, and these terms, "Born again," and "Are you saved" were commonly used by Baptists and other evangelical churches in Igboland before the Nigerian civil war.

87   Achunike, *Dreams of Heaven*, 56–57.

88   Vincent Orih, Area Traveling Secretary, Scripture Union, Imo State, Owerri, in-
     terview by author, 23 January 1996, Owerri, Nigeria, tape recording.

89   Isichei, *A History of the Igbo People,* 160.

Chapter 5

Current Practice of Christianity Among the Igbo

This chapter will address the present condition of the church in Igboland, with particular reference to Owerri Igbo. We will use the findings of field research to assess the current nature of religious consciousness in Igboland. In presenting this, we will consider relevant historical events which contributed to the present state of Christianity in Igboland.

One of the striking things about the early Christianization of Igboland is the fact that the Igbo were receptive to, but suspicious of, the Christian faith at the beginning. The adherents of indigenous Igbo religion were suspicious of the new faith, and considered conversion to it an abomination to their belief system.

> Little progress was made through mere preaching. The natives resisted Christianity which they considered inferior to their native religion. Similar rejection attended all aspects of Western culture. Early converts were ridiculed and ostracised. Slaves and outcasts were the first converts.[1]

However, Igbo people did not kill foreign missionaries as was the case in some parts of the world. Before the missionaries came, most Igbo communities had contacts with white people by trade transactions; first "in ordinary mercenaries and later it extended to slave-trade."[2] Almost all the communities had been exposed to the European rule of law. There were already District Commissioners (D.C.s) serving in strategic Igbo locations, since Igboland was part of the British colony of Nigeria. Owerri is a good example of those locations.

> By 1900, . . . the British administrators had arrived in Owerri and had chosen the town as a garrison for the soldiers who carried out the Aro Expedition of 1902.[3] When this operation was accomplished, two companies of soldiers were

still left at Owerri to help Government control the area. Mr. Harold M. Douglas (Udongalash) became the first District Commissioner in Owerri, but the whole area of Southern Nigeria was under the Acting High Commissioner in Calabar, Mr. Leslie Probyn. And it was actually Probyn who brought the initiative for religious expansion to Owerri.[4]

The Christianization of Owerri Igbo began in the context of colonial control.

Following the success of this expedition, missionary activities in Igboland began in earnest. Penetration into the villages became easier, and many people began to request modern amenities from the missionaries. This situation afforded the missionaries opportunities to preach the gospel of Jesus Christ, and to help the people by establishing hospitals and schools. However, rivalry among major foreign mission agencies sowed the seeds of suspicion and discord among Christian converts. Denominationalism and the provision of social services rather than Jesus often became the primary issue. The aftermath of this initial sentiment still lingers with most Igbo Christians today. F. K. Ekechi observes:

> Perhaps without clearly distinguishing the doctrinal differences between the Catholics and the Protestants, and judging almost solely by results, many Igbo towns and villages seemed quite receptive to whichever Christian mission more readily provided school teachers to educate their children. . . . Roman Catholic preoccupation with reconverting former Protestants was indeed aggravating.[5]

While the early missionaries meant well for the Igbo through the propagation of the message of Christ, it is important to note that the spiritual benefits of their endeavors eluded many Igbo converts. As a result, the average Igbo Christian today still struggles with the existential implications of Christianity. There are beautiful church buildings all over Igboland, and people flock to these buildings for "worship." But the day-to-day lives of these people often betray the tenets of the faith they seem to hold so dear.

> The churches have not been the same . . . . , and the malaise in the church was a reflection of the deeper malaise in society, a society in which the basic ethics of morality have been trampled upon with impunity. If the churches themselves which are expected to stand guard over morality of their members found themselves so helpless, where was the salvation for society? It did seem as though many Nigerians have been paying only lip service to religion, preferring to ignore the tenets which ought to be the code of conduct for everyday life.[6]

The 1990 Imo State *Historical Handbook* states that more than 90% of the population of Imo State is Christian.[7] The question is, how did the compilers of this statistic come up with this staggering figure? And what is their definition for "Christian"?

These statistics seem to be based more on assumption rather than verifiable data. Again, the word "Christian" has been misunderstood by most of those who use it, especially secular writers. In most cases, they use "Christian" to mean all who attend one church or the other. Its biblical meaning, a follower of Jesus Christ whose life has been transformed to reflect the life of Christ, is rarely implied. This is one of the major problems of Christianity in Igboland. Orlando E. Costas identifies four major areas of holistic church growth:

1. Numerical: recruitment of persons for the kingdom of God by calling them to repentance and faith in Jesus Christ.
2. Organic: the internal development of a local community of faith.
3. Conceptual: the degree of consciousness that a community of faith has with regard to its nature and mission to the world.
4. Incarnational: the degree of involvement of a community of faith in the life and problems of her social environment.[8]

Costas argues that the saved, who constitute the church, should not only come to the church on Sunday. They should also give witness to others about their faith. Judging from the views of most of the people interviewed, along with the result of the survey forms, the lifestyle of many Igbo church-goers does not match with Costa's definition of church growth.

It appears that during the early Christianization of Igboland, missionaries emphasized charity, formal Western education, and Western civilization for communities more than they did the salvation of individual souls. Denominationalism was the major motive for the provision of social services, education and medical services. Both the Protestants and Catholics conformed to this initial practice. They each scrambled for people to fill up the pews in their churches, often neglecting essential Biblical teachings required for genuine Christian conversion.

> The medical care which the Catholic missionaries gave to the natives was by no means entirely without ulterior motive. Pruned of its humanitarian trappings, the dispersing of medicines and gifts was conceived to influence the people to the Catholic religion. Nor were medicines given to the sick without any obligation from the recipient. As a condition for treating the children, the missionaries demanded that they be baptized first. . . . The CMS became increasingly apprehensive of the effects of the Catholic charitable approach to evangelization. The offering of gifts and medicines to the Africans, they contended, was a calculated attempt to hire converts to their church.[9]

There is nothing wrong in using the avenues of charity, social services, education and medical services. The problem is the application of these avenues in the evangelization process. They should not serve as the end, but as means to the end—salvation of souls. The improper application of these avenues may explain the lack of spiritual commitment which one sees today in the lives of most mission-trained teachers, civil servants, and business people in Igboland. Much is still to be desired in the lives of these "converts." Many see the church as a social club which meets every Sunday, and the church building as a place where everybody "greets one another with, 'How's the car behaving"?[10] Many people in this category do not understand the difference between Western education and Christian conversion. They think that to be educated in the Western form is synonymous with salvation. In the early years of Christianity in Igboland, most missionaries used educated non-Christian members of their churches as Sunday School teachers, lay preachers, Catechists, and church officers. The primary qualification was the ability to read, write, and interpret for the missionaries. Isichei contends that "the Christianization of Igboland is a question of depth and sincerity," exhibiting a contradiction, involving fervency on one hand and lawlessness on the other.[11] She comments that

> The inconsistencies of the early Igbo Christians occurred in a context where the churches claimed much control, of a rather legalistic kind, over their members' lives, and where infringements were especially vulnerable to this kind of sanction. Too many of them, having cut themselves off from one world and being imperfectly accepted in another, were forced to live, in the imagery of the Onitsha Christians, in the air.[12]

These were some of the conditions which led Igbo Christianity to where it is today.

The state of Christianity today in Igboland is one of both joy and sadness. There is a special move of God in many churches. Spiritual renewal is taking place, and new churches are springing up as a result. On the other hand, greed, avarice and commercialism have given rise to the proliferation of churches and ministries. Most people who watch these two trends in Igbo Christianity are confused. They do not know whom to believe, what to believe, and where to go. Crusades, spiritual retreats, and Bible study sessions are conducted almost every day, everywhere in Igboland. This is especially true in Owerri.

> If we were to judge from the religious fervor we see around us, the number of people that attend church on Sundays and fellowships during the week, and the crusades that are conducted in and around Owerri in these later days, I would say

there is vibrant religious consciousness. . . . . At times I begin to question the validity of these crusades, and church attendances, whether really Christianity and the tenets of Christianity permeate into the consciousness of those who attend churches because we notice in Owerri now once it is 8 o'clock, people are afraid to come out. They are afraid to come out not because NEPA[13] is not on, or because any wild animal will devour them, but because they are afraid of their fellow human beings. There is hardly any night you won't have incidents of robbery in Owerri. . . . A round June/July of last year, there were so many kidnappings of children . . . some of the people who do these things or the people behind them, are not people who haven't heard the Christian message, but to put it directly, they are Christians. [14]

On September 24 and 25, 1996, many residents of Owerri took to the streets, protesting the strange happenings in Owerri. According to the Government White Paper on the disturbances, the following were immediate causes:

1. The beheading of Ikechukwu Okonkwo
2. The death of Innocent Ekeanyanwu in police custody
3. The Snake saga in Owerri[15]
4. The Exhumation of the headless body of Master Ikechukwu Okonkwo at Otokoto Hotel
5. The discovery of the roasted body of a human being in Damaco's[16] house.[17]

A very unfortunate aspect of the disturbances was an apparent involvement of one of the new Pentecostal churches in Owerri. The leaders of the church were accused of aiding and abetting fraudulent practices by "nouveaux riches."[18] They were also accused of ritual killing of human beings because of a television program in which the leader of the church, Overcomers Christian Mission, Alexander Ekewuba, showed a human skull on the television screen. In another incident involving this same church, a newspaper story, captioned, "Condom in Church," ran thus:

An Owerri-based Pentecostal church, razed down by irate youths protesting against ritual murders and advanced fee fraud ("419") last week, had a strange consignment in its sanctuary. Two cartons of condoms and two human skulls were allegedly raked up from the ruins of the church. The youths who were combing the hitherto quiet town of Owerri razed down the church when information reached them that the church was also involved in ritual killings.[19]

Today the average Christian congregation in Igboland is under serious scrutiny. Most people find it very difficult to trust church leaders because of the flamboyant life-style which many of these leaders exhibit. These leaders often show an intense craving for mundane things. They often take advantage of the credulity of the people, and in some cases fabricate false programs to extort money from their parishioners. Often by use of the Bible, they take undue advantage of their people's physical, emotional, economic and psychological needs. They promise to heal peoples' sicknesses, and bring them out of poverty. They promise children to barren women, husbands to spinsters, and employment to the unemployed. Unfortunately, they do not lay much emphasis on the salvation of individual souls. Eze Nnanna Oparaechekwe makes the following comments:

> Our people say, "as you grow, your ears widen." The type of Christianity we see in Igboland today is beyond our understanding. We do not know those who are telling the truth; we do not know those who are telling lies. As the English people say, "do not praise a newcomer until he shows you his attitude." This uncertain situation disturbs us. We are therefore tempted to say that our grandparents' religion (Igbo religion) is better than the so called Christian religion. Today, almost everybody wants his or her own church....We are confused.[20]

Christianity in Igboland is under fire. Since the end of the civil war, many strange things have happened. Prominent among those happenings are:

1. The emergence of Social Clubs (1970–). Social Clubs are social organizations which people form for their own benefits and those of their community. Most of these clubs engage in philanthropic activities, especially the development of communities through the provision of infrastructural facilities. They take care of the economic needs of their members by making job placement contacts for them and by giving out monetary loans to those who desire to go into business. However, many of these social clubs became avenues for easy money during the mid-1970s through the early 1990s. "Funeral Benefits"[21] became a phenomenon in these clubs.

2. Ogwu Ego (literally, medicine for money). The 1980s saw the beginning of this ugly trend in Igboland. Some misguided individuals were making use of magic and hypnotism to deprive people of their money and other material belongings. Some of those who performed these acts, dressed like pastors and priests. In most cases they used the Bible while they prophesied and prayed for their victims. The 1980s were difficult years for genuine pastors and priests because of the fraudulent activities of the "Ogwu ego" group.

3. The robbing of churches and clergy (1990–). Robbers have visited most churches and parsonages in Owerri area. They robbed, raped and brutalized individuals. As a result, terrible fear has gripped the entire province. The government of the day was apathetic to the situation. Little or no help came from law enforcement agents. Citizens became frustrated, dejected and helpless.

4. Advance Fee Fraud (419) became pronounced in the early 1990s. Those who were involved in this practice were also referred to as "nouveaux riches." Between 1993 and 1994 a group of young men who suddenly acquired enormous wealth in circumstances that were either unexplained or unexplainable thronged the capital city of Owerri with their wealth. Their activities were, however, not challenged and called to order by the authorities which ordinarily should challenge them. The result was that the group became emboldened, wild, unruly, lawless and started to intimidate, over-awe and torment the citizenry. For example, they lived such flamboyant life-style that were far out of tune and touch with the prevailing economic situation in the country. In most cases they drove in long convoys of flashy and expensive siren-fitted cars accompanied by uniformed policemen. They frequently terrorized law abiding citizens by shooting indiscriminately into the air....The activities of this group were watched by people in agonizing and painful mood.[22]

5. 1994 saw the kidnapping of children. Kidnapping incidents within the city of Owerri between 1994 and 1995 were not taken seriously by the police. The period of the tenure of the former Police Commissioner in the State, Mr. David Abure, was the most offending period when the activities of the group were at their peak. The police under his command either connived with the fraudsters or refused to act in spite of public outcry.[23]

6. The sixth thing that has happened in Igboland since the end of the civil war is the proliferation of churches and para-church groups. The changing roles of secular musicians has become a part of this phenomenon. Many musicians have become "converted" to the Christian faith because "Christian music" has become popular and lucrative.

Eze Oparaechekwe believes that greed is the reason for the proliferation of churches and ministries. He also holds that position-seeking is another reason for the multiplication of churches. Akagha attributes the proliferation of churches to the present hard economic situation in Igboland.

He states: "These churches springing up are not really churches. They are associations where people make money. Money is the motivating factor."[24] Eze Eric Osuji pictures the nature of Christianity in Igboland as "water which is ready to spill away because money has become the motive for every venture, even the founding of churches. Money has become our people's god."[25] He laments the lack of justice in most indigenous courts and the way kings, chiefs and respected community leaders now pervert justice in order to acquire enormous wealth. He asserts that unfortunately, most of these people are prominent church people.

Survey Results

The writer distributed 400 survey forms regarding the state of Christianity in Igboland to the clergy and members of various churches and ministries in Owerri Province (see appendix 1). Two hundred fifty people returned their forms. Their response to the questions in the form were varied and interesting. It seems clear that each respondent acted alone. There appears to be no group consultation involved, and there was no consensus among members of the same church or ministry. Though the forms asked for some information regarding denominational affiliation and local church responsibilities, the main thrust of the survey was to discover how independently Igbo Christians think and act. The result of the survey does not reflect responses along denominational lines. They do reflect how the Igbo, as a people, view Christianity and its practice in Igboland. Of the 250 forms returned, 170 (68%) respondents believed that most Igbo church-goers do not understand what it means to be a Christian; 75 (30%) believed that Igbo church-goers understand, while 5 (2%) had no opinion. Responding to the question about the effect of integrating any part of Igbo culture into the church, 145 (58%) said it will negatively affect the essence of the Christian faith; 100 (40%) said it will not, while 5 (2%) expressed no opinion.

The Igbo Church Today

This section will highlight the current status of the churches of Igboland. Churches in Igboland interact, forming national and international associations with other churches. It is pertinent to observe that most Igbo churches reflect their counterparts in other parts of the world. At the beginning, the mission churches tended to be more concerned with institutional development than individual evangelism. On the other hand, indigenous churches made prayer, healing and simple evangelistic preaching the mainstay of their religious life. The mission churches have deep roots in Euro-American culture, while indigenous ones see great value in the Igbo culture and endeavor to create an indigenous Christianity.

In recent years the trend in most Christian communities has been moving toward interaction and acceptance instead of distance and hostility. Most mainline churches are now prepared to interact positively with Evangelical, Pentecostal and indigenous groups. The reverse is true also. Associations, such as Christian Council of Nigeria (CAN) include almost every Christian church in its membership. The Christian Council of Nigeria admits all mainline Protestant, Evangelical and almost all other willing Christian groups. While interaction and cooperation is commendable, there have been a few problems and challenges emanating from it. The most significant issues are: the emergence of splinter groups from mainline churches, Charismatic and Pentecostal tendencies in non-Pentecostal churches, and doctrinal conflicts.

Charismatic and Pentecostal trends have gradually become important parts of the worship expression of most mission and indigenous churches in Igboland. The indigenous consciousness and the pressure towards greater contextualization have helped to foster this trend.

The first Pentecostal forms of Christianity in Nigeria appeared rather more than fifty years ago, in the form of spontaneous and independent prophetic or "spiritual" movements in communities where non-Pentecostal missions had already planted churches. It was not till 1932 that a Western Pentecostal church established mission work, so that the first developments were peculiarly African in form and local in origin. Like their Western counterparts, they were both revivals within and then reactions from older African churches which had no special Pentecostal emphasis.[26]

Nigerian Pentecostalism is not necessarily the same as its Western counterpart. Also, it is not congregationalist. There is far less interest in millennial adventism, and it does not tend to lay much stress on personal holiness. However, there is a great emphasis on "believers" baptism by immersion, the importance of prayer, and above all the presence and power of the Holy Spirit made evident in charismatic gifts and visible signs and results.[27]

The Charismatic movement in Nigeria began during the early years of the 1970s. This time marked the beginning of a vigorous Christian awakening in Nigeria.

Charismatic churches have attained much social prominence in Nigeria because of their adroit use of the media, the attention to them by the secular media, and their attracting a large membership among educated youth. Today, Charismatic Christians are the most dynamic element in Nigerian Christianity, affecting millions of educated young people.[28]

The Nigerian Charismatic[29] movement does not share the same roots with its Western counterpart. While the root of Western charismatic movement is the 1906 Azuza Street revival in Los Angeles, USA, the Nigerian expression has an indigenous origin.

The pioneers and early leaders were Nigerians without any previous contact with American Pentecostalism. Nigerian charismatics share similar doctrinal emphasis and practices like baptism of the Holy Spirit, speaking in tongues, and healing. In addition, the mass media, charismatic literature, and the common use of the English language have helped to forge close links between the Western and Nigerian movements. Nevertheless, the Nigerian movement is essentially indigenous, and it has succeeded in adapting the Pentecostal faith to the Nigerian contemporary milieu, thus making it contextually meaningful.[30]

Matthews A. Ojo recognizes the influence of two international Christian organizations, the Student Christian Movement (SCM) and the Christian Union (CU), on the emergence of the Nigerian Charismatic movement. Before the 1970s, these two organizations were well-established in most educational institutions in Nigeria. The Student Christian Movement and the Christian Union entered Nigeria between 1937 and 1955, mainly from Britain. "It was among these students, already exposed to liberal and conservative evangelical Christianity, that the charismatic revival gained root."[31]

This Charismatic consciousness led a small group of student members of the Christian Union at the University of Ibadan to claim baptism of the Holy Spirit. They made this claim in January 1970 after they had had some contact with a Pentecostal church in Ibadan. They also spoke in "tongues." In May 1970 these students established a new group and named it World Action Team for Christ (WATC). The aim of this organization was to spread Pentecostal beliefs throughout Nigeria. In about five years, the charismatic revival which began at the University of Ibadan assumed national scope. One reason for this spread was the efforts of the WATC. They went everywhere in Nigeria, "organizing evangelistic outreaches and mobilizing students for evangelism."[32] By 1975, all the six Nigerian universities at the time felt the touch of the revival. The University of Nigeria, Nsukka[33] was one of the universities where this revival took place. The Nigerian charismatic movement started as an indigenous initiative. In 1972, the influx of free American Pentecostal literature helped to alter certain aspects of the indigenous charismatic revival, and also introduced new dimensions. "Nonetheless, the charismatic organizations remain clearly indigenous because they are evolving new traditions of Christianity contextually relevant to contemporary Nigeria."[34]

The winds of Pentecostalism and the Charismatic movements are blowing very hard in almost all the churches in Igboland. While the majority of Pentecostal churches promote these movements, few orthodox and evangelical churches accommodate them. There is an exceedingly strong emphasis on speaking in tongues and divine healing. The movement has seen a startling proliferation of churches and ministries. Most of those who establish these organizations take on titles such as "President, and Overseer;" "Founder and President," "Apostle," or "Bishop."

> What happens today is that once an individual discovers God's gift in his life, he will begin to build his own ministry around that gift, and will begin to gather people who will support him. People are running after signs and wonders, and because of this charismatic expression, people gather easily around the charismatic leader. . . . There are also personality problems associated with this proliferation phenomenon. Some individuals find it difficult to humble themselves under others. They want to be heard and be known, so they branch out and form their own. . . . There is also the current emphasis on social status. People who never went to secondary school want to become Reverend Doctors. They will just go to one hotel in Lagos[35] and buy this thing, and will start to answer Rev. Dr. . . .[36]

The church has become big business in Igboland. Many of those who establish churches and ministries of their own look for international connections with Western Christian organizations. While a few of those who affiliate their churches or ministries with foreign Christian bodies have good intentions for the spread of the gospel of Jesus Christ among the Igbo, it would appear that many of them look for these affiliations to provide personal material gain. This is a disturbing trend, and many well-meaning Igbo Christians frown at this fraudulent practice.[37] The average Igbo man or woman is enterprising. Normally, the Igbo person is industrious, and loves to be self-supporting. Individuals support themselves, and communities embark on self-supporting civic ventures. They do not necessarily depend on the government. These same self-supporting individuals and communities tend to have a different view of the church and its activities. At the beginning of Christianity in Igboland some communities built buildings, both for Christian worship and for schooling and then invited the Christian missions to take over and administer worship and education. Most of the early Igbo seekers of Christianity paid their church and school teachers out of their meager agricultural incomes. They did this proudly.

Unfortunately, the tide has changed. Today most people desire what the church will do for them, and not what they will do for the church. It is difficult to offer an adequate explanation for this change of attitude, but the civil war is a factor. The Igbo lost a great deal of their "Igboness" in the trauma of that war. As a result, some of their cherished values, such as self-pride, were damaged or destroyed. For the first time in their history, the Igbo depended on handouts from Christian and humanitarian relief agencies for survival. The war deprived them of their farmlands. Schools were closed. Their young men were drafted into the army. The sick, the elderly and the women were left alone to fight hunger and disease. Many young women became widows because their husbands were killed in the war. Prostitution became rampant in places where it had never been practised. The established churches had little or no power over their members because of the effects of the war. Many of the churches met under trees and bushes for worship because of the fear of bombardments. The few which met in their normal places of worship did not have most of their members because of frequent movements.[38]

> Before the civil war the established churches had attained stability but they began to lose grip of their members who moved from one town to another due to the pressures of the war. There were many refugees in this war period. Many people went into hiding in the thickets. Thus hardship, social tensions, dreadful sicknesses like kwashiorkor, refugee lifestyle and psychological problems which the mainline churches could not offer solutions[39] to, diverted the response of many Igbo towards the Aladura churches and prayer houses which were springing up at an alarming rate at this time; and promised to offer solutions to some of the problems mentioned above.[40]

Though the leaders of the Aladura churches and prayer houses established their centers of worship close to most refugee camps, they did not necessarily outdistance the leaders of the established churches in the work of evangelism. Baptist groups conducted evangelistic outreaches from one safe town to the other. Basil Ibejiuba Nwaosu was the recognized leader of the Baptist people of Igboland at that time. J. B. Durham directed the relief efforts of the World Council of Churches (WCC). He was a Southern Baptist missionary to Nigeria. The Catholics, the Anglicans and a few other churches were also meeting people's physical and spiritual needs through the distribution of relief materials and evangelistic efforts.

The Baptist people of Igboland did not rest during that war. They went from village to village, distributing relief materials, building sick-bays, and establishing churches in many villages. These efforts resulted in more than 100 new churches. The International Red Cross Society was a major relief agency during the war. The International Red Cross, Caritas and the WCC worked together to supply the people of Biafra with food, clothing, drugs, and in some cases, shelter. God kept the Igbo nation through the war. They lost the war, and many of them felt disappointed in God. Some of these felt from the beginning that God was not on their side. However, they did not stop worshipping Him. They held on to their Christian faith. Achunike asserts, "Becoming a Christian is one thing and responding meaningfully to Christianity is quite another."[41] While it is encouraging to hear that Igboland is a melting-pot for all kinds of Christian expression, it is equally important to examine the authenticity of these groups.

A close examination of the religious behavior of Igbo Christians will show that the mainline mission churches are the ones which have maintained established liturgical and doctrinal structures. They operate with constitutions and by-laws, and tend to appoint their leaders through committees, based on genuine call of God. They do not normally have self-appointed leaders, and power is not concentrated in the hands of one person. On the other hand, most of the new churches and ministries are a "one person show." Some of them run as a family business, and the bulk of the membership does not participate in decision-making. They generally have no set doctrinal affirmations and no strong constitutional guidelines for both the leaders and the members. The Holy Spirit is made responsible for everything that happens. "I am led by the Holy Spirit to . . ." is a common refrain.

God's Children Fellowship Ministry is a vivid example of these new movements. *Beaton,* an Owerri-based newspaper, reported a situation in this church under the heading: "Trouble in Bro. Peter's Church? Mis-use of Church's fund alleged; accused of using 'juju' (conjuring medicine or magical power); and on war path with trustees." Peter Ozigbo of Owerri, leader of this church, was interviewed by *Beaton.*

> On the allegations that he was running the church as his personal property, Bro. Peter said, "If I have 100 buildings, it is nobody's business. It is to the glory of God. Whether I am running my fellowship as personal property, it is not anybody's concern. I am not subject to anybody's scrutiny."[42]

However, the more established churches have their own problems too. These include leadership rivalry, embezzlement of church funds, marital infidelity amongst leaders, and the tendency towards accommodating popular culture. In most cases, unhealthy rivalry among the clergy results in polarization of membership support. Leaders mount heavy campaigns for ecclesiastical positions. For example, the issue of successors to pastors, priests, bishops, Moderators, General Secretaries or Executive Secretaries, has led to all kinds of strife, divisions and in some cases open fights among the various churches. Some church leaders have been accused and found guilty of using church money for their private businesses.

> It is not something new. In the past and recent times, churches of God have turned themselves into a babel of tongues; as they are engulfed by ecclesiastical feuds. Sad enough, these ecclesiastical feuds are now causing serious cracks in the walls of many churches. Some years ago (1976 precisely) the introduction of the Patriarchal constitution in the Methodist Church of Nigeria which set the retirement age of the Patriarch at 70 caught the late Patriarch, Prof. Bolaji Idowu in a web of controversy with the radical members of the church.

> After his retirement, two leaders emerged to succeed him: Sunday Mbang from the Patriarchal fold and Adeolu Adegbola from the laity. Other churches had in the past, passed through the agonising experiences. The Anglicans have had leadership crisis many of which resulted in court cases. The Cherubim and Seraphim, the Bapitst, the Catholics had, at one time or the other, had this baptism of crisis.

> Today, the story is not different. Churches which are supposed to be the house of God have been turned into the house of discord. . . . If the church leaders are now involved in the scramble for wealth, what lesson do they have to teach their followers...?[43]

In some cases, they co-opt some of the most influential and outspoken members of their churches. As a result of their involvement in these vices, they become morally and spiritually incapacitated. They cannot condemn sin any more. They cannot play the role of "Odoziobodo," one who shapes society and keeps it morally pure.

The picture is not totally bleak for the church in Igboland. However, there is a serious and unfortunate situation, a lack of moral and spiritual authenticity in many churches. There are many Igbo who have had genuine personal encounters with Jesus Christ. These are living their lives, based on their understanding of Jesus as their Savior. On the other hand, there are too many who do not personally know Jesus, though they attend church. In some cases, the church makes it difficult for this latter group to know Jesus, because the church has failed to use the Bible as the basis for moral and spiritual conduct. Situation ethics has gained influence, and many people feel free to behave the way they like, provided they feel happy.

Materialism has raised its ugly head in the churches today. One can observe flamboyant and very expensive weddings and funerals which some church leaders permit. The indiscriminate conferment of chieftaincy titles[44] has become a common practice among many Igbo communities. The church has knowingly or unknowingly given its approval for this practice by participating in services of "Thanksgiving and dedication" for title-holders. Most of these title-holders donate large sums of money to the church to show appreciation. Some of those who receive these titles are not Christians; but because the church conducts services of Thanksgiving for them, most have the impression that they are Christians. In most cases, these services are conducted inside the church building on Sunday mornings. The celebrants normally invite their relations, friends and well-wishers to the church. In the presence of members of the church and the invited guests, they announce special donations for the church. In some cases, the motive for these donations is to buy the pastor's conscience, so that the pastor will not condemn their sins. Achunike writes,

> We have a big problem to solve and it borders seriously on morality. Money and what money can buy continues to dominate minds and hearts . . . Squandermenia at celebrations is a problem in Nigeria. Nigerians also invest their money in expensive cars, summer holidays in Europe or America for the whole family, and social club epicurean sessions. . . . The total disregard for uprightness in our society which has enthroned wealth by all means is quite worrisome to me. Thus, not only are those who defraud our public treasuries honoured, even robbers and drug barons are able to buy respectability. Rampant corruption and get-rich-quick mania therefore have become cankerworms in all spheres of our national life.[45]

Achunike calls on the church to face "this national malaise headlong." The church must begin this work now. The church must make its members hold tenaciously to the principle of wrong and right in human affairs and recognize the enduring Christian values, of honesty, truth, personal integrity, neighborly love, kindness, simplicity, poverty of spirit and humility.[46] What is the nature of the church relative to materialism? Achunike answers with reference to the Catholic church,

> Sodalities and societies in the Nigerian church today—knights, papal and non-papal, youth and women's organizations of kinds and colours, the lifestyle of the clergy of all ranks—have long assumed a materialistic outlook; even prayer and healing houses tend to be very much materialistic and worldly too. This is merely to establish the fact that this great plague of low, secular moral standards in our values has invaded the very lifestyle of the church in Nigeria. . . . Materialism

is dangerous. It can wreck an entire nation. It had done some damage of great magnitude in Igboland.[47]

The Catholic Church is not alone. This cankerworm of materialism has also affected Protestant, Evangelical, Pentecostal and indigenous churches in Igboland.

While great problems face most Christian churches of Igboland, it is also encouraging to know that some are designing programs and activities to address these issues. The adequacy of these programs remains uncertain. Let us briefly look at a few of them.

Evangelical Movements

Evangelistic organizations and independent churches are the two main groups which have emerged out of mission churches in Igboland, as a reaction against the probable coldness and deadness in these churches. The Evangelical Fellowship of Anglican Communion (EFAC) and the Catholic Charismatic Renewal (CCR) are the two most prominent examples of evangelistic organizations within the mission churches. Each of these organizations emphasizes Bible study, religious rallies, holiness and the expression of charismatic gifts within the established church. Dan Onwukwe, D. Nkachukwu, and Joe Anyanwu began the EFAC organization at Christ Church, Owerri, in 1981. They initially called it Anglican Christian Fellowship, but changed the name to Evangelical Fellowship of Anglican Communion about 1985. At the beginning, EFAC encountered difficulties with the heirarchy of the Anglican Church. The organization intentionally or unintentionally encouraged splinter groups and fragmentation within the church by carving out a "kingdom for themselves without reference to church authority."[48] In the Catholic church, the charismatic Renewal is less than welcomed by church authorities. While some charismatics are loyal to the church, some are disobedient.

> Some charismatics indulge in excesses, and criticize the doctrines of the church, Mariology and the sacraments...some charismatic Movements are loyal to the churches and need genuine and proper direction.[49]

This need for proper direction necessitated a statement from the Catholic Bishops' Conference of Nigeria.

> On 22 February, 1986 the Catholic Bishops' Conference of Nigeria issued a document signed by Bishops G. G. Ganaka and E. S. Obot outlining some directives on how the Charismatic Movement must be operated within the Catholic Church in Nigeria. It has eleven points. The first point reads . . . "No Catholic

Charismatic Renewal group should operate in Nigeria without a chaplain appointed by the Bishop of the Diocese." In 1991 the same Catholic Bishops' Conference of Nigeria published the Guidelines for the Catholic Charismatic Renewal of Nigeria.[50]

One of the Catholic Renewal movements in the Owerri Dioceses has become a separate entity. Its new name is Catholic Watchman, and it has no ecclesiastical or organizational ties with the mainline Catholic church. Its mode of worship is totally different from the traditional Catholic Mass. It operates more like an independent evangelical organization.

Baptist, Methodist, Presbyterian and Assemblies of God churches have evangelistic groups within their churches. However, the groups in these churches are not as confrontational to their church leaders as the Anglican and Roman Catholic Communities. For example, First Baptist Church in Owerri has an evangelism committee which plans, oversees, and supervises evangelistic programs for the church. The Church's Youth Fellowship is very active in evangelism geared toward church growth. This church has a prayer band, which is open to everyone, even non-members of the church. The pastor of the church supervises the activities of the Prayer Band and makes sure that the group functions well, and in accordance with Biblical injunctions.

The Second Category (independent churches) comprises groups of individuals who pull out of their churches and denominations and form themselves into separate churches and denominations. Most of these churches emphasize prayer more than other components of the Christian life. They practise healing and engage in simple evangelistic preaching, adopting the style of verse-by-verse interpretations most of the time. Making Christianity relevant and meaningful to the Igbo is the main goal of these indigenous groups. However, the realization of this goal appears uncertain.

Outreach Programs
Almost every church in Igboland engages in one kind of outreach program or another. These programs include street preaching, market Bible study and prayer, student holiday programs, crusades, prison ministry, and many others. During the civil war, many churches helped the International Red Cross Society, Caritas and the World Council of Churches to distribute food, clothing and other needed materials to the needy. The war adversely affected most residents of Igbo towns and villages. This situation paved the way for churches to meet the material needs of people, and at the same time share with them the gospel of Jesus Christ. The churches took the food, the clothing and the gospel to homes and refugee

camps. They also used town halls and village squares as centers for food distribution and gospel proclamation. This practice helped to intensify the efforts of the churches which normally embarked on outreach programs, and opened the evangelistic eyes of those which were apathetic to evangelism and missions.

Many mission groups helped the refugees, both during the war and after the war. Missionaries and nationals teamed up to minister to people's needs. For example, the Baptist denomination's pastors and missionaries worked with refugees all over the eastern part of Nigeria. During the war they were distributing food and clothing and were also attending to the medical needs of the people. After the war, they helped to transport refugees to their villages and also helped to settle them in their homes. Most of them had lost their homes, their farm crops and other essentials. Robert Williams was the first Southern Baptist Convention missionary to work in the Owerri area after the war. He worked with the International Red Cross Society. He stayed about six months, then left. Emogene Harris[51] was the second SBC missionary who came to Owerri. At the time, she was living in Port-Harcourt, a city about 80 miles west of Owerri. During the early months of 1970, she would visit the Baptist people of Igboland, attend their Igbo Union meetings, and encourage all who were recovering from the effects of the war. She visited people in their homes, and gave gifts of money and material things to those in need.

These efforts by mainline churches helped to light the fire of evangelism and church planting in Igboland immediately after the war ended. During the war

> Darkness rolled, tears flowed, widows mourned, old men moaned, young men groaned, children died, evil danced. Brother rose against brother. . . . The dying children cried, "God save us." The weeping widows cried, "God help us." Old and young alike cried unto God for His salvation. And from a distance the Lord looked down with pity upon the affairs of men in that part of the world and He sent Revival![52]

That revival began in 1970 and its ripples have continued till today. It resulted in the multiplication of churches and ministries. While most of the churches which were established as a result of the revival are Pentecostal and Charismatic in form and style, a few are Evangelical. Still, the ideal of authentic Christianity remains a distant hope. Most of the leaders of these new groups preach like Euro-American evangelists and preachers. They depend heavily on foreign Christian literature and tracts for their evangelism and Bible Study. They solicit for and, in most cases depend on, foreign financial support for their programs. A majority of these leaders neglect sound theological training because of the "anointing of the Holy Spirit."[53] This situation has led to near anarchy and confusion in the practice of Christianity in Igboland. Non-Christians listen to many preachers on the streets and on crusade grounds, but often find it difficult to make a genuine decision for Jesus Christ and commit themselves to Him because of the types of messages they hear. In some cases, preachers denounce other churches and condemn their leaders. They use their pulpits to promote their own churches and condemn others. They concentrate so much on the negatives that the non-Christians and the weak ones find excuses to keep distance from deep commitment to the Christian faith.

Though this state of confusion exists, there are a few churches which concern themselves primarily with evangelism, instead of the promotion of churches and denominations. One finds these churches among established denominations, especially Evangelical ones. Some Pentecostal churches, especially the Assemblies of God and the Deeper Life Bible Church[54] are also working very hard in the areas of evangelism and church planting. Each of these two have strongly-constituted evangelism teams which work among students in high schools, colleges and universities. They also extend their evangelistic efforts to government offices, market places, and rural communities. Their major method of evangelism is crusade. In Owerri, these two groups are active in evangelism. The Assemblies of God emphasizes their "Decade of Harvest."[55] Charles Osoueke[56] made the following statements about Decade of Harvest and Missions,

> With the successful execution of "Operation '90: Mission Ife," "operation 91/92: Missions Gongola, Kwawa and Kafanchan," and "operation '93: Mission Bida," the Decade of Harvest Programme is right on course. The enthusiasm this programme has generated among our people is most encouraging, and this year, we are strengthening our base spiritually, numerically and materially, for a greater offensive in 1995. As a result 1,573 churches were planted in the past four years, bringing our total number of churches to 5,119 as is shown in the statistics.[57]

The Deeper Life Bible Church has a different number of evangelistic programs. Crusades are the primary method. Others include holiday retreats, Bible Studies and camping. Most of their retreats and camping activities are held in public places, such as school compounds and civic centers. The church gives invitations to non-members, and promises them free food and free lodging. Bible Study, singing of songs, testimonies, preaching and "altar call"[58] form the core of retreat and camping activities. The church vigorously follows up non-members who respond to its invitations, and especially those who respond to altar calls. Members of the church who do the follow-up strongly urge the new "converts" to become Deeper Life members. As a result of their aggressive style, some Deeper Life Bible Church members experience resistance and mild abuse during door-to-door witnessing and other types of one-on-one evangelism.

The Church of Nigeria (Anglican Communion) has its own program of evangelism, "Decade of Evangelism." The Baptist churches in Igboland have their own programs of evangelism and missions also. They generally adopt the Nigerian Baptist Convention programs of evangelism, which are in most cases organizationally oriented. Despite the existence of cooperative programs,[59] local churches use structured church organizations to carry out their outreach programs. These organizations include Women's Missionary Society (married women), Men's Missionary Union (married men), Girl's Auxiliary (ages 13–16), Lydia Auxiliary (young women ages 17 till marriage), Royal Ambassadors (boys ages 12–25), and church-based Baptist Students' Fellowship (BSF, high school, college and university students). Another organization which the local church uses is Youth Fellowship. This is an organization which combines young adults, males and females, ages 17 till marriage. In some cases, males who marry while they are members of the Youth Fellowship, retain membership in this organization up to age 50. Females do not; they go over to the Women's Missionary Society (WMS) as soon as they marry.

These church organizations resemble those of Southern Baptist Convention churches in structure and functions. In some cases, churches still order literature materials from Nashville, Tennessee, USA. Most of the churches still function organizationally like Southern Baptist Convention churches, differences in culture notwithstanding. There is a strong sentiment among some old members, "We want to do things the way the early missionaries taught us." This creates obvious difficulties for any attempt at indigenization. Currently, the Nigerian Baptist Convention has a missions strategy for cities, towns and villages in Nigeria, and some neighbouring West African countries. This program, Operation Reach All (ORA) by A.D. 2000, is similar to the Assemblies of God Decade of Harvest. The only difference appears to be success. While Decade of Harvest seems to be functioning well and producing quantifiable results, Operation Reach All seems to be struggling. There is a consensus among many Nigerian Baptists that Operation Reach All (ORA) is still miles away from actualizing its goals.

One of the major goals of ORA is to reach every person and every community in Nigeria with the gospel of Jesus Christ by A.D. 2000. In the few cases where people are making some effort to achieve this goal, they employ two primary methods: open air preachings and simultaneous revivals in local Baptist churches of the same geographical location. Again, the method of outreach here is mass evangelism. In its 1994 annual Convention session in Aba, the Nigerian Baptist Convention Operation Reach All department stated:

> Aba convention has come and gone. But its effects will continue to linger on in the memory of our brethren from Aba in particular and in the generality of the Convention family. It is all because the Evangelism Explosion witnessed a dramatic change at Aba. It was initially planned that preaching would be done to achieve two objectives:
> 1. To reach the messengers.
> 2. To reach the people of Aba with the gospel of our Lord Jesus Christ. We mapped out five centres around the city where preaching was to take place for three nights. But to our dismay, no adequate preparation was made for the centres. Devil planned to jeopardize our efforts, but glory be to God, Holy Spirit led us to employ greater strategy which resulted in a bountiful harvest. These messengers were led in one-to-one witnessing around the city. . . .[60]

Person-to-person witnessing is commendable, but the issue here is lack of follow-up. Let us believe that the "Evangelism Explosion" at Aba, which took the form of person-to-person witnessing resulted in the conversion of some souls. However, the ORA Committee of the Nigerian Baptist Convention demonstrated little follow-up of the new converts. Mass evangelism is not adequate; person-to-person witnessing without strongly organized follow-up is equally inadequate. The Nigerian Baptist Convention Operation Reach All co-ordinators are yet to come up with workable follow-up plans for their outreach programs. Until they do, ORA will remain a laudable idea but a non-productive outreach program. New Christian converts need to understand what it means to become a Christian. Those Christians who witness to non-Christians need to know how to witness effectively. The effectiveness of witnessing does not lie in the number of converts, but in the quality of converts. Statistically, the number of Christian converts which come from crusades, open air services, retreats, camps, and holiday programs is high.

> Christians thinking of or planning for A.D. 2000 or 2025 must be supplied with accurate, objective data indicating whether or not the whole Christian enterprise is progressing toward its stated goals. . . . After undertaking a detailed religio-demographic analysis over last year, we have come up with statistics that indicate both progress and setbacks. . . . Each day some 234,200 hitherto

unevangelized individuals become evangelized. However, unevangelized individuals are increasing every day through births by 257,800 persons.[61]

But in most cases, the life these "converts" live is often inconsistent with a profession of faith in Jesus Christ. This is the central problem facing Christian evangelism in Igboland.

Today, in a number of places, there is a strong spiritual battle amongst Christians. Deception has come in amongst them and is causing havoc. This new deception is even more difficult to detect. I believe that the Devil has learnt that Christians look for error of beliefs about Jesus Christ, His death and resurrection, and can fairly easily spot the error in these areas. So he has become even more clever. People are being allowed to believe in Jesus, to have zeal for God and for the gospel. But the deception comes in what they are being asked to do; their rebelliousness and the way they are attacking and destroying the ministry of other Christians.[62]

Little, if any co-operation exists among Christian denominations in Igboland in matters of evangelism and witnessing. In some cases, there is unhealthy rivalry. The scramble for converts, which began with the early missionaries, still exists. Many new converts take undue advantage of this unfortunate situation. They live whichever way they like, irrespective of what the church says. However,

True conversion is not mere adhesion and it is not just having one leg in the church and another leg outside it. Real conversion is total and radical transformation; a right-about-turn from the former belief to the new faith. A proper understanding of conversion is important for a genuine conception of religious change and missionary enterprise.[63]

Many new converts lack spiritual depth and strong commitment to the person of Jesus Christ. They may attend church regularly, and become active in church activities, but they do not have a strong relationship with Jesus Christ. Many of them fall back on traditional Igbo religion when they face personal problems and difficulties.[64]

Education

The Igbo love Western education. Parents work very hard to make money to send their children to school. A well-known Igbo teacher and clergyman said,

An Igboman is intellectually excellent. He always wants to carry his ego with him. Within our cultural settings as Igbos, a typical Igboman has a lot of pride to defend, even in the midst of staggering ignorance. . . . Those who did not

acquire Western education, while they were young, will do everything to get it, even if they have to attend night school, in order to boost their ego. They do this after they have made money, but discover that they cannot discuss intelligently with the educated ones during social gatherings. They regard lack of western education a deficiency. . . . A typical Igboman will do two things to make up this deficiency:
1. Adult education classes.
2. Make sure that his children receive sound Western education.[65]

This is one of the reasons most early missionaries used schools to evangelize Igboland. Almost all the major denominations built schools. On the other hand, the colonial government saw the training of Africans as a way to make labor cheap. Isichei asserts,

To the missions, the schools were an invaluable way to influence the young in their impressionable years, and government subsidies a precious supplement to their meagre budgets. The government needed a large cadre of Africans who were literate and numerate to staff the railways, postal services, police force, and fill a large number of clerical posts; the expatriate commercial firms, likewise, needed the same type of personnel. It was cheaper to subsidize mission schools than to start their own, or to import educated Africans from further afield.[66]

The C.M.S. and the R.C.M. built primary schools as a major avenue of their evangelistic outreach to the Igbo. The Baptists, the Presbyterians, the Methodists, and the Qua Iboe, who came later, built their own primary schools. The C.M.S. was the first mission to provide post-primary education to the Igbo. Its first endeavor was a training school for catechists in Lokoja, a non-Igbo city Northwest of Enugu. Most students of this school were Igbos. There is no record about the date this school began in Lokoja. The school moved to Asaba, Inyienu and finally to Awka in 1904. Asaba, Inyienu, and Awka are Northern Igbo towns. In Awka, this school developed two branches: a teachers' training college, and a theological school for ministers.[67] The Catholic denomination established its own college and seminary in the remote rural village of Igbariam in 1913. The mission chose this village site to avoid the supposedly corrupting influence of city life. In 1918, the mission stopped operating the school in Igbariam. We do not have any records about the reason for this abandonment. However, in 1928, the mission refounded the school as St. Charles Training College, Onitsha.

These mission training colleges, together with those the government opened, filled an invaluable role in Igbo education. Before secondary schools were set up in Igboland, they provided the only avenue to post primary education.[68]

The Primitive Methodist was the first mission to establish a secondary school in Igboland. Uzuakoli Methodist School opened in 1923. This school soon combined secondary and teachers' training sections. The C.M.S. Mission established Dennis Memorial Grammar School in 1925 at Onitsha. The Colonial Government opened Government College Umuahia in the same year. The Catholic Mission founded Christ the King College, Onitsha in 1932, and Queen of the Rosary College for girls, Enugu, in 1942. The first Baptist secondary school in Igboland was Baptist Girl's Secondary School, Enugu. The school was established in 1967. This school has ceased to exist because of the Nigerian civil war.

At the present time, the state governments own most of the schools all over Nigeria, including Igboland. However, churches own a few secondary schools, primary schools and most nursery/kindergarten schools. In the Owerri area, the Catholics, the Church of Nigeria, the Baptists, and the Assemblies of God operate some of these schools. The Catholics, the Church of Nigeria and the Assemblies of God call their secondary schools junior seminaries.[69] In 1994, the Baptist people of Igboland established their first secondary school since the end of the civil war. The name of the school is Baptist Commercial Secondary School, and it is located about ten miles southeast of Owerri. Almost all the mission and indigenous churches in Igboland today own their own nursery and kindergarten schools. A few of them own primary schools. In addition to the commercial intent for the founding of these schools, these churches use these schools as avenues of evangelism. Some parents, who like how and what their children are learning at a particular church school, change churches. They become members of the churches which operate the schools where their children attend. Most of these schools, though denominationally owned, have open-door admission. They admit pupils from non-Christian families, as well as those from different denominational backgrounds.

The educational landscape is quite different from what it was at the beginning of Christianity in Igboland. Then, most missionaries admitted only the pupils whose parents attended their own denominational churches. This more open admission policy is helping to swell the population of church schools. Other factors responsible for the phenomenal growth of church schools include: good quality education, moral discipline, and teacher availability. Since the end of the civil war, and following the federal and state take-over of schools, both the academic and moral standards of most Nigerian schools have fallen tremendously. Government teachers do not receive their salaries on a regular basis, and as a result, teachers embark upon periodic strikes. Schools close, and students go home.[70] As an alternative to this uncertain situation, those parents who can afford the money, send their children to private schools. They are especially attracted to church ones where teachers receive their salaries regularly and classes go on uninterrupted.

Social Ministries

Most Igbo churches engage in social programs which benefit the needy. The Catholic church is the champion in this endeavor. Igbo Catholics run a good number of orphanages and Motherless Babies' Homes. Okwelle Motherless Babies' Home, located about eleven miles north of Owerri, is a fine example. This home takes care of orphans. The Catholics, members of the Church of Nigeria, the Baptists, the Methodists, the Assemblies of God members, the Presbyterians and the Qua Iboe members are active in prison ministry in Owerri township. A few indigenous church groups and para-church groups such as the Scripture Union, also do some prison ministries in Owerri. These churches and groups conduct regular Bible study sessions and occasional worship services for the prisoners.

Here again, competition manifests itself; each denomination ministers alone. There is no co-operative ministry in the areas of Bible study and worship. Prison officials allocate to each denomination its own time and day for ministry. They make up a roster of churches and schedule each church either weekly or monthly as the case may be. These churches and groups go beyond Bible study and worship. They donate money and other material things for the upkeep of the prisoners. Some of the churches obtain permission from the prison authorities to hold crusades and revival services in the prison premises for prisoners and their officials. The first Baptist Church, Owerri, held a four-day open air preaching at the Owerri Central Prison, Okigwe Road in 1991. The program was successful; some of those who attended gave their lives to Jesus, including two prison officers. The following year, two of those prisoners were released, and they came to First Baptist Church to testify to the goodness of God.[71]

Theological Education

Theological schools abound in Igboland. The levels of these schools range from Bible schools to theological seminaries. Only a few of them are accredited by nationally accrediting agencies. The Catholics have a good number of junior and major seminaries. The Anglicans, the Methodists and the Presbyterians jointly own a divinity college, Trinity Theological College, Umuahia. The Baptists operate a Bible College in Obinze, while the Assemblies have the Assemblies of God Divinity School, Old Umuahia.

Many inter-denominational Bible Colleges exist in Igboland. In Owerri, the two most outstanding ones are Wesley Theological Seminary and Cornerstone Theological Seminary.

Medical Ministries

The Presbyterians, Methodists, Roman Catholics and Anglicans have strong medical missions in Igboland. Francis Akanu Ibiam[72] was the first indigenous Christian doctor in Igboland. Some writers refer to him as an Igbo medical missionary. He was a pioneer medical missionary with the Church of Scotland Mission in the southeastern part of Igboland. Around the late 1930s and early 1940s, the C.M.S., the Methodists and the Presbyterians jointly founded the Queen Elizabeth Hospital, Unmuahia.[73] The C.M.S. alone had built Iyi-Enu Hospital at Ogidi in 1907. This mission also built Oji River Leper Settlement in 1936. The Presbyterians, in their pioneering efforts had built a hospital at Uburu, near Okigwe in 1915, and a leper settlement at Itu in 1928. The Methodists built a hospital at Amachara in 1929 and a leper colony at Uzuakoli in 1930. The Catholic Church had made an initial effort in the area of medical missions in Onitsha during the early years of 1900, but failed to carry through. In 1935, the mission established its first hospital in Igboland: Holy Rosary Maternity Hospital Onitsha. In the same year the mission built its second hospital, but the first in Owerri Igbo: Mount Carmel Hospital Emekuku.[74] Then others followed. The only medical institution which has a Baptist name in Igboland is Baptist Dental Center, Enugu. The ownership, management and operation of this center are still in the hands of the Baptist Mission of Nigeria.[75] Nationals have little or no say in its operation and administration.

The newer church groups, foreign and indigenous, rarely go into medical missions. Medical services are still the exclusive reserve of the major missions in Igboland. Some of these hospitals and medical institutions have mission-trained chaplains who provide pastoral care to patients and their families. These chaplains preach sermons during scheduled chapel services. They also visit in-patients in their rooms, talk with them, and provide needed counseling to their family members. The chaplains are few in number. They cannot adequately minister to the spiritual needs of their in-patients, much less their out-patients. In most cases, they lose contact with their counselees as soon as the patients go home from the hospitals. Telephones are not common, and only a few of the chaplains own means of transportation, such as motor-cycle or motor-vehicle. It is also very difficult to locate people's residences, especially those who live in the villages. There are no street names, and no house numbers. These factors mitigate against effective evangelism through medical institutions.

It appears that the quality of treatment and care in many mission hospitals has fallen in recent years. Generally, patients and their families complain about the inadequate attention they receive from some staff members. They claim that a lot has changed in the way hospitals are now run. The slogan: "*Inwekwara Abraham n'nna?*" (Do you have Abraham as your father?)[76] has also become a common saying in church institutions. Generally, most people are disgusted with this trend. On the surface, Igbo Christianity may look vibrant if one considers the number of crusades which take place each day, and the number of "conversions" which these crusade organizers report. To the contrary, the day-to-day lives of most Christians in the land tend to betray the statistics. What is wrong? I agree with some of my interviewees that there may be many professions, but very little commitment. Surface Christianity is different from permeation.

This book aims at providing an answer for this nagging phenomenon in Igbo Christianity. Crusades and revival meetings have been over-done in Igboland. Most people now tend to "tune off" whenever they see posters on billboards, or hear radio or television announcements about crusades and revivals. People have become tired of attacks and counter attacks by churches and ministries against one another on crusade grounds and at revival meetings. They are disgusted with pious clichés and theological jargons which some preachers use, which in many cases, neither the preacher nor their hearers understand.

Many Igbo are struggling with spiritual problems which crusade and street preachers do not address. These struggling people need someone to draw closer to them, share with them the true nature of God, and explain how God works in the lives of individuals. They need someone who will help them understand the true meaning and purpose of life, and the direction God wants them to take. These preachers must give way, and allow the Holy Spirit to touch the lives of individuals and give solutions to their spiritual dilemmas. Those who share, must share from the standpoint of personal experience, and not mere book knowledge. The Holy Spirit must take the place of programs. Dialogues must become a constant method of sermon presentation to Igbo listeners.

Notes

1 Uzodimma Nwala, "Some Reflections on British Conquest of Igbo Traditional Oracles, 1900–1924," *Nigeria Magazine* (1982): 31.

2 Ibid.

3 The Aro Expedition was the 1901–1902 British government's attempt to establish its colonial administration, to maintain "law and order" so that legitimate trade would flow. Opposition to British rule was based on the desire of the natives to defend their own civilization. It was strongly suspected that the missionaries helped to instigate the Expedition in order to subdue the natives and make them accept Christianity. Sir Ralph Moore was the British High Commissioner in Calabar at the time of this Expedition. He gave the British soldiers the following "Memorandum of Instructions:"

4 Put a stop to slave-raiding and the slave trade.

5 Abolish the juju hierarchy of the Aro people, which by superstition and fraud causes much injustice among the coast peoples generally and is opposed to the establishment of government.

6 Hillary C. Achunike, *Dreams of Heaven* (quoted from *Newswatch*, 14 July 1986): 35–36.

7 Ministry of Arts and Culture, Imo State, Nigeria, *1990 Historical Handbook* (Owerri: Ministry of Arts and Culture, 1990), 15.

8 Orlando E. Costas, *The Church and Its Mission: A Shattering Critique from the Third World* (Wheaton, Ill: Tyndale House Publishers, Inc., 1974), 90.

9 Ekechi, *Missionary Enterprise and Rivalry in Igboland,* 75.

10 Chinua Achebe, *No Longer at Ease* (London: Heinemann Educational Books, 1960), 96.

11 Elizabeth Isichei, *A History of the Igbo People* (New York: St. Martin's Press, 1976), 183.

12 Ibid., 184.

13 NEPA is Nigerian Electric Power Authority. This is the company which supplies electricity to Owerri residents.

14 Kevin C. Akagha, Editor, *The Leader* (Catholic Newspaper) Owerri), interview by author, 11 January 1996, Owerri, Nigeria, tape recording.

15 There occurred in regular pattern and quick succession a phenomenon whereby snakes of identical species swallowed up those of other kinds. The Igbos have an old adage which ascribed doom and ominous consequences to a situation where

one snake swallows another. When people saw the adage in practical reality they were alarmed and believed that some calamity was imminent unless something was done to forestall it.

16 Damaco is a prominent Owerri-based business man. His real name is Dominic Egbukwu.

17 "Report of the Judicial Commission of Inquiry into the Disturbances of 24–25 September 1996," *Imo State of Nigeria, Government White Paper* (Owerri, Nigeria: Office of the Secretary to the State Government, Owerri, 19 February 1997), 15–18.

18 Nouveaus riches were persons who were considered to have acquired their wealth through illegitimate, fraudulent or dubious means or through the abuse of their office. Some of them were accused of gruesome acts such as ritual killings of human beings. They were also known as "419" people ("419" is number of the penal code in the Nigerian constitution for those who obtain material things by tricks or fraud).

19 "Condom in Church," *National Post* (Nigerian Newspaper), 30 September–6 October, 1996, 13.

20 Nnanna Oparaechekwe, His Royal Highness, Eze Ebubedike 2 of Ulakwo, Owerri, interview by author 16 January 1996, Owerri, Nigeria, tape recording.

21 "Funeral Benefits" are "compensations" which bereaved individuals, especially spouses, receive from the social clubs, for losing their loved ones. If a man dies, his wife will receive some large amount of money and other material things from her dead husband's social club, and vice versa. As a result, it has been alleged that some husbands and wives secretly poison their spouses in order to receive funeral benefits.

22 *Imo State of Nigeria, Government White Paper*, 19 February 1997, 6.

23 Ibid., 7.

24 Akagha, interview.

25 Eric Osuji, His Royal Highness, Eze Duruojinnaka I of Umudim; Chairman, Ikeduru Council of Kings, interview by author 17 January 1996, Umudim, Ikeduru, Nigeria, tape recording.

26 Harold W. Turner, "Pentecostal Movements in Nigeria," *Orita* 4, no. 2 (December 1970): 39.

27 Ibid.

28 Matthews A. Ojo, "The Charismatic Movement in Nigeria Today," *International Bulletin of Missionary Research* (July 1995): 114.

29 In the Western world the term "Charismatic" is generally applied to Christians within Protestant and Roman Catholic churches who testify to the Baptism of the Holy Spirit, who experience its accompaniment of speaking in tongues, and who

exercise the gifts of the Holy Spirit, principally the gift of healing. Charismatic Christians in Nigeria share these features with their Western counterparts. (See Matthew A. Ojo, "The Charismatic Movement in Nigeria Today," *International Bulletin of Missionary Research* (July 1995): 114.

30   Ibid.

31   Ibid.

32   Ibid.

33   Nsukka is a town in Igboland. Majority of the students of UNN at this time were Igbos.

34   Ojo, "Charismatic Movement in Nigeria Today," 115.

35   Lagos is a prominent city in Nigeria. It was until the late 1980s, the capital of Nigeria.

36   Orih, interview.

37   Oparaechekwe, interview.

38   Achunike, *Dreams of Heaven*, 55–57.

39   The mainline churches definitely addressed the needs of the refugees by working through two main relief agencies: Caritas (Catholic) and World Council of Churches (Protestant) to supply food, clothing, drugs and other medical needs to the needy. The churches also built sick-bays in many locations for the very sick, especially those who were suffering from Kwashirokor.

40   Achunike, *Dreams of Heaven*, 55–56.

41   Ibid., 60.

42   "Trouble in Bro. Peter's Church," *Beaton* (Nigerian monthly Newspaper), August 1991, 5.

43   "Crisis in the House of God," *Sunday Sketch* (Nigerian Weekly Newspaper) 20 October 1996, 8–9.

44   Chieftaincy titles are social honors which Ezes of different communities confer on certain members of their citizenry or some outside of their communities for their recognizable achievements in education, commerce, industry, politics and so on.

45   Achunike, *Dreams of Heaven*, 96–97.

46   Ibid.

47   Ibid., 98.

48   Ibid., 61.

49   Ibid.

50   Ibid.

51   Emogene Harris, an SBC missionary, worked among the Igbo for twenty-nine years (1965–1994) of her thirty-four years (1960–1994) in Nigeria. During the civil war, she worked among refugees, mostly Igbo, in Port-Harcourt and Igrita. Dearly beloved by most Baptists of Igboland, she lived in three Igbo towns: Enugu, Onitsha and Owerri.

52   Frances Lawjua Bolton, *And We Beheld His Glory: A Personal Account of the Revival in Eastern Nigeria in 1970/71* (Harlow, Essex: Christ the King Publishing, 1992), 1.

53   Most of the leaders of the new Pentecostal/Charismatic churches and ministries believe that the anointing (call) of the Holy Spirit is the only thing it takes a person to become an effective pastor or evangelist. They claim that formal education, including theological training, is not necessary.

54   Deeper Life Bible Church is an indigenous Nigerian Church. W.F. Kumuyi, a one-time mathematics teacher at the University of Lagos, Nigeria, is its founder. The church began in 1973 as a Bible Study group in Kumuyi's apartment. Fifteen people, most of them students, attended every Monday evening. In 1983, Kumuyi declared the group a full church because of its phenomenal numerical growth. The church has about 700,000 members, and 1000 branches all over Nigeria. In Africa, Deeper Life Bible Church has work in about 30 countries. It has also expanded its work to the United States of America, United Kingdom and the Philippines. The International Conference of Pentecostal and Evangelical Churches has given this church the recognition of being the largest single congregation in Africa and the fourth largest in the world. (See *West Africa*, 27 December 1993–6 January 1994.)

55   Decade of Harvest is a plan which the Assemblies of God Church, Nigeria, has initiated to commit itself to the task of planting: "A church for every unreached people autonomous community in Nigeria and foreign missions program in 30 African countries by the year 2000 A.D." Its targets are:

Increasing church membership by 5,000,000 persons
Planting 6,451 new indigenous local church distributed among the unreached autonomous communities
Training of 10,000new pioneer ministers, 10,500 new lay workers, 2,000 cross-cultural missionaries
Establishing National Assemblies of God Church in 30 African countries in co-operation with other National Assemblies of God churches and Inter Mission Agencies
Mobilizing 150,000 volunteer prayer warriors
Raising N1.5 billion to finance the whole program
Providing 5,000,000 Bibles for the new converts in the language they can understand
Establishing auxiliary projects
Primary and secondary schools; Primary Health Care and specialized ministries...(See *General Council Assemblies of God Nigeria Decade of Harvest Update, Operations '90-'93*, September, 1994, 1).

56   Charles O. Osueke is the General Superintendent of the Assemblies of God, Nigeria.

57   Charles O. Osueke, "General Superintendent's Tri-ennial Report: 1991–1993," General Council, Assemblies of God, Nigeria, Rivers Bible College, Eleme, Port-Harcourt, 23–27 May 1994, 21–22.

58   Altar call is the invitation which preachers extend to those who have listened to their sermons to give their lives to Jesus Christ or to accept Jesus as their Lord and Savior. In most cases, this invitation comes at the end of the sermon.

59   Co-operative programs are combined evangelism and missions efforts of the churches of the Nigerian Baptist Convention on national and international levels.

60   Ajao Banjo, "New Wine Burst the Old Wineskin during Aba '94 Evangelism Explosion," *The Nigerian Baptist* (June 1994): 17.

61   David B. Barrett, "Annual Statistical Table on Global Mission: 1993," *International Bulletin of Missionary Research* (January 1993): 22.

62   Bolton, *And We Beheld His Glory,* 25.

63   Achunike, *Dreams of Heaven,* 63.

64   Ibid.

65   R.O. Uwadi, Methodist Bishop of Owerri, interview by author, 9 January 1996, Owerri, Nigeria, tape recording.

66   Isichei, *A History of the Igbo People,* 185.

67   Ibid., 186.

68   Ibid.

69   "Owerri District Tri-ennial Report," *General Council, Assemblies of God, Nigeria* (23–27 May 1994): 103.

70   O.A. Onyeagocha, Community Leader, interview by author, 10 March, 1997, Obinze, Owerri, Nigeria, tape recording.

71   Christian Obijuru, Deacon, First Baptist Church, Owerri, interview by author, 17 January 1996, Owerri, Nigeria, tape recording.

72   Dr. Francis Akanu Ibiam (born 29 November 1906 and died 1 July 1995) was an outstanding Igbo Christian. He was one of the first Igbo medical doctors of note. He was a Presbyterian and was very instrumental in the pioneering work of medical missions in Igboland. He built Abiriba Hospital from 1936–1945. He held many posts both nationally and internationally. He was a former civilian governor of Eastern Nigeria (1960–1966) and President of Christian Council of Nigeria (1955–1958). See *The International Who's Who: 1995–1996* 59th ed. London: Europa Publications, 1995, 728–729.

73   Isichei, *A History of the Igbo People,* 170.

74   Achunike, *Dreams of Heaven*, 48.

75   "Baptist Mission of Nigeria" is the official name for the organization of Southern Baptist Convention missionaries working in Nigeria. This organization is separate from the Nigerian Baptist Convention. However, both bodies are partners in missions and evangelism.

76   "Do you have Abraham as your father?" practically means do you have anyone who will act for you and see that you receive needed attention?

Chapter 6

Inculturation Theory

A number of African and Western theologians have expressed the need for authentic African Christianity. They argue that until Christianity becomes truly African, most Africans, especially those who receive Western education, will continue to regard Christianity as a foreign religion. In order to solve the problem of "foreignness," these scholars have suggested various models of indigenous Christianity in Africa. We will briefly examine seven of these models from their definitional standpoint, as a background for developing an authentic Igbo Christianity.

Indigenization

Indigenization is a process in mission methodology which aims at evolving and maintaining a culturally integrated Christianity. The adjective, "indigenous," connotes the ideas of native, aboriginal, originating in, characteristic of, or endemic to. In the context of the African culture, some African scholars have suggested the term "Africanization" as a way of making Christianity native or endemic to the African peoples. In most cases, when secular and religious African scholars refer to Africanization, the issue of cultural revival comes up. They argue that for Christianity to be authentic in Africa, African ways of life must replace Western ways of life. They assert that Africans must look at Christianity with the African "eye" and understand its tenets with the African "mind."

    Gwinyai Henry Muzorewa, an African scholar from Zimbabwe, calls for a moratorium on a Western theology of mission, which according to him, carries its superiority baggage. In *An African Theology of Missions*, Muzorewa focuses mainly on Protestant mission theologies and uses the various conferences organized by the World Council of Churches as his frame of reference. He contends that the twentieth century development of traditional Protestant theology is too narrow because it is primarily the work of Europeans and Americans whose theological lenses are colored by Western bias. He defines Christian theology as "a reflection of a people's experience of God and what God is doing for them."[1] Muzorewa maintains that it is not consistent with the nature of reality for a person to borrow other people's[2] theological perspectives in order to express his or her own reflection. An individual's theological perspectives are normally based on that individual's experience and social context. He uses the term "pre-church faith" to describe an African theology of mission which according to him, sees continuity between faith in God and belief in God through Jesus Christ.

> The church in Africa is redefining mission theology in order to recapture their vision of the will of God in pre-church times. The African church itself is being sent and is responding in obedience to the Lord, but it needs to hear God's voice in its original chord, not through the Western "theological mufflers" which distort truth.[3]

G. C. Oosthuizen,[4] commenting on indigenization, highlights some of the features of African Independent churches, with regard to indigenization. He asserts that African Independent churches stress the importance of African indigenous culture. They expose the degree to which Western ideology and scholarship often undervalue African cultural heritages and see "African things" as insignificant. They perceive African thinking as "prelogical because it does not fit the secular intellectualist approach." The West sees Africa as "primitive" and "traditional," while they perceive themselves as "civilized" and "modern."

> . . . for many years the typical missionary and anthropological literature has presented African religion in a negative manner, characterizing it as pervaded with irrational beliefs in magic, fetishes, spirits, ancestors, and so forth. Indigenous values and sociomoral injunctions based on African cultural and religious inheritances have been underestimated and misrepresented. In this intellectual climate, it is little wonder that Western theological constructs and ecclesiastical models were imposed on South African Christians. As a result, the positive contributions of traditional African culture were smothered.[5]

The recent wave of revival of culture in various parts of Africa is a direct reaction to this smothering of everything African. Many Africans want to recapture their past. Hence the cultural regeneration in all areas of their life, especially in religion. Religion is the hub which connects all aspects of African life. However, as in almost all situations where people have been oppressed and humiliated, reactions take various forms. In the case of

Christianity in Africa, there are two main reactions: complete abandonment of Christianity or the indigenization of Christianity.

Obviously, most African Christians favor indigenization over abandonment. They call for Africanization of Christianity. The call for Africanization accelerated following World War II and the liberation of most African nations from direct Western colonial control in the 1950s and 60s. It intensified during the 1960s and the 1970s, as a component of Pan-Africanism.[6] The 1970s saw an intensive pursuit of the revival of African culture, which culminated in the 1973 Festival of Arts and Culture (Festac) in Lagos, Nigeria, for all African nations.

Toward the close of the nineteenth century, Nigerian Nationalism was shaking off the chains of colonial oppression. The churches, many of which had supported British rule in Nigeria, began to withdraw that support.

> The church became the cradle of Nigerian nationalism, the only forum of nationalist expression until the beginnings of the Nigerian-owned press after 1879, and the main focus of nationalist energies after 1914.[7]

It is important to note that the first generation of educated Nigerians "were pre-eminently equipped for a nationalist task by their learning and the circumstances of their age."[8] These educated Nigerians had free access to the Bible and became aware of its conceptions of equality, justice and non-racialism. These educated, early converts to Christianity saw the Bible as a valid weapon with which to confront those missionaries who brushed Biblical ideals aside in church administration and in their relations with their converts. Some of the converts, especially the church leaders, had studied the classics and the history of the struggle of oppressed peoples against their imperial masters. They "believed they had heroes worthy of emulation."[9]

The early Nigerian nationalists believed themselves to be "Ethiopians."[10] Ethiopianism became an important component of African identity.[11] The implication of the term in the minds of educated Africans included eventual conversion of Africa to Christianity and the establishment of a Christian theocracy.

> Conceived in the Biblical sense the term "Ethiopia" came to have a deep sentimental connotation; it whipped up Negro racialism and became the beacon of hope and promise which educated Africans believed would be fulfilled at some future date. They looked forward to the day when Africa would become the cynosure of the world and the Negro race the model for other races . . . In practical terms Ethiopianism expressed in terms of racial antagonism between the white

missionaries and their wards represented the African struggle for power and position in church government. It also had a parallel in the struggle by Africans for
the higher positions in the civil service, and it awakened the dream of a nation
state to be controlled ultimately by Africans.[12]

While this "Ethiopian" mentality was being propagated, the educated
Africans did not regard the Western missionaries as their enemies. Rather,
they saw the missionaries as their benefactors. They were grateful to the
missionaries because the missionaries were the ones who created the
educational environment which produced these pastors, clerks, teachers,
catechists, traders, politicians and so on. The churches held a virtual
monopoly over education. The missionaries were the ones who provided
them with the Bible from which they learned the principles of freedom
and equality. Therefore they decided not to abandon Christianity, but to
propagate it, and struggle to take up leadership with it. Ethiopianism,
according to Ayandele, was the bedrock for Nigerian nationalism.

Ayandele suggests Henry Venn, Prebendary of St. Paul's London, was
the originator of Nigerian nationalism. Venn was Secretary of the Church
Missionary Society for thirty years (1842-1872). He singlehandedly and
deliberately "urged Africans to be prepared to assume the leadership of
their countries."[13] Ayandele observes:

> Why and how he became the spokesman of the Africans he answers in a letter of
> September 1871. His love for Africans, he said began about 1800, at the age of
> four, at Clapham Common, where he was a playmate to African children brought
> up by Governor Zachary Macaulay of Sierra Leone. He grew up in the environ-
> ment of the Chapham Sect and was an evangelical of the deepest hue. His cast of
> mind is illustrated by the fact that among his correspondents were William
> Wilberforce, the liberator of the Negroes, and Lord Shatterbury, the great nine-
> teenth-century reformer.[14]

Venn is a celebrated personality in mission history, especially for his principles of church government. The principles entail an evolutionary process, in three stages, by which churches in Africa and Asia would become
indigenous. These stages are: self-supporting, self-governing, and self-
extending. He called this process the "euthanasia" of missions, stating
that "once the European missionary had set the churches on their feet his
work was done, for he was not to be a pastor. He should move on to a
virgin field."[15]

In a paper entitled, "Indigenous Church Principles: A Survey of Origin
and Development," Hans Kasdorf raises the issue of the meaning of "indigenous Church Principles," and asks whether or not "self-support,"

"self-government," and "self-extension" adequately express the full meaning of an indigenous church. He adds four other "selfs" to these three: "self-amplifying," "self-teaching," "self-functioning," and "self-determining." He gives the impression that even these seven are inadequate to define an indigenous church.[16] Jacob Loewen, an anthropologist and translation consultant for the American Bible Society, notes that the term "indigenous" is almost exclusively akin to missions and the development of younger churches. "When thus used it is colored by overtones of the local, the independent, the distinctive, the unique, and the separatist."[17] Kasdorf observes that when Henry Venn conceived the ideas of the principles of the indigenous church, his primary target was the "euthanasia of a mission." His thought in "subjecting the mission to a painless death was indigenization of the national church on one hand and the devolution of the mission on the other."[18] He contends that "devolution" for Venn meant "full transfer of all responsibilities from the foreign mission to the national church at the earliest possible date in order to free the mission for pioneer evangelism and church planting."[19] He understands Venn to have believed that when the national church has reached the tripartite selfhood, "it has become autonomous and independent."[20] This autonomy and independence suggest that the national church has become free of any external ecclesiastical control.

Kasdorf brings us to consider the difference between an indigenized church and an indigenous church as conceived by Venn. An indigenized church is one which foreign missionaries planted, but which later came under the leadership and support of national people, without foreign domination. On the other hand, an indigenous church is a church which nationals founded in their own locality, exclusive of any direct foreign influence or control. In *The Indigenous Church*, Melvin Hodges defines the indigenous church: "The word indigenous means that, as a result of missionary effort, a native church has been produced which shares the life of the country in which it is planted and finds within itself the ability to govern itself, support itself, and reproduce itself."[21] "Indigenous" and "indigenized" are kin terms. However, their major difference lies on who established or establishes a church. While "indigenous" churches refer to those churches which nationals establish in their own land and support with their own resources, "indigenized" churches are those which foreign missionaries establish in a land to which they go as missionaries, and which later fall under the governance of national leaders, with or without foreign support. It could be that Venn and his contemporary, Rufus Anderson[22] conceived the idea of the indigenous church only in terms of the "euthanasia of mission," arising from self-supporting, self-governing and self-extending characters and functions of the national church.

It seems that self-supporting, self-governing and self-extending presuppose indigenous theology. While Muzorewa calls for an African theology of mission, V.E. Devadutt sheds more light on an indigenous theology, citing India as his frame of reference. He suggests self-expression; revelation, theology and experience; the interpretation of history; the Holy Spirit; the church and uniqueness as essential features of indigenous theology.

A time will come when every people will grow up. They will no longer be fed by somebody else; they will feed themselves. Writing from an Indian perspective, Devadutt cites the opening speech of the chairman of the Committee on the Indigenous School of Christian Theology during a theological conference in India. The chairman used two words, "absorption" and "reaction," to describe the condition of Christian teaching and learning in India.

> Hitherto Christianity has been "absorbed" from the West, but now the Indian Christian mind is beginning to react naturally to what it had absorbed. Christian theology is no longer the gift of others but is now becoming India's own possession, natural to her own culture and traditions. Just as there was a Roman theology and an Anglo-Saxon theology, so there must be an Indian Christian theology.[23]

What is so obviously true of India is also true of Africa. But, is the Western church prepared to accept theological creativity and theological independence in India or Africa? It would appear not. It seems that "euthanasia of mission" in the minds of most Western theologians and missiologists does not include theological independence for the indigenous church. It appears to focus only on administrative freedom while attempting to maintain the theological status quo. This is the real challenge of indigenization. The growth and maturity of the national church appears to be limited by already-established and approved church dogmas. Theology and dogma become "no go" areas for the leaders of the so-called indigenous churches. Though most of these leaders of the African church attended the same theological schools and received the same education as their Western counterparts, these national leaders are still regarded as incapable of genuine theological creativity. They are expected to depend on commentaries and insights of their Western colleagues in order to interpret the Bible correctly. Many national leaders agonize over this situation, especially when they consider the type of reception and acceptance which greet their views at international conferences.[24]

As a result, many nationals over-react to this kind of treatment in their indigenization attempts. Many of these leaders go to extremes in their attempt to localize Christianity through unnatural native forms of worship and synthesis of theological beliefs. In Africa, this over-reaction against Western Christianity has become most pronounced. Osadolor Imasogie describes this "Christ of Culture Attitude" as an unfortunate extreme.

> For those in this camp Christ is a cultural hero; hence, in their opinion, the distinction which people make between Christianity and culture is artificial and even unchristian. As far as those in this group are concerned, there should be no tension between customary laws and the laws of the Gospel. In fact, they see no difference between divine grace and human effort, no demarcation between salvation and social conservation. Their main concern is to accommodate Christ to culture, "selecting from his teachings and actions as well as from Christian doctrines such points as seem to agree with what is best in civilization," as defined by particular culture. In the process, any elements of the Gospel that are discordant with the specific culture are to be jettisoned. Christ is here seen only as a great philosopher, an excellent moralist and a reformer of culture but never as the divine Savior of man.[25]

Imasogie observes that since Pierre Abelard's[26] death, there have been persons throughout the Christian world who have held and propagated this view. Imasogie terms this view "unChristian," and calls for a rejection of it. Imasogie does not believe that the "Christ of Culture Attitude" should enter, much less dominate, the religious dimension of African cultural revival. He illustrates his point in the case of a Nigerian clergyman—sociologist, S.S. Iwe, whose lecture on "The Role of Religion in a Developing Culture," was reported in *Sunday Times*, a prominent Nigerian newspaper. Iwe contended that "polygamy should be revised in favor of Nigerian culture, because polygamy is one of the honest institutions of our forefathers."[27] Iwe also argued that

> to be progressive, organized religion or the church must see that its concepts, authority and service to the people are in keeping and comparing favourably with the achievements of humanity in this twentieth century—in terms of law, liberty, justice, human rights and democracy.[28]

Imasogie disagrees very strongly with Iwe on this issue. He gives three reasons why polygamy should not be accepted by the church on the basis that it is an African institution: the institution of polygamy is not reconcilable with the achievements of humanity in the twentieth century; there is no harmony between polygamy which "regards women as a chattel to be owned" and the twentieth century sense of liberty, justice and human rights, especially when this institution does not encourage polyandry; and it is a falsification of history to suggest that polygamy is endemic to the Africans. Polygamy is a part of universal human culture, though some segments of human society have discontinued it because of its obnoxious characteristics to "a developed sense of justice, human rights and democracy."[29] Imasogie posits that another reason why polygamy should not be accepted by the African church is that the argument by Iwe that polygamy is part of African culture is weak. Most Africans have done away with slavery, human sacrifice and the "osu" system, which could as well have been integral parts of the African ethos. Since African societies have discontinued these practices because of their negative features, why suggest a retension of polygamy?

Imasogie regards the "Christ of Culture Attitude" as inadequate for the process of indigenization. He observes:

> It is true that such a call for indigenization as this is a psychological reaction against the moribund apologetic method forged under the subtle influence of a lopsided "Christ Against Culture" mentality. I call it lopsided because, while inexcusably unaware of his own culture colouring of the Christian faith, the apologist demanded that the African renounce his culture "wholesale" and in its place embrace Western culture if he was to be saved. . . . This mentality was the underlying presupposition behind the assumption of foreign names at baptism, and, in a few instances, the barring of worshippers from certain churches in Lagos and in Calabar on the grounds that they were not properly dressed. Proper dress here is interpreted as Western suits! Today the position is reversed, and if we are not careful we may find ourselves on the other extreme pole which interprets Christ and Christianity only in terms of African culture. Two wrongs do not make one right; hence, we must be careful not to explain Christ in terms of a particular culture in our attempt to make Him acceptable.[30]

When we come to consider the indigenization of Christianity within the Igbo culture, what are we talking about? We agree with Imasogie that both the "Christ Against Culture" and "Christ of Culture" mentalities are insufficient. But how do we present Christ and the Christian faith to the Igbo so that they will have an indigenous understanding and an indigenous expression of both Christ and Christianity, whose origins were not Igbo? First, we contend that the Igbo must perceive Jesus Christ as a universal divine personality. The Igbo must use the Igbo language, Igbo symbols and Igbo metaphors to postulate authentic Biblical affirmations.

As a first step, the Igbo translation of the Bible must be based on the original Hebrew and Greek manuscripts, and not on any English translation, most of which have Western cultural colorings. We also contend that the Igbo church needs to re-examine some of its current liturgical practices, and not feel hesitant to make suitable cultural changes. Certainly priests or pastors of Igbo churches do not have to put on ecclesiastical robes or Western suits to play their priestly or pastoral roles. They do not have to use Latin or English language to "say mass" or conduct worship services. They do not have to use bread or wine from the fruit of the vine to observe the Lord's Supper. These elements are only symbols, pointing to the fact that Jesus Christ was crucified and His blood was shed for the remission of the sins of the whole world, including the Igbo. Any applicable local element can substitute for bread and wine where these are not available.

However, an honest evaluation of Igbo Christianity will surely reveal that the "Igbonization of Christianity," the genuine incarnation of Christianity within the Igbo society, is still miles away. It is true that most Igbo regret the unnecessary loss and disparagement of their cultural norms by most of the early Euro-American anthropologists, sociologists, historians and even Christian missionaries. Yet many still feel guilty today when they want to effect some necessary changes. The master-servant relationship which existed, in the case of the church, between the missionaries and the national church, still lingers on today. Frank A. Salamone and Michael C. Mbabuike contend:

> Reflecting colonial class distinctions, the belief persists among many Igbo that a priest should be aloof, wealthy, deal primarily with the rich, and be condescending in discussing matters with the community. For these people, a priest cannot be at home with the people or eat what they do. It is crucial to note that this behavior is not an aspect of the role of traditional religious practitioners. The changeover to Catholic priests from traditional priests freed Igbo priests from traditional controls, leading to their isolation. Because they are set apart from their parishioners, modern priests are able to do things traditional priests were not able to do. Their vows of celibacy and consequent lack of legitimate wives and children further isolate them and snap essential ties with the community.

> It is imperative to remember that Catholicism is a foreign missionary religion that came with colonialism. The model for Igbo Catholic priests remains the white missionary who established himself away from the people. Numerous indigenous Catholic priests continued the colonial model . . . In fundamental ways they are more Roman than the Roman Catholic Church.[31]

This situation is not limited to the Catholic Church and its priests in Igboland. Some mainline Protestant Churches and their pastors, along with many independent churches and ministries which have foreign affiliations, tend to operate in much the same way. This situation is a real limitation to genuine indigenization of Christianity in Igboland.

Salamone and Mbabuike provide examples of two Catholic priests and two Catholic communities in Igboland, Martin Maduka and J. C. Akunna, and Ekwulobia and Umuleri respectively, who are indigenizing Christianity. Maduka's basic premise is that those African beliefs and practices which do not contradict Christian practices, but complement them, should be introduced into the church. He believes that every religion should be adapted to local understanding and that "Christian liturgy should reflect African culture just as Christianity once reflected Jewish culture and more recently European culture."[32] Akunna and his Umuleri parish have Africanized Catholic rites, ceremonies and liturgy. "The result has been a happy syncretism between Catholic worship and Igbo cultural beliefs and practices."[33] There are no more religious and denominational barriers in public worship in Umuleri. From time to time, Catholics, Protestants, and adherents of indigenous Igbo religion worship together.

> Sunday mass has become a village theatrical performance. Traditional music and dance play prominent roles in the liturgy. Dancers from different age groups perform in turn—women singers and dancers, young men and their drummers, titled men of the village—each in turn perform and take turns officiating. From time to time, the parish priest leads the choir, sings a solo, and performs dance movements reminiscent of those of the traditional high priests and singing masquerades of the past.[34]

In my own opinion, Maduka and Akunna may have good intentions for their own styles of indigenization, but they have not fully faced the problem of compromise. In their attempt to react against the "Christ Against Culture" of Western missionaries, they have taken "Christ of Culture" to an unfortunate extreme. In their public worship, they have failed to heed to the Biblical injunction,

> Do not be yoked together with unbelievers. For what do righteousness and wickedness have in common? Or what fellowship can light have with darkness? What harmony is there between Christ and Belial? What does a believer have in common with an unbeliever? What agreement is there between the temple of God and idols?[35]

The Igbo are proud of their cultural heritage. While they respect their culture and endeavor to keep it, they also remain liberally open to other cultures. They are always willing to associate and interact with people from other cultural backgrounds. We regard this quality as a major key to indigenization. Their open-mindedness helps them "Igbonize" these foreign cultural practices which enhance their style of living.

Perhaps the most outstanding quality of the Igbo is his innate receptivity to new ideas and adaptability to change which, under the stimulus of Christianity and Western education imported into Nigeria by the modern government, readily triggered in him an obsessive desire for self-improvement and modernity through education. . . . The Igbos were quick in grasping the value of Western education. The drive for education thus became the driving force in the Igbo society.[36]

Thus indigenization will give rise to authentic Igbo Christianity in the context of open educational and cultural interactions.

Contextualization

Contextualization is a relatively new term in the arena of Christian missions and church growth. Shaki Coe and Aharon Sapsezian, directors of the Theological Education Fund (TEF) were the first to use this term in early 1972.

The TEF report for that year, *Ministry and Context*, suggested that "contextualization" implies all that is involved in the familiar term indigenization, but seeks to press beyond it to take into account the process of secularity, technology and the struggle for human justice which characterized the historical movement of nations in the Third World. The report introduces the TEF's Third Mandate as a response to the widespread crisis of faith, and search for meaning in life; the urgent issues of human development and social justice; the dialectic between a universal technological civilization and local culture and religious situations.[37]

Bruce J. Nicholls asserts that contextualization is a "theological necessity demanded by the incarnational nature of the Word."[38] Contextualization is closely related to "contextuality," the "capacity to respond fully to the gospel within the framework of one's own situation."[39] Contextualization is a process, just like indigenization. While contextualization suggests the process of bringing out something from within, indigenization connotes the idea of taking something which is external or foreign and making it authentically indigenous. "Contextualizing takes place in *every* form of faith, Christian or non-Christian, liberal or conservative, revolutionary or nonrevolutionary."[40] However, in the context of Christianity, contextualization has become a major part of a wider theological debate since its first use. Cultural contextualization and theological contextualization are the two main levels of contextualization. Cultural contextualization deals with "the institutions of family, law, education and the observable level of cultural behavior and the use of artifacts."[41]

Theologians concern themselves with the world view and cosmology, and the moral and ethical norms, the deeper levels of culture.[42] Anthropologists and theologians have never been at ease with one another.

> They speak different languages, approach culture from different perspectives and look for different sets of results. The Consultation of Gospel and Culture at Willowbank, Bermuda, January 1978, was an attempt to help evangelical theologians and anthropologists begin to talk and, more appropriately, to listen to each other.[43]

It is important to note that in theological circles, the term contextualization does not carry the same meaning for everyone. Hence Nicholls differentiates what he calls existential contextualization from dogmatic contextualization. Existential contextualization involves the interactions of the principle of "the essential relativity of text and context, and the dialectical method of the search for truth."[44] Nicholls notes that Western existential theology presupposes that:

> all theology, including biblical theology, is culturally conditioned and therefore in some sense relative. Theologizing is understood as a human fallible process, so that no theology is perfect or absolute.[45]

On the other hand, dogmatic contextualization "begins with an authoritative biblical theology whose dogmatic understanding is contextualized in a given cultural situation."[46] Some Western and non-Western theologians feel that the Christian message which the missionaries took to Asia and Africa was highly dogmatic and militant. They suggest that this kind of message made the Gospel of Jesus Christ appear to be negative and exclusive both to religious beliefs and to people's cultural expressions.[47] Nicholls contends that this attitude toward the Gospel of Jesus Christ which the missionaries brought fostered an "inability to distinguish between biblical theology and Western theology."

Adaptation

Adaptation is more of a sociological term than it is theological or missiological. Adaptation, as a sociological term, "refers to the process of interaction between changes made by an organism on its environment and change made by the environment on the organism."[48] Humans are organisms. They react to environmental, sociological and religious changes. Their reactions may be positive or negative. When they react positively to a given innovation, they may develop a tendency toward adaptation, which "establishes a moving balance between the needs of a population and the potential of its environment."[49] In the arena of missions, adaptation encourages a borrowing of foreign ideas and practices by the national church. The goal of adaptation is mainly to change existing ideas and practices in the minds of nationals and in the ecclesiastical behavior of the national church, so as to bring conformity in these areas with those of the foreign mission boards. It would appear that adaptation may diagnose the problems of the national church, administer some anesthetic solutions, but may fail to offer authentic solutions which may ease the pains of cultural imposition and identity crisis.

> "Adaptation" implied a peripheral, superficial or non-essential activity within a culture. Its concept encoded Western cultural superiority complex and domination. This was soon realised and African theologians have long fought against it and rejected it.[50]

Adaptation may suggest the mere Christianization of cultural practices, which lacks depth and meaning. For example, the changing of one's Igbo name to either a Biblical or English one at baptism does not necessarily make that individual a Christian. It may satisfy the missionary, but not the individual who is baptised. The Igbo are good at adaptation. They can survive any situation of life and any social and religious changes. Other cultures do not intimidate them. They know how to react with other cultures. But the question is how deep is their adaptation to other cultures? The adaptation appears to be shallow. This is the case with some Igbo adaptation of some Christian practices and forms. Adaptation stops at the surface level. It does not get to the root. On the other hand, some Igbo look at adaptation with disdain and contempt. They contend that adaptation carries the baggage of insult for the Igbo culture, superiority and cultural imposition by the missionary, and dependence on the foreign mission agency.

Incarnation

The theory of Incarnation derives from the coming of God into the world in human form. Jesus is the incarnation of God. He came into the world as a human being so that He would understand the human condition better and respond to it appropriately. The Incarnation of God in Jesus is a mystery and it will continue to be. Incarnation, if it is not properly explained to the average Igbo mind, may suggest the meaning of reincarnation—the second, third or fourth etc. of a dead relative. In the Bible the birth of Christ is mysterious. Incarnation is subject to misunderstanding by most Igbo. Proponents of the theory of Incarnation in mission endeavor contend that as an inculturation model, Incarnation goes back to God. God is the originator of mission. God knows how best to do mission, hence incarnation.

> The way in which the analogy of the Incarnation was first used suggests that it served what is called a Christology from above. The purpose of inculturation was compared to the Son of God taking human flesh and adopting a human culture as a necessary concomitant of his human nature.[51]

Shorter notes three corollaries from this view of inculturation:

1 This model was Christ's own enculturation. It was Christ's cultural education as a first-century Jew who lived in Galilee.
2 This view indicates Christ's need of other cultures so that He could effectively spread this Good News of the kingdom and share His life with humanity.
3 This cultural education and Christ's adoption of a specific human culture, placed the earthly Jesus "into the whole historical process of communication between cultures."[52]

Shorter observes that Jesus accepted the dynamics of cultural exchange as a consequence of his own inculturation, and encouraged missionaries to follow His example anywhere they went. However, Shorter notes some problems with this concept of Incarnation. First, this concept is limited to the cultural education of the earthly Jesus. He contends that with this understanding of cultural education, which gives the impression of the "first insertion of the Gospel into a culture," one will overlook the ongoing dialogue which takes place between Gospel and culture. The second problem he sees in this view is that it "encourages in practice a one-way view of inculturation" because "it is a Christology from above." The third problem is that this "incarnation model may encourage people to succumb to the temptation of culturalism."[53] Shorter calls for a more inclusive approach to the "mystery of the Word made flesh" in order to remedy the defects of the incarnation-model.

> This is, in fact, the main theological criticism that has to be made of the analogy between Incarnation and inculturation. One cannot use only one aspect of the Christ-event to illuminate the dialogue between Gospel and culture. The whole mystery of Christ, passion, death and resurrection, has to be applied analogically to the process of inculturation. It is only when this is done that a Christological understanding of inculturation becomes possible.[54]

The late David J. Bosch, a native of South Africa and a prominent Protestant missiologist, asserted that Protestant churches have "an underdeveloped theology of the incarnation," while the "churches of the East, Roman Catholics and Anglicans have always taken the incarnation far more seriously."[55] He cites the case of the Eastern church which tends to lay emphasis on the Incarnation "within the context of the preexistence, the origin, of Christ."[56] Liberation theology views the mission of the church in terms of the incarnate Christ. The human Jesus, who lived in Nazareth and walked the dusty roads of Palestine, had compassion on the down-trodden and the marginalized. Jesus is today perceived as one who walks on the side of the poor of the world, especially by those in Brazil and South Africa.

> In this model, one is not interested in a Christ who offers only external salvation, but in a Christ who agonizes and sweats and bleeds with the victims of oppression. One criticizes the bourgeois church of the West, which leans toward docetism and for which Jesus' humanness is only a veil hiding his divinity. This bourgeois church has an idealist understanding of itself, refuses to take sides, and believes that it offers a home for masters as well as slaves, rich and poor, oppressor and oppressed. Because it refuses to practice solidarity with victims, such a church has lost its relevance. Having peeled off the social and political dimensions of the gospel, it has dematured it completely.[57]

The Incarnation has its beginning in Jesus Christ. In Jesus, God demonstrates His love for humanity. The Incarnation tells the story of God who gets involved in the human condition without minding the decay and the suffering. Through the Incarnation, God comes down to the level of humankind with salvation—the ultimate solution for the human condition. In Incarnation, God feels and loves. In Incarnation, God lives in solidarity with the oppressed and the marginalised. It is a fact that Jesus befriended the poor and the weak and cared for them. The circumstances of His birth, His temptation experience, the composition of His twelve disciples, His relationships with women, His love for children, His identification with the sick, the outcasts and the excluded from the mainstream of society, give testimony of the real meaning of Incarnation.[58]

Acculturation

No culture is static. Since creation, human societies have been characterized by movement and interaction. When people move, they normally move with their culture. When they come into contact with people of other cultures, they relate to these new people through the instrumentality of their own culture. One of the major vehicles of cultural inter-change is language. Every people's language is unique because there are symbols and concepts which are unique to each cultural group in the world. Every group of people guards its cultural heritages with care. No group desires to be deprived of its culture in any form or shape.

However, cultural changes do occur as a result of movements and consequent interaction with other cultures. Acculturation involves major changes which may occur as a result of prolonged inter-cultural contacts.

> Acculturation occurs when groups having different cultures come into intensive firsthand contact, with subsequent massive changes in the original culture patterns of one or both groups. It always involves an element of force, either directly, as in the case of conquest, or indirectly, as in the implicit or explicit threat that force will be used if people refuse to make the changes that those in the other group expect them to make.[59]

In the arena of Christian theology, the term acculturation is closely related to the concept of inculturation. However, acculturation is functionally a sociological concept. Judging from its sociological meaning, acculturation appears to be a misfit in Christian missionary endeavor. It gives the impression of internal manipulation of a given culture. In principle, it is the "communication between cultures on a footing of mutual respect and tolerance,"[60] but in practice it is manipulative. This manipulative cultural interplay appears to be unChristian because it is an abuse of one culture on another culture. However acculturation may have a positive side if, in Christianity, missiologists become aware of the fact that Christianity is a universal religion and its authenticity is not limited to one culture, whether it is Hebrew or Western. "Being human demands not only insertion into one's own culture, but openness towards other cultures."[61] Shorter continues:

> Intercultural contact, especially when it is multiple and rapid, as is the case at the present day, precipitates structural change, and structural change is typically associated with inculturation in its first stage, the first insertion of a faith into a given culture.[62]

The Igbo culture is a case in point. Much has happened to the Igbo since the introduction of Christianity in the land. In most communities today the Christian priest or pastor plays the roles of the juju priest. Many people go to the church both for worship and for fellowship. The priest or the pastor is expected to lead in the people's worship experience. He or she is also expected to ignite the fire of fellowship among worshippers.

The expectations which Christian worshippers have of their leaders are similar to those which adherents of the indigenous religion have of their leaders. However, on close examination, one will discover that

> . . . many (some would argue most) African Christian priests and ministers are more culturally European in their Christianity than many, if not most, Euroamerican missionaries.[63]

This situation appears to be one of the effects of acculturation. It also appears not to be working well for the growth of the church in Africa, particularly in Igboland.

Enculturation

Enculturation is another sociological term.. Every society in the world has its own culture. People who are born into a given society learn the culture of that group of people through the process of socialization. Culture is not genetic. Rather culture is transmitted to people. This transmission is a process. This process may be termed enculturation. "Enculturation is the process by which a society's culture is transmitted from one generation to the next."[64] Sociologists claim that people learn the socially appropriate way of meeting their biologically determined needs through the process of enculturation. They also claim that there are human needs which are not learned. These biological needs are food, shelter, companionship, self-defense, and sexual gratification. "Each culture determines in its own way how these needs will be met."[65] In recent years, the use of enculturation among theologians is beginning to gain acceptance. Church growth experts as well as missiologists are using this term to convey the notion of inculturation.[66]

> Enculturation refers to the cultural learning process of the individual, the process by which a person is inserted into his or her culture. It is a concept that is closely related to that of socialization . . . while the process obviously includes formal teaching and learning, it is very largely an informal, and even an unconscious, experience. To a great extent the individual teaches himself through a process of adaptive learning, the rules of which are given by society. The images or symbols of a culture are in themselves didactic, and they teach the individual to construct his own categories and even to transcend them in the very act of constructing them.[67]

Shorter observes that language is not the only thing that has grammar. "There is also the imaginative grammar of the culture."[68] He claims that every culture has its own signs which are comparable to language. The grammar of culture is a configuration of images, concepts and interpretations. "Through the process of enculturation, this grammar is acquired unconsciously by the individual member of society."[69] The point Shorter is making has some validity for the practice of Christianity in Igboland. There is a parallel between enculturation and inculturation. This parallel lies in "insertion of an individual into his or her culture and the insertion of the Christian faith into a culture where Christians were not previously present."[70]

Inculturation

Joseph Masson, professor at the Gregorian University in Rome, was the first to use the term "inculturation" in a written document at the opening of the Second Vatican Council in 1962.[71] "Today there is a more urgent need for a Catholicism that is inculturated."[72] However members of the Society of Jesus seemed to be responsible for the introduction and popularization of this term.[73] "Inculturation" has become a popular term among Catholic and Protestant theologians, especially those in Two-Thirds World countries. Shorter defines inculturation as:

> The on-going dialogue between faith and culture or cultures. More fully, it is the creative and dynamic relationship between the Christian message and a culture or cultures.[74]

Shorter then shares Father Pedro Arrup's definition of inculturation:

> The incarnation of Christian life and of the Christian message in a particular cultural context, in such a way that this experience not only finds expression through elements proper to the culture in question (this alone would be no more than a superficial adaptation) but becomes a principle that animates, directs and unifies the culture, transforming it and remaking it so as to bring about a "new creation."[75]

Shorter observes three points about the functionality of this term: Inculturation is not only the first insertion of the Christian message into a non-Christian culture or cultures; it is also a relevant phenomenon in the evangelized West. He sees the need for inculturation in Europe and North America because many countries in these areas "have been Christianized and now de-Christianized."[76] He states: "As long as faith is present to a culture, the dialogue must take place. It is a process that never comes to an end."[77] The second point Shorter makes about inculturation is that the Christian faith exists in a cultural form.

When we speak of Christian faith or Christian life, we are necessarily speaking of a cultural phenomenon. It is a distinctive way of life that can only operate culturally.[78]

Shorter argues that inculturation involves "a dialogue between a culture and the faith in cultural form."[79] The implication here is interaction between cultures, that is between the Christianized culture of the missionary and the unChristianized culture to which the missionary comes. In other words, Shorter's use of inculturation is synonymous with "acculturation." Shorter's third point about inculturation is that it is a fact of life which goes beyond mere acculturation. It is the point at which the Gospel of Jesus Christ enlivens the culture of a given people from among them. The result of this internal enlivening and spiritual sensitivity is reformulation or reinterpretation of cultural values and norms.[80]

Justin S. Ukpong, an African theologian, observes the newness of "inculturation" in the field of Christian theology and maintains that the meaning of this term is still developing. However he gives the following definition:

It is . . . an approach in mission/evangelization, and involves evangelizing a culture from within, that is to say, proclaiming the Good News to people from within the perspective of their culture.[81]

Ukpong mentions three characteristics of this approach in evangelism and Christian witness:

1 The utilization of the resources of the culture which is being evangelized in expressing the Christian faith.
2 The Good News of Jesus is pronounced to challenge and animate the culture.
3 This challenging and animating are done from the perspective of the culture and through the agency of an insider or insiders in the culture.[82]

David J. Bosch, writing about relevant missiology, sees mission as inculturation. He argues that models such as accommodation, indigenization and adaptation are inadequate for contextualizing theology. He observes that "Western colonialism, cultural superiority, and 'manifest destiny' exercised on the Western missionary enterprise . . . compromised the gospel."[83] He further cites ways in which these conditions affect Western missionary enterprise in the Two-Thirds World countries.

By the time the large-scale Western colonial expansion began, Western Christians were unconscious of the fact that their theology was culturally conditioned; they simply assumed that it was supra-cultural and universally valid. And since Western culture was implicitly regarded as Christian, it was equally self-evident that this culture had to be exported together with the Christian faith. Still, it was soon acknowledged that, in order to expedite the conversion process, some adjustments were necessary. The strategy by which these were to be put into effect was variously called adaptation or accommodation (in Catholicism) or indigenization (in Protestantism). It was often, however, limited to accidental matters, such as liturgical vestments, non-sacramental rites, art, literature, architecture, and music.[84]

Though the term inculturation is new in Christian theology and mission methodology, the theory itself is not new. We believe that this theory is as old as when God first conceived it in His mind. God is the originator and also the source of mission. The sole purpose of the Incarnation is to reach humans for salvation where they are.

The Word became flesh and made his dwelling among us. We have seen his glory, the glory of the One and Only, who came from the Father, full of grace and truth.[85]

Since the coming of Jesus into the world, God has been sending missionaries to mission fields all over the world. Many of these local or/and foreign missionaries do effective evangelistic work, others perform poorly, depending on the level of their commitment to God and the strategy they employ. Indigenization, Contextualization, Adaptation, Incarnation, Acculturation, Enculturation, and Inculturation are among the models which missionaries have used over the years. We prefer Inculturation to any of the others for effective evangelization of non-Christian Communities or even for a re-evangelization of apostate communities. Our reason for this preference is not because of the currency of the term, but because of its suggested meaning.

Therefore, for a better understanding of the intent of this book, we define Inculturation as cultural interchange which freely and openly allows the non-Christian community or the apostate community the opportunity to interpret the Biblical message of salvation within their cultural, conceptual and symbolic frameworks, with a view to attaining authentic faith and practice.

The next chapter will present dialogue as a specifically effective model of inculturation in Igboland, and show why it is the most effective model for authentic Christianity in Igboland.

Notes

1 Gwinyai Henry Muzorewa, *An African Theology of Mission* (Lewiston, NY., Edwin Mellen Press, 1990), 31.

2 By "other people," Muzorewa is referring to any person or persons who do not share one's experience, culture, faith, struggle and aspiration.

3 Ibid., 82.

4 G. C. Oosthuizen, "Indigenous Christianity and the Future of the church in South Africa," *International Bulleting of Missionary Research* (January 1997): 8. G. C. Oosthuizen was director of the Research Unit for New Religious and Independent/indigenous churches, University of Zululand, South Africa. He is Professor Emeritus in the Department of Science of Religion at the University of Durban-Westville, South Africa.

5 Ibid., 8, 9.

6 Pan-Aficanism is the quest for African identity by Africans. It is a movement of ideas similar to capitalism, socialism, World Federalism or Zionism. See Colin Legum, ed., *Africa: A Handbook to the Continent* (New York: Federick A. Praeger, reprint 1967), 413.

7 E. A. Ayandele, *The Missionary Impact on Modern Nigeria: 1842-1914* (London: Longmans, Green and Co.. 1966), 175.

8 Ibid., 176.

9 Ibid., 177.

10 "Ethiopianism" was one of the terms which described African nationalism expressed through the medium of the church. Ayandele observes that in Nigeria, and most of West Africa, Ethiopianism acquired a different meaning from its meaning in South and Central African settings. Whereas the term in these territories was fundamentally racial because of the color-bar policy of the white rulers in those places, in West Africa, Ethiopianism was also fundamentally racial, but in a peculiar way. In South and Central Africa, the mission churches did not raise up an African agency early enough which would have introduced African leadership into church life. As a result, the churches did not provide freedom and scope for Africans to express their own personality. The only option for Africans was secession. They seceded and founded their own churches. Therefore, secession became a necessary ingredient of Ethiopianism. The racial policy of the white rulers drove these "separatist" churches into becoming media for anti-government movements, and often-times for explosive subterranean organizations. In West Africa Ethiopianism never became anti-government. Though it was anti-white, it was not on the same scale as in South and Central Africa. In West Africa, there were no white settlements and nothing like the kind of economic exploita-

tion which took place in South and Central Africa. The most important difference is the fact that mission churches in West Africa raised up early an African agency and missionaries' wards found sufficient scope within the churches to express their natural desire for responsibility and leadership. The term "Ethiopianism" derives from Psalm 68:31. "Ethiopia shall stretch forth her hands to God." (See Ayandele, *Missionary Impact on Modern Nigeria: 1842-1914*, 177–178).

11 Ibid., 178.

12 Ibid.

13 Ibid., 180.

14 Ibid.

15 Ibid., 181.

16 Charles H. Kraft and Tom N. Wisley, eds., *Readings in Dynamic Indigeneity* (Pasadena, Calif: William Carey Library, 1979), 72.

17 Ibid., 73.

18 Ibid.

19 Ibid., 74.

20 Ibid.

21 Ibid., 73.

22 Rufus Anderson was a theoretician and administrator of the American Board of Commissioners for Foreign Missions (ABCFM).

23 Ibid., 314.

24 See Gwinyai H. Muzorewa, *The Origins and Development of African Theology* (Maryknoll, N.Y.: Orbis Books, 1985), 57–74.

25 Osadolar Imasogie, "A Christian Attitude to Cultural Revival," *Ogbomoso Journal of Theology* 7 (December 1992): 6–7.

26 Pierre Abelard was a notable champion of this view. He lived during the Middle Ages and was condemned as a heretic. His Christ was only a moral teacher who "in all he did in the flesh...had the intention of our instruction, doing on a higher degree what Socrates and Plato had done before him." See Samuel Baker, "The Races of the Nile Basin," in *Transactions of Ethnological Society of London* (1891): 423–424.

27 Ibid., 7.

28 Ibid.

29 Ibid.

30 Ibid., 7–8.

31 Frank A. Salamone and Michael C. Mbabuike, "The Plight of the Indigenous Catholic Priest in Africa: An Igbo Example," *Missiology*23, No. 2 (April 1995): 166–167.

32 Ibid., 169.

33 Ibid., 170.

34 Ibid.

35 2 Cor. 6:14–16a NIV.

36 Ben O. Nwabueze, "The Igbos in the Context of Modern Government and Politics in Nigeria: A Call for Self-Examination and Self-Correction," *The 1985 Akiajoku Lecture* (Owerri, Nigeria: Ministry of Information and Culture, 1985), 6.

37 Bruce J. Nicholls, *Contextualization: A Theology of Gospel and Cutlure* (Downers Grove, Ill: InterVarsity Press, 1979), 21.

38 Ibid.

39 Ibid.

40 Ruy O. Costa ed., *One Faith, Many Cultures* (Maryknoll, N.Y.: Orbis Books, 1988), 129.

41 Nicholls, *Contextualization: A Theology of Gospel and Culture*, 24.

42 Ibid.

43 Ibid.

44 Ibid., 24–25.

45 Ibid., 25.

46 Ibid., 24.

47 Ibid., 28.

48 William A. Haviland, *Cultural Anthropology*, 5th ed. (New York: Holt, Rinehart and Winston, 1987), 140.

49 Ibid., 141.

50 Oliver A. Onwubiko, *Theory and Practices of Inculturation: An African Perspective* (Enugu, Nigeria: SNAAP Press, 1992), 47.

51 Aylward Shorter, *Toward a Theology of Inculturation* (Maryknoll, N.Y.: Orbis Books, 1988), 80.

52 Ibid.

53 Ibid., 81–82.

54 Ibid., 82.

55 David J. Bosch, *Transforming Mission: Paradigm Shifts in Theology of Mission* (Maryknoll, N.Y.: Orbis Books, 1994), 512.

56 Ibid.

57 Ibid., 512–513.

58 John W. de Gruchy and Charles Villa-Vicencio, eds., *Doing Theology in Context: South African Perspectives* (Maryknoll, N.Y. Orbis Books, 1994), 63.

59 Haviland, *Cultural Anthropology*, 373.

60 Shorter, *Toward A Theology of Inculturation*, 8.

61 Ibid.

62 Ibid., 47.

63 Salamone and Mbabuike, "The Plight of the Indigenous Catholic Priest in Africa" *Missiology*, 170.

64 Haviland, *Cultural Anthropology*, 31.

65 Ibid., 32.

66 Shorter, *Toward a Theology of Inculturation*, 5.

67 Ibid.

68 Ibid., 6.

69 Ibid.

70 Ibid.

71 Ibid., 10.

72 Ibid.

73 Ibid.

74 Ibid., 11.

75 Ibid.

76 Ibid., 12.

77 Ibid.

78 Ibid.

79 Ibid.

80 Shorter, *Toward a Theology of Inculturation*, 11–13.

81 Rosino Gibellin, ed., *Paths of African Theology* (Maryknoll, N.Y: Orbis Books, 1994), 40–41.

82   Ibid., 41.

83   Bosch, *Transforming Mission*, 448.

84   Ibid.

85   John 1:14 NIV.

Chapter 7

Dialogue: An Inculturation Model for Christianity in Igboland

The Igbo love to talk; they enjoy dialogue as a group. Though the family is the basic social unit in Igboland, the Igbo have a superb sense of broader community. They have a type of village government which has been described as a "segmentary pattern of government."[1] Family and religious ties hold this government together. "It is a spectacular achievement of the Igbos in political organization."[2]

One of the major benefits of this type of government is that it makes government small and allows people both the freedom of participation and the responsibility of involvement in the administration of their government. Though families may delegate authority to their first-born males who make up the Council of Elders, a major community decision will normally require the consensus of the members of the community, especially males. The Igbo have autonomous communities which are

> linked with other communities by ties that could be blood, trade, marriage, etc., with age grades, titled men, wealthy citizens and the poor, all playing some part in the community affairs, in village decision-making. The Igbo fully articulated this organization which gives full rein to individual participation and offers a value for the restless energy of the villager. . . . Igbo culture can . . . be described by its emphasis on individual achievement and initiatives, alternative prestige goals and paths of action, a tendency towards equalitarian leadership. While the social structure is termed "flexible," it does not imply a structural weakness; rather it gives the individual the opportunity to work through and across the groups to achieve desired goals and freedom to select alternatives.[3]

The average villager enjoys freedom of speech and action, provided the exercise of this freedom does not interfere with another person's freedom. Since no individual exists alone, persons are expected to be sensitive to the feelings and needs of others in the community.

The individual villager is expected to remain loyal to the community not only because it provides collective security, both moral and psychological, but also because the community safeguards all that is precious to the individual citizen, especially land.[4]

The average Igbo cherishes both individualism and corporateness. While the Igbo react negatively to the deprivation of their individual freedoms, they also have a strong identity with the corporate body, the community. They feel that *igwe bu ike* (crowd is strength), *otu onye anaghi ebi* (no one person lives alone).

It has been pointed out that the Igbo universal ideal of relations is a harmonious alignment of dynamic entities. Igbo philosophy is only the Igbo elaboration of African philosophy, and the ideal of that philosophy in the area of organization has been said to be holism. So the ideal for organization in Igbo philosophy is into "harmonious wholes." This is clearly reflected in the Igbo choice of kolanut, eagle's feather and "Omu nkwu"[5] as sacred symbols of relations. These are all objects with parts made up of disparate shapes and sizes that fold harmoniously into wholes.[6]

The "harmonious alignment" which exists in the Igbo organizational structure fosters conversation and dialogue. Village squares and town halls are common sights in every Igbo community. Males and females, both young and old, constitute themselves into groups. These groups, which could be religious or social, provide avenues for people to interact with one another. When they meet, they talk and even solve difficult problems through conversation and dialogue because *nwayo nwayo ka eji aracha ofe di oku* (it takes little sips to consume hot soup). Dialogue is an important aspect of Igbo life.

This chapter will define dialogue and deal with some aspects of the dialogical method of communication. We will also define communication, and relate that definition to the communication of the gospel of Jesus Christ to the Igbo of Nigeria. We will consider a few examples of the present methods of gospel communication in Igboland and suggest dialogue as the most effective method of communicating the gospel message to the Igbo. The chapter will close with a comparison of some Biblical teachings and some basic Igbo beliefs, with a view to suggesting effective points of contact for the gospel communicator.

Dialogue: Definition

"Dialogue" is a word derived from the Greek noun *dialogos*. Its verb form, *dialegomai*, means "to converse, reason, talk with . . . to discourse, argue."[7] According to Leonard Swidler, dialogue is "a conversation on a common subject between two or more persons with differing views, the primary purpose of which is for each participant to learn from the other so that he or she can change and grow."[8]

Chinua Achebe notes the Igbo flair for dialogue in his book, *Things Fall Apart*. A white missionary was visiting the Igbo town of Mbanta. Most of the people in Mbanta had not seen a white person. They gathered in their village square to see the white missionary and hear him speak.

> . . . the white man began to speak to them. He spoke through an interpreter who was an Ibo man, though his dialect was different and harsh to the ears of Mbanta. Many people laughed at his dialect and the way he used words strangely. Instead of saying "myself" he always said "my buttocks." But he was a man of commanding presence and the clansmen listened to him.[9]

The white missionary, continuing his preaching, "told them they worshipped false gods, gods of wood and stone. A deep murmur went through the crowd when he said this."[10] The missionary continued his preaching and spoke about God as one who lived above and that every one would meet Him at death for judgment.

> Evil men and all the heathen who in their blindness bowed to wood and stone were thrown into a fire that burned like palm-oil. But good men who worshipped the true God lived for ever in His happy kingdom. "We have been sent by this great God to ask you to leave your wicked ways and false gods and turn to Him so that you may be saved when you die," he said.[11]

At the close of the white man's message someone from the crowd made a derogatory remark about his interpreter. The crowd laughed. They also discussed excitedly the white man's intention to live among them.

> At this point an old man said he had a question. "Which is this god of yours," he asked. "The goddess of the earth, the god of the sky, Amadiora of the thunderbolt, or what?" The interpreter spoke to the white man and he immediately gave his answer. "All the gods you have named are not gods at all. They are gods of deceit who tell you to kill your fellows and destroy innocent children. There is only one true God and He has the earth, the sky, you and me and all of us." "If we leave our gods and follow your god," asked another man, "who will protect us from the anger of our neglected gods and ancestors?"

> "Your gods are not alive and cannot do you any harm," replied the white man. "They are pieces of wood and stone."

> When this was interpreted to the men of Mbanta, they broke into derisive laughter. "These men must be mad," they said to themselves. How else could they say

that Ani and Amadiora were harmless? And Idemili and Ogwugwu[12] too? And some of them began to go away.[13]

This dialogue is a typical example of how the early missionaries shared the gospel with the Igbo in the beginnings of Christianity. Many indigenous preachers still present the gospel the same way today. In many instances, these preachers do not really answer the people's questions. Rather, they become condemning and judgmental. They find it easier to condemn the people's religion and religious expressions than to explain to them who God truly is and how he desires that they worship Him. This attitude makes dialogue difficult, if not impossible.

John B. Taylor observes that

Dialogue may involve a rediscovered theology of Incarnation and participation which urges us as adopted sons to try, perhaps belatedly, to do what our Lord did in identifying with the world's joys and sufferings. It may be a theology of mission which leads us to go first to where our neighbour stands rather than summoning him to our position and leaving him alone if he cannot come. It may be a theology of hope which expects the Spirit's activity in the most unlikely places and believes that all things work together for good.[14]

Though maintaining a specialty in Islamic Studies, Taylor suggests that "in the intentions and principles of dialogue which we apply to the Muslim situation, we may find tools to explore other possibilities for the Christian conscience to serve in fields where Christ has been hitherto unknown, unrecognized, unpreached, or rejected."[15] He outlines five considerations for meaningful dialogue in gospel communication:

1. Meeting for dialogue. Mutual cooperation is essential for meaningful dialogue: "If we wish to talk together, we must talk with each other, not against or about each other."[16]
2. Dialogue for learning: We must be sensitive to the other person's religious tradition. We must be willing to hear the other person's theological language which may be unfamiliar and be also willing to recognize the spiritual values of its symbols and rituals.

Dialogue encourages us to penetrate into each other's spiritual experiences, to achieve sympathy with that which is sought after by our neighbour, and to realize the priorities within our own tradition. When we learn the religious terminology of the other man's faith; when we try to communicate to him our own experience of God, we are rethinking, re-expressing and, perhaps, rediscovering truth about God.

If we start by being ready to learn about our neighbour's faith and tradition, rather than by rushing in to teach our own, we may already be making an effective witness and may also be preparing for communication and even proclamation at a later stage.[17]

3. Dialogue for service: Christians and people of other faiths work together, go to school together and do other secular things together. "Each needs to win the other's confidence to further their cooperation with each other."[18]

4. Dialogue . . . with God? "The chief justification for our encounter and dialogue is that it may lead us closer to responding to God's dialogue with men."[19]

5. Dialogue . . . in the World?

Religious values are becoming more and not less necessary in many parts of the world to challenge at the deepest level complacency over material inequalities, to provoke compassion for vast suffering, to bring reconciliation and non-violent resolution to obdurate racial tensions. It is especially urgent that religion be reconciling rather than divisive when one recalls how religion may be misused within situations of tension, and how it may be distorted into self-righteousness and prejudice.[20]

Swidler, in addition to defining "dialogue," suggests ten "commandments" of dialogue:

1   The primary purpose of dialogue is to change and grow in the perception and understanding of reality and ... act accordingly.

2   Interreligious dialogue must be a two-sided project—within each religious community.

3   Each participant must come to the dialogue with complete honesty and sincerity.

4   Each participant must assume a similar complete honesty and sincerity in the other partners.

5   Each participant must define himself. Conversely—the one interpreted must be able to recognize himself or herself in the interpretation.

6   Each participant must come to the dialogue with no hard-and-fast assumptions as to where the points of disagreement are.

7   Dialogue can take place only between equals.

8   Dialogue can take place only on the basis of mutual trust.
9   Persons entering into interreligious dialogue must be at least minimally self-critical of both themselves and their own religious traditions.
10   Each participant eventually must attempt to experience the partner's religion "from within."[21]

Swidler mentions three areas in which interreligious dialogue operates: "the practical, where we collaborate to help humanity; the cognitive, where we seek understanding and truth; and the spiritual, where we attempt to experience the partner's religion 'from within.'"[22] Paul Knitter maintains that participants in interreligious dialogue must enter into dialogue with no biases if meaningful dialogue is to be attained.[23] Similarly, Donald K. Swearer asserts that "if we believe that our particular perception of religious truth is the *only* correct one, then genuine dialogue does not take place at all."[24]

There are different kinds of religious dialogue. There is dialogue between religions, for example Islam and Christianity or Christianity and an African religion. This type of dialogue is generally referred to as interreligious dialogue. There is also "inner dialogue." The Catholic Church engaged in this kind of dialogue with some African Christian communities in the early 1970s. It is still going on today. Inner dialogue is "not between Christians and representatives of traditional African religions, but between African Christians and their own traditional religious heritage."[25]

At the close of one of such dialogues in Yaounde, Cameroon, in 1976, Pietro Rossano, a Catholic priest, described this type of dialogue in a radio interview:

> Here [in Africa] dialogue takes on, I would say, a peculiar aspect which in English circles today has come to be called "inner dialogue." It is an interior dialogue in which a Christian alone or from within a community confronts his or her cultural environment, his or her cultural, religious, spiritual, and ancestral heritage.[26]

Adherents of African religions did not participate in this dialogue. "Christians who shared the religious spirit of Africa and who were thus influenced by the general outlooks and symbols of African spirituality,"[27] were the ones who did. They were indeed the ones who probably initiated and promoted this kind of dialogue.

> The purpose of such dialogue was to form a truly African Christianity . . . the message of Christ assumes the values of a particular culture and transforms them.

God's redeeming activity, in other words, builds upon the already existing moral and religious substratum and brings it to fulfillment.[28]

The third kind of dialogue is one that takes place between the Christian witness and the non-Christian inquirer. This type of dialogue is not necessarily organized. It does not have to involve more than two persons. Its goal is neither ecumenism nor contextualization. Its goal is genuine salvation of the individual and a culturally authentic Christianity. This is the kind of dialogue which is the goal of this book. This dialogue is a process, but it is one which is different from "the bilateral . . . instance of Christian theologising in general and of ecumenical theologising in particular.[29] Rather, it is the type of dialogue which necessitates the Christian witness to truly and genuinely aspire "to have as much knowledge and experience about [for example] African heritage before a real dialogue of understanding can ensue."[30] Kofi Asare Opoku observes that

> one of the most vital features of the African heritage is the sense of community. The community has a religious foundation and goes beyond the limits of its visible members to include God, often regarded as the First Grand Ancestor of the community, or the Overlord or Chief; the ancestors who are forebears of the community and who uphold communal unity and co-operation as well as those yet to be born. The divinities, who sustain social institutions as part of their assigned responsibilities from the Creator, also form part of the community. The invisible members of the community wield an immensely sacred influence in setting every living person on the path to righteousness and justice. . . . The community is . . . an integrated entity which is undergirded and kept alive by extended relationships, the purpose of which is to enhance unity and promote greater and greater friendly co-operation. The structure of the community is divinely given and community loyalty has a religious dimension, for everyone is under obligation to be loyal to one's family or clan and family and clan loyalty is social value with tremendous implications.[31]

Therefore the Christian witness must be prepared to adequately address matters and concerns regarding the various visible and invisible components of the community which the inquirer may meet.

The Dialogical Method of Communication

Dialogue means communication. When two or more people meet, there is the tendency for them to talk to one another. Exchange of greetings is a form of dialogue. Conversation or dialogue is a common feature of all social formations. "Like twittering birds, man has a need to express himself."[32] Communication is important for the survival of humanity.

"Conversation creates a union, a collective, a social relationship."[33] People converse with those whom they have interest in. There are various kinds of conversation. However, four stand out in almost every human society: social, political, academic and religious. Each of these types of conversation could be entertaining, informative or educative. In most cases, when people engage one another in conversation, they understand one another better. No meaningful or helpful conversation can be unilateral; helpful or meaningful conversations are usually bilateral. In this type of conversation, participants normally respect one another and one another's views.

This dialogical form of conversation gives room for exchange of ideas and opinions because of the process of communication which is taking place. Communication is a basic human need. One of the important elements of human communication is the use not only of words, but also of symbols.

> Among living creatures only man has the creative capacity to live simultaneously in two realms of experience, the physical and the symbolic. The sound, sight, taste, smell, and touch of people, events, and objects comprise the raw data of our physical world; and the composite assumptions and hunches about the way things "really are" make up our sense of the symbolic. It is not man's nature to participate totally in either world to the exclusion of the other. In neither can he remain an aloof bystander. Physical facts, after all, do not speak for themselves. They carry no automatic or proper significance. We have no way to divorce our participation in the physical realm from the way we represent our experience in the abstract, for the two are inexorably intertwined. Similarly, symbolic meaning does not spring full-blown from the sheer course of events; it must be created. And in human affairs it is created only by placing the particulars into some larger frame of reference, an image or model through which the specifics can be interpreted in abstract form.[34]

This certainly is a major reason for communication so that dialogical partners will be able to understand one another well and respond appropriately to one another. Communication will become fuzzy or distorted when the sender and the receiver of communication cues have different frames of reference. C. David Mortensen observes the contextual nature of effective communication, stating that

> Communication never takes place in a vacuum; it is not a "pure" process, devoid of background or situational overtones; it always requires at least one's minimal sensitivity to immediate physical surroundings, an awareness of setting or place that in turn influences the ebb and flow of what is regarded as personally significant.[35]

Donald K. Smith, in *Creating Understanding*, defines communication as "involvement." He observes:

> Those whom we don't know always seem different, sometimes even frightening. But as we become acquainted, we are astonished to learn how similar our needs and fears really are. Strangers become friends through steadily increasing involvement. . . . Those we have been trained to dislike or even hate are changed in our eyes to "good people" when we share in the same activities.[36]

Smith further observes the inseparable nature of "involvement" from "communication," stating that *communis*, is the root word for communication. Involvement is sharing something in common. "From that root *communis* come many related words: common, commune, community, communism, communion, and communication."[37] Sharing is a key element of each of these conditions of human relationship. "All these are occasions of "communication," a constantly broadening involvement that finds and builds more and more commonness, more areas of sharing."[38] Therefore, communication means trying to establish "commonness with someone."[39]

Emphasizing the importance of human involvement in effective communication, Smith draws a distinction between "transmission" and "communication."

> Technology may lead merely to transmission, which should not be confused with communication. Transmission occurs without involvement. It is a spreading out of words and symbols that does not take into account the responses of the audience. Once the message is transmitted, responsibility appears to have been discharged .... Thereby everything is seemingly explained.[40]

To buttress his argument, Smith quotes David Augsburger,

> communication is co-response. To communicate with you is to respond to you and to recognize your response to me. Being in each other's presence is communicating .... Communication is co-responsibility. To communicate effectively is to honor the mutuality of our relationship and to respect our equal privilege to respond to each other.[41]

He suggests "bonding" as the starting point of involvement and lists four "overlapping phases" for bonding:

1. Learning the other person's language.
2. Sharing in the other person's experiences.
3. Participating in the other person's culture.

4. Understanding the other person's beliefs.[42]

The core of Smith's argument in defining communication is that

Communication is a relationship. We do not get involved in order to communicate. We communicate by being involved. Involvement is the foundation of all communication. Cultural differences only emphasize its importance.[43]

Smith proposes more principles for creating understanding through effective communication:

1. Communication is a process.

   Communication cannot be treated as an isolated act, but is a process for which there is no clear beginning or ending. Effective communication requires awareness of the past, present, and future dimensions for all involved in communicating.[44]

2. In communication, meaning is internal and individual.

   Meaning is always personal and unique to each individual. Similar meanings are held by different people, but precise meanings are personal. There is no way to transfer meaning directly from teacher to student, from employer to employee, or from preacher to congregation. Meaning is developed indirectly. The person sending a message can only give information—BITs, Binary Information Units. The receiver of a message assembles the BIT of that message into a meaning, using a mental model that seems related to the new message. That mental model, which has been formed from earlier experiences, acts something like an interpreter, giving a sense (meaning) to signals that are otherwise just noises and images.

   If the mental models are similar in sender and receiver, and if an adequate amount of information has been given, the meaning developed in the receiver's mind will be close to the meaning in the sender's mind.

   Thus emphasis must be on the transfer of the right kind of, and enough, information from the sender to the receiver. When that is achieved, they will share similar meanings—and they have successfully communicated. Understanding is being created between the participants.[45]

3. Communication is what is heard and not what is said.

> Communication is a transaction during which understandings are shared and developed. The exchange involved in this transaction is listening and speaking; one party listens, another speaks, and then response reverses the flow. Through this reciprocity, understanding, but not necessarily agreement is developed.

> Good speaking is a matter not simply of pleasant words, but instead, of words and symbols chosen so that the hearer will develop the intended meaning. Senders must be aware that many filters always exist between themselves and their hearers—experience, culture, mood, personal needs, physical environment. Even with the best of intentions and the greatest of care, the message heard will seldom be the same as the message spoken.[46]

4. Clarification of goals increases the possibility of effective communication.

> Goals give broad direction but should be reduced to a series of objectives. Objectives are the steps that lead toward accomplishment of a goal. They are relevant to the goal, measurable, time-limited, and manageable with expected resources, (sic) and they require a significant effort to achieve.

> Objectives provide a standard against which to evaluate work and consider desirable changes so that the overall good will be reached. Without goals and objectives, intercultural workers can become so baffled by culture stress that nothing is achieved. Objectives help translate high ideals into necessary daily tasks.[47]

5. The communicator's personality and experiences modify the form of a message.

> A message changes as the messenger changes. Though the content is basically the same, the way it is expressed will be different with different bearers of the message. The communicator's personality, social group, personal spiritual life—in fact, all that he or she is—shapes the message.[48]

6. The communicator's image of the audience and understanding of the context are primary factors in shaping the form of the message.

> It is not the reality but the image of the audience that determines how communication occurs. The communicator chooses both content and communicative style based on his or her ideas about the audience—who they are, what they are interested in, and how they will respond. . . . Often the communicator's image of the audience is a shadowy distortion of reality, even though it is a controlling factor in the selection of content and presentation.

> A first step in improving communication is to gain a more accurate understanding of the audience. Identify where your image differs from the reality through formal study, supplemented by careful observations and involvement with the life of the audience. As these steps bring the image closer to the reality, communication effectiveness increases.[49]

7. Communication increases commitment.

> Commitment to an idea or a person is not static, but increases or diminishes over time. It is strengthened by public statement of the commitment, increasing inward commitment.

> Attitude includes belief, feeling, and knowledge. It is part of living, not separable from activity. Belief is reinforced when it is communicated, allowing it to involve emotion and relationships actively.

> Failure to communicate a new belief will weaken commitment to it. Lacking emotional and relational involvement, the belief becomes increasingly irrelevant and may eventually be given up. On the other hand, active participation in communication can lead to change of attitude and acceptance of new beliefs.[50]

These elements of communication will certainly find relevant expression in any Igbo community, and will also enhance the effective communication, and the consequent understanding, of the Christian message. These elements of communication share strong similarity with Charles H. Kraft's theory of "Dynamic equivalence." Commenting on the prerequisites for the effective planting of indigenous churches, Kraft forms six recommendations:

1. Each language and culture has its own genius, its own distinctiveness, its own special character, its own patterning, its own strengths, weaknesses and limitations. The effective church planter . . . must recognize this distinctiveness.
2. To communicate effectively in another language and culture one must respect and work in terms of this uniqueness.
3. In general, meanings that are communicable in one language and culture are communicable in another, though in different forms and always with some loss and gain of meaning.
4. "To preserve the content of the message the form must be changed" when that message is translated into another language with its own unique genius.
5. Available evidence and perspectives strongly suggest that we should not regard the languages and cultures of the Bible as too sacred to analyze and relate to as we do to other languages and cultures. They appear to be subject to the same limitations as other languages and cultures.
6. "The writers of the biblical books expected to be understood". . . . God expects to be understood through his church as well as through his Word. The church . . . is meant to be maximally intelligible to the world around it, conveying to it meanings equivalent to those conveyed to their cultures by scripturally recommended examples of churches.[51]

Looking at Smith's and Kraft's recommendations for effective communication of the Christian faith across culture and considering the nature of Christianity in Igboland, it appears that much of the early Christian work in Igboland lacked these tools. It appears that communication was monological and Western cultural imposition on the Igbo culture was strong. Involvement in the process of communication was minimal if not totally absent on the part of the Igbo inquirer. This cultural imposition by both the British colonial government and some of the early missionaries, coupled with the lack of dialogical involvement by the Igbo Christian convert, resulted in surface level Christianity and lack of commitment to the Christian faith.

The Igbo took to education as a means of acquiring new ways, jobs, promotion, wealth, knowledge, and adjustment to the colonial fact. When a missionary body could no longer run schools or used insufficient indigenous teachers who could hardly speak English, communities defected to another missionary body. All these give a certain ironical twist to the many letters from missionaries alleging that the field was ripe for harvest when the gospel was surely not the fruit. In mass baptism strategy, they were satisfied with a harvest of mere adherents.[52]

Effective communication of the gospel message to the Igbo must be dialogical. The "bridge-building" nature of dialogical evangelism cannot be over-emphasized.

We must approach dialogue as equals, listening as much as we speak. If we believe in the truth of the gospel there is nothing wrong in our desire for others to come to Christ. Integrity demands that we share what is most precious to us in dialogue, with the hope and prayer that the other person will be drawn to the same truth.[53]

In practical terms, evangelism and dialogue are interrelated. The Catholic Church's 1991 Pontifical Council for Interreligious Dialogue and Congregation for the Evangelization of Peoples in its statement, supports the evangelistic view of dialogue:

"Dialogue" can be understood in different ways. Firstly, at the purely human level, it means reciprocal communication, leading to a common goal or, at a deeper level, to interpersonal communion. Secondly, dialogue can be taken as an attitude of respect and friendship, which permeates or should permeate all those activities constituting the evangelizing mission of the church. This can appropriately be called "the spirit of dialogue." Thirdly, in the context of religious plurality, dialogue means "all positive and constructive interreligious relations with individuals and communities of other faiths which are directed at mutual understanding and enrichment, in obedience to truth and respect for freedom." It includes both witness and exploration of respective religious convictions.[54]

Judging from the meaning of "dialogue" which has its root in the "Platonic tradition," and the relationship between dialogue and evangelism, especially in the New Testament, we observe that "dialogue" is an essential model for authentic Christianity in Igboland.

"Dialogue" is both an old word and a new word. In the Western intellectual tradition, "dialogue" has roots in the Platonic tradition. There it refers to a method. In Plato's dialogues, Socrates is portrayed as one who uses a method of question and answer; through dialogue, he hopes to arrive at a better understanding of truth. The concept of dialogue, then, has a distinguished and ancient intellectual pedigree.[55]

David Lochhead observes that dialogue is a new word in theological discussions, stating that "dialogue" appears "as a subject heading only in the mid 1960s,"[56] during the time when the Roman Catholic church, under Pope John XXIII, entered "into the mainstream of ecumenical discussion."[57] In the context of gospel communication to the Igbo, "dialogue" becomes a new word, though an old word. We are using it here to mean "conversation" which is necessary for a better understanding of the Igbo worldview. A genuine conversation with a non-Igbo Christian will lead to a better understanding of his or her beliefs, spiritual condition, social and religious circumstances, and future spiritual aspirations by the Christian witness.

> In Plato, dialogue is a method for conducting a search for truth. In the *Dialogues*, Socrates appears as one who makes no claim to knowledge but who, through entering into conversation with others, exposes the falsity of what we think we know and through question and answer, leads us into a deeper understanding of truth.[58]

A vivid illustration of this Socratic method of dialogue is the conversation between Socrates and the slave boy in *Meno*.

> By a process of only asking questions, Socrates leads the boy to a knowledge of a geometrical proposition that the boy was not able to recognize at the beginning of the conversation. The conclusion that Socrates draws from this example is that, because Socrates did not tell the boy the truth but only asked questions, the truth had to be "in" the boy, albeit in a forgotten form. Learning, for Socrates, is a remembering of a truth that is already in us. The educator through the art of dialogue, enables the truth to emerge.[59]

Plato uses his "idealistic metaphysic" to support this dialogic philosophy of education. He believes that the realm of the universal is the domain of truth. Truth lies in the abstract and in the rational. Goodness, Beauty and Truth are the universal ideals; they are genuinely real and genuinely true. Universal realities express themselves imperfectly in the concrete, the particular and the empirical. Plato believes that the empirical world, the world of appearance, is not the real world, the world of universals. "According to Plato, we know the real world prior to birth. Birth is a forgetting and dialogue is the method by which we remember forgotten truth."[60]

While there are merits in the Socratic method of dialogue, we are concerned that Plato seems to locate the source of truth in humans. It appears that Plato believes that humans have the truth in themselves, "waiting to be appropriated by the proper method."[61] For Plato, the process of this appropriation of truth is dialogue, and specifically, question and answer. This view of Plato appears to dismiss revelation as the source of truth. Many Christian thinkers suggest that Plato's epistemology is different from Christian epistemology because while Plato believes in the innateness of truth, "Christ communicates a truth that is not already 'in' the learner in a forgotten or potential way."[62] As a result, many Christian thinkers have overlooked dialogue as a source of truth. Instead they look for truth in the Scriptures and in the natural world. "Even where Christians have understood truth to be immanent to the soul, either by virtue of its created goodness (the image of God) or by virtue of the indwelling of the Holy Spirit, the way to truth has been seen as prayer, meditation, reflection, or introspection, not as dialogue."[63]

Platonic philosophy has elicited two main responses from Christian thinkers: rejection of any notion of innate truth, and the articulation of a theology of revelation; a marriage between revelation and reason.[64] In the context of this work, however, we will suggest that Plato's legacy of the dialogical method of conversation should not be totally brushed aside.

> Dialogue has been described as a way of sharing truth or as a way of communicating it. In these descriptions it is assumed that the truth that is communicated or shared is a truth that one or both parties to the dialogue already possesses. The Platonic legacy points us to the possibility that dialogue may be a condition of truth, a way of knowing truth that is not possessed by any one of the dialogical partners alone. If this possibility is real, the truth to which dialogue leads may not be so completely opposed to revelation as the traditional debate has assumed.[65]

Lochhead brings Martin Buber's theology of the "I-Thou" relationship into the dialogical arena. He observes that for Buber, dialogue is a way to truth. According to Buber, dialogue exists in terms of the I-Thou relationship.

> The terms themselves suggest a model of dialogue that is primarily a person-to-person encounter. Although it is true that the one-to-one relationship is the paradigm that Buber refers to most frequently, the reality to which Buber wishes to point by his use of the concept transcends the paradigm. Many of the things that Buber has to say about the I-Thou relationship illuminate the nature of dialogue between communities and between traditions. All dialogue is dialogue between people.[66]

Lochhead posits that Buber's philosophy has influenced Christian theology a great deal during the twentieth century. However, Christian theologians have taken only part of Buber's philosophy of dialogue—the I-Thou relationship. They emphasize Buber's understanding of God and the individual's relationship with God more than they do his understanding of the nature of dialogue in a general sense.

To understand Buber, we must appreciate that "I-It" and "I-Thou" are not compound words. They are primary words. To speak of a world to which the self relates, we must distinguish between "It" and "Thou." The world is an abstraction from one of the primary words. The world we know as "It" can never, therefore, be equated with the world we encounter as "Thou." The world exists in, and not apart from , one of these attitudes. Similarly, there is not independent self that relates now to "It," now to "Thou." Like the world, the self is an abstraction from a primary word. The "I" of "I-It" cannot be equated with the "I" of "I-Thou."

The "I-It" and "I-Thou" can be distinguished by where, in the two structures, reality is centered. In "I-It," reality is centered in the self. "It" is the world as it is known, experienced, and used by a subject. . . . In the "I-Thou" relationship, I do not experience. I do not know. I am addressed. I encounter. In the spatial image of a center, the cosmos centers not in me, but in a point between I and Thou.[67]

The impression one gets from Buber is that the possibility of dialogue does not depend on "a prior valuation of the other. Dialogue is not based on whether the Thou is intelligent enough or worthy enough to relate to me. In dialogue, there is not a priori decision that the other is qualified to speak to me and to be heard by me before dialogue can begin."[68]

We note some problems with Buber's theology in the "I-Thou" relationship. Lochhead portrays Buber as believing that truth is a relationship, which is closely related to the doctrine of God. Buber paints the picture of God as the "eternal Thou." For him, God is "the Thou that by its very nature cannot become it. The eternal Thou, Buber holds, is encountered in every particular Thou. Consequently, for Buber, there is no such thing as seeking God for there is nothing in which he could not be found."[69] This Pantheistic view poses a problem for Christian apologetics. If this theory aims at proposing a universal theology of revelation, we disagree with Buber. However, both Plato and Buber present dialogue as a way to truth.

Both support their view of dialogue with a theory that accounts for the power of dialogue to convey truth. Plato's theory of dialogue involves the postulation of an eternal world of universals which can be "recollected" by a dialogical method. Buber's theory rests on the identification of God as the eternal Thou who is encountered in every particular Thou.[70]

While we respect the views of both Plato and Buber on dialogue, we suggest that the attainment of truth goes beyond dialogue. Dialogue alone does not contain truth. Truth, especially spiritual truth, can be attained when the Holy Spirit of God acts on dialogical conversations and enables persons to see things the way God sees them. "But when he, the Spirit of truth comes, He will guide you into all truth."[71]

Jesus Christ was good at dialogue. He used dialogue on various occasions to lead people into the deeper knowledge of divine truth. The following incidents are some of His dialogical encounters:

1. Jesus' engagement with religious leaders of His day (Luke 2:6,).
2. Jesus' engagement with the devil (Matthew 4:1–11,).
3. Jesus' engagement with a teacher of the law (Matthew 8:18–22,).
4. Jesus' encounter with Nicodemus (John 3:1–21,).
5. Jesus and the Samaritan woman (John 4:4–42,).
6. Jesus, the Pharisees and the woman caught in adultery (John 8:2–11,).

Paul's use of the dialogical method of evangelism was extensive. He conversed with both individuals and groups of individuals. He reasoned with some, and argued and disputed with others as the occasion warranted. Examples include:

1. Paul and Felix, the Roman governor (Acts 24:24–26,).
2. Paul's visit to Thessalonica and the consequent establishment of the church there. "As his custom was, Paul went into the synagogue, and on three Sabbath days he "reasoned" with them from the Scriptures . . ." (Acts 17:2–4,).
3. Paul with some Jews and a group of Epicureans in Athens. "So he "reasoned" in the synagogue with the Jews and the God-fearing Greeks, as well as in the market-place day by day with those who happened to be there. A group of Epicureans and Stoic philosophers began to dispute with him. Some of them asked. . . ." (Acts 17:17–34,).
4. Paul in Ephesus. "Paul entered the synagogue and spoke boldly there for three months, arguing persuasively about the kingdom of God. But some of them became obstinate; they refused to believe. . . ." (Acts 19:8–10,).

Authentic Igbo Christianity requires dialogical evangelism.

Monological witness implies superiority and imperialism. Dialogue is between equals. It is unChristian to want to convert others to one's own particular creed, denomination or culture. It is Christian to share the universal Gospel and to hope that in total human freedom the other acknowledges Christ as Lord and Savior. In monological witness we are sometimes tempted to identify our victory in logical argumentation or presentation with the victory of Christ. In dialogical witness the concern is that the truth of God may appear, and any victory may be his alone.[72]

When there is dialogue, parties are likely to understand one another better, appropriate beliefs better, and commit more deeply to the new faith. This is where the challenge for authentic Igbo Christianity lies.

Authentic Faith: What is it?

Authenticity is both a philosophical word and a socio-religious word. Ronald E. Santoni, writing about philosopher Sartre's concept of authenticity as documented in *The War Diaries*, states that authenticity

> can be understood only in terms of the human condition, that condition of a being into a situation . . . Through the authentic realization of the being-in-situation, one brings to plenary existence the situation on the one hand and human reality on the other. To be authentic . . . is to realize fully one's being-in-situation, whatever this situation may happen to be.[73]

Also Jacob Golomb reflects on Soren Kierkegaard's notion of authenticity. He states:

> Kierkegaard reveals a fundamentally religious personality. In his actual life, however, he did not always feel or live religiously, and was diverted many times on to different paths. His personal solution to this conflict was to return to or recover an abandoned religious "Self." Hence his insistence on connecting authenticity with genuine faith and his appeal to his readers to return to the origins of Christianity, to original, authentic faith.[74]

Kierkegaard's determination was "to entice his readers to leap into and embrace passionately the genuine religious sphere of existence, to become Christian and live intensely, fulfilling all the demands of a faith that can transform the whole of life."[75] For Sartre, authenticity is a negative term and for Kierkegaard and Camus, "any positive definition of authenticity would be self-nullifying."[76] In spite of the philosophical understanding of authenticity or authentic phenomena, and for the purpose of this work, we will define authenticity as something which is real, genuine, true, original or actual. From this definition, authentic faith is one which is genuine, true, real, bona fide or original. Authentic Igbo Christianity is one which becomes part and parcel of Igbo life in such a way that Igbo Christians can claim ownership of it in a real and genuine way. It is one which allows Igbo Christians to relate to God through Jesus Christ by means of the Igbo culture, language and institutions, without feeling guilty of offending any "parent" foreign body. Religion is of ultimate concern to the Igbo. Therefore, Christianity must be authentic to them if it is to claim their ultimate attention. "An ultimate concern which points to that which is truly ultimate is authentic. A faith which stops short in a concern for the penultimates of culture is inauthentic."[77] Alland A. Galloway makes a distinction between authentic and inauthentic faith. The clear difference comes at the point where "the interest of theology is clearly and unambiguously distinguished from that of anthropology."[78] He observes that the *de facto* ultimates of cultural concern, ordinary things of human social behavior, are important. There are many such *de facto* ultimates and many people live their lives on the basis of them without feeling a need for "a transcendent, unifying centre of concern."[79] These people may function in the society, experiencing wholeness and good psychological health.

> The degree of wholeness, the degree of healthy functional reciprocity with environment, the degree of meaningful personal existence that can be found in the plural "de facto" ultimates of cultural concern is not to be despised. None of us, except the mentally ill, do despise them in our daily lives—whatever our theology may say about them. To despise these things is to despise the daily bread which the Father gives to his children. We must honour grace where we find it.[80]

However, it is important to note that "these *de facto* ultimates of secular culture are essentially precarious and insecure."[81] Hence a necessary search for a higher concern, "Ultimate concern."[82] Describing "Ultimate concern" and its relationship to real faith, Galloway states:

> It is at the level of existential understanding that the concept of ultimate concern can disclose the distinctive character of faith which sets it in dialectical tension as well as creative co-operation with culture. A clear perception of the radical distinction between the empirical and the existential understanding of ultimate concern provides a basis on which one can elucidate the distinction between authentic and inauthentic faith in its formal, logical and epistemological aspects.[83]

This criterion is necessary to avoid subjective preferences, based on content alone. Galloway suggests that in order to arrive at "ultimate concern," the "pyramid" (scale of preference) model must be left out.

> Ultimate concern, understood existentially, is not a specific concern distinguished from other concerns subsumed under it only by the fact of its being the highest. Paul Tillich himself consistently uses the concept of ultimate concern at an existential level of understanding. . . . He makes the point quite explicit in his last publication:

"But you see, the unconditional or ultimate should not be viewed as part of a pyramid, even if its place is at the top. For the ultimate is that which is the ground and the top at the same time, or the embracing of the pyramid."[84]

Galloway observes that to survive within culture, humans must choose from among a plurality of *de facto* ultimate concerns. As a result, the issue of essential and unessential ultimate concerns comes up. This will lead to deliberation, consideration and eventual choosing of that concern which is perceived to be more fundamental, ultimate, than the other. The process of arriving at the most ultimate concern is a difficult one. It is indeed a process which takes place in all human societies on a daily basis, if not moment by moment. "It is the logical basis of all cultural self-determination."[85] He maintains that "ultimate concern," when "used in its transcendental, existential sense turns out to be thoroughly paradoxical."[86] He regards this condition as "the source of all the paradoxes of faith," but "not an arbitrary contradiction."[87] A person can evade this contradiction, only if he or she inhibits the questions which drive him or her to it.

Human culture, in contrast with animal culture, is characterized by intentionality. It has orientation towards meaning and coherence. Every culture has a relationship to ultimate concern.

In a *Confession* Leo Tolstoy says: Whatever faith may be, and what answers it may give, and to whomsoever it gives them, every such answer gives to the finite existence of man an infinite meaning, a meaning not destroyed by sufferings, deprivations, or death. This means that only in faith can we find for life a meaning and a possibility.

What then, is faith?. . . Faith is a knowledge of the meaning of human life in consequence of which a man does not destroy himself but lives. Faith is the strength of life. If a man lives, he believes in something. If he did not believe that one must live for something, he would not live.[88]

Galloway argues that "faith as ultimate concern is a universal aspect of human existence and a universal source of culture."[89] The faith he is arguing about here "may not be overly religious. But it has a form which points beyond the immediate content of experience and forces thought out of the objective, empirical mode."[90] Again, there is a paradox here. Actual faith exists only in the concrete concerns of culture. But authentic faith exists "only in relation to that which is essentially and unassailably ultimate and therefore transcends the finite concerns of culture."[91] Again, paradox manifests itself and may lead to despair, but not despondency. "So the dialectic is maintained."[92] This dialectic is "the inescapable tension which persists at the heart of every culture."[93]

As part of the world's community of religious beings, the Igbo may experience these paradoxes in the daily expression of their faith, especially in their concern for the ultimate. However, as in all African communities, the Igbo community makes no sharp demarcation between secular and religious concerns. Almost every choice they make has a religious implication. This means that the paradox or tension which Galloway is bringing out in his attempt to differentiate between authentic and inauthentic faith is less pronounced in Igbo culture. Our concern in this work is how to find ways in which the Igbo can appropriate Christianity in such a way that Christianity and culture can co-exist authentically. We suggest dialogical inculturation.

> The church, in the exercise of its universal mission, can enter into contact and communion with diverse forms of human culture. Christ can incarnate himself in all of them. God does not discriminate against peoples and cultures. Any cultural partiality would be in contrast to the nature of the Christian message itself which can be implanted in any form of healthy human culture.

> When the gospel dialogues with cultures, it does not destroy them. To believe does not mean renouncing one's unique individual and social personality. Christian faith does not imply a renunciation of any human value.[94] Because if a value is authentic, it is already Christian.[95]

Notes

1   Pius N. C. Okigbo, "Towards a Reconstruction of the Political Economy of Igbo Civilization," *1986 Ahiajoku Lecture* (Owerri, Nigeria: Ministry of Information and Culture, 1986), 13.

2   Ibid.

3   Ibid.

4   Ibid., 14.

5   "Omu nkwu" is the Igbo name for palm leaf.

6   Chidi G. Osuagwu, "Erima—Concept of the Organic Community in Obowu," *ANU: A Journal of Igbo Culture*, No. 5 (February 1989): 52–53.

7   Henry George Liddell, *Greek-English Lexicon*, abridged from *Liddell and Scott's Greek-English Lexicon* (Oxford: Clarendon Press, 1980), 163.

8   Leonard Swidler, "The Dialogue Decalogue: Ground Rules for Interreligious Dialogue," *Journal of Ecumenical Studies* 20 (Winter 1986): 1.

9   Chinua Achebe, *Things Fall Apart* (London: Heinemann Educational Books, 1958), 102.

10 Ibid.

11 Ibid.

12 Ani and Amadiora are the respective deities in charge of land and lightning. Idemili and Ogwugwu were two other powerful deities.

13 Achebe, *Things Fall Apart*, 102–103.

14 John B. Taylor, "Inter-Faith Dialogue," in *Christianity and Change*, ed. Norman Autton, (London: S.P.C.K., 1971), 63.

15 Ibid., 66.

16 Ibid.

17 Ibid., 70.

18 Ibid., 71.

19 Ibid., 72.

20 Ibid., 75.

21 Swidler, "The Dialogue of Decalogue," 1–3.

22 Ibid., 4.

23 Paul F. Knitter, *No Other Name? A Critical Survey of Christian Attitudes Toward the World Religions* (Maryknoll, N.Y.: Orbis Books, 1985), 211.

24 Donald K. Swearer, *Dialogue: The Key to Understanding Other Religions* (Philadelphia: Westminster Press, 1977), 41.

25 Robert B. Sheard, *Interreligious Dialogue in the Catholic Church since Vatican II: A Historical and Theological Study* (Lewiston, N.Y.: Edwin Mellen Press, 1987), 94.

26 Ibid.

27 Ibid., 95.

28 Ibid.

29 Nills Ehrenstrom and Gunther Gassmann, *Confessions in Dialogue: A Survey of Bilateral Conversations among World Confessional Families 1959–1974* (Geneva: World Council of Churches, 1975), 130.

30 Constantine D. Jathanna, ed., *Dialogue in Community: Essays in Honour of Stanley J. Samartha* (Balmatta, India: Karnataka Theological Research Institute, 1982), 154.

31 Ibid., 154–155.

32 Joost A. M. Meeloo, *Conversation and Communication: A Psychological Inquiry Into Language and Human Relations* (New York: International Universities Press, 1952), 3.

33 Ibid.

34 C. David Mortensen, *Communication: The Study of Human Interaction* (New York: McGraw-Hill book Co., 1972), 3.

35 Ibid., 20.

36 Donald K. Smith, *Creating Understanding: A Handbook for Christian Communication Across Cultural Landscapes* (Grand Rapids: Zondervan Publishing House, 1992), 23.

37 Ibid., 24.

38 Ibid.

39 Ibid., 25.

40 Ibid.

41 Ibid.

42 Ibid., 30–36.

43 Ibid., 39.

44 Ibid., 49.

45   Ibid., 43–64.

46   Ibid., 80.

47   Smith, *Creating Understanding*, 96–97.

48   Ibid., 115.

49   Ibid., 123.

50   Ibid., 143.

51   John Stott and Robert T. Coote, eds., *Gospel and Culture: The Papers of A Consultation on the Gospel and Culture, Convened by the Lausanne Committee's Theology and Education Group* (Pasadena, Calif.: William Carey Library, 1979), 300–303.

52   Ogbu U. Kalu, "Color and Conversion: The White Missionary Factor in the Christianization of Igboland," *Missiology* 18, no. 1 (January 1990): 68.

53   Sriganda E. M. Arulampalam, "Toward an Exclusivistic Model of Dialogue in a Religiously Pluralistic World" (Ph.D. diss., The Southern Baptist Theological Seminary, 1994), 197.

54   *Dialogue and Proclamation* (Rome: Pontifical Council for Interreligious Dialogue and Congregation for the Evangelization of Peoples, 20 June 1991), para. 9, *New Directions in Mission and Evangelization I: Basic Statements 1974–1991,* ed. James A. Scherer and Stephen B. Bevans, eds. (Maryknoll, N.Y.: Orbis Books, 1992), 180.

55   David Lochhead, *The Dialogical Imperative: A Christian Reflection on Interfaith Encounter* (Maryknoll, N.Y.: Orbis Books, 1988), 46.

56   Ibid.

57   Ibid.

58   Ibid., 47.

59   Ibid.

60   Ibid.

61   Ibid.

62   Ibid.

63   Ibid., 48.

64   Ibid.

65   Lockhead, *The Dialogical Imperative*, 48.

66   Ibid., 48–49.

67   Ibid., 49.

68 Ibid., 50.

69 Ibid., 51.

70 Ibid., 52.

71 John 16:13 NIV.

72 Arulampalam, "Toward an Exclusivistic Model of Dialogue in a Religiously Pluralistic World," 208-209.

73 Ronald E. Santoni, *Bad Faith, Good Faith, and Authenticity in Sartre's Early Philosophy* (Philadelphia: Temple University Press, 1995), 89–90.

74 Jacob Golomb, *In Search of Authenticity: From Kierkegaard to Camus* (London: Routledge, 1995), 35.

75 Ibid.

76 Ibid., 7.

77 Alland D. Galloway, *Faith in a Changing Culture: Keer Lectures Delivered at Glasgow University, 1966* (London: George Allen & Unwin, 1967), 24.

78 Ibid.

79 Ibid., 25.

80 Ibid., 26.

81 Ibid.

82 Ibid., 27.

83 Ibid., 28.

84 Ibid.

85 Ibid., 30.

86 Ibid.

87 Ibid.

88 Ibid., 32–33.

89 Galloway, *Faith in a Changing Culture*, 33.

90 Ibid.

91 Ibid.

92 Ibid.

93 Ibid.

94 Unless the individual and social personalities, and the human values conflict with Biblical values.

95   Frederick E. Chiromba, *Evangelization and Inculturation* (Gweru, Zimbabwe: Mambo Press, 1989), 24.
     There may be some human values which may not agree with biblical values. A person needs to be conscious of those in the evangelization process. The following principles of inculturation may serve as a guideline:

1. It is always necessary to distinguish clearly between faith and culture, between the message itself and its cultural expression.
2. Given its universality, the gospel message cannot exclude any particular culture. The Gospel is perfectly adaptable and expressible in any type of human culture.
3. A good knowledge of the culture is necessary, that is, those cultures in which one wished to incarnate the Gospel ...
4. There is need for openness and readiness to accept human values, be they spiritual or religious, embodied in human cultures.
5. The Christian message should be taken as it is and as a whole, without seeking to take only those elements that agree with one's culture while neglecting those that may point to the contrary, which may involve sacrifice and the cross.
6. The transcendental character of Christ, his Word and his church must be preserved. Christianity is not a humanism nor a symposium of culture.
7. The gospel message cannot be divorced from the culture in which it was diffused right from the beginning with the incarnation of Christ. On the other hand, the message shows a transforming and regenerating power everywhere.
8. The work of inculturation demands great theological knowledge, spiritual discernment, wisdom and prudence which are the gifts of the Holy Spirit. The Holy Spirit is the principal agent of evangelization and, therefore, also of inculturation (See Chiromba, *Evangelization and Inculturation*, 21).

Chapter 8

Some Current Methods
of Evangelism in Igboland

Christian preachers and teachers of the gospel in Igboland employ various methods in their attempt to reach the Igbo for Christ. Five of these methods stand out: sermons, crusades, drama, group Bible study, and Christian literature.

Sermons

Sermon delivery is the most popular form of communicating the gospel to Igbo hearers. The foreign missionaries used this method at the beginning of Christian work in Igboland. They used this method everywhere they went, in people's homes, at village squares, in the schools and in the houses of worship. The format of the delivery was monological. People listened and responded to the preacher's invitation to either join the church or get baptized. The process of sermon delivery did not give room for questions and so, in many cases, the preacher did not necessarily have to clarify the points he raised during the sermon delivery. Listeners were expected to abandon their Igbo religion and declare allegiance to Jesus Christ. Many who heard the missionaries preach did what the missionaries told them to do—joined the church. Many joined the church, but not all who joined the church understood who Christ was. One of the reasons for this lack of knowledge of the person of Christ appears to be the absence of questions in sermons. Many people had doubts about the new faith, but they joined the church any way because

. . . in as much as it (the gospel) inculcated that the only way to human dignity and full-grown personality was to be in everything like Europeans and despise their own culture. It was in this way that Christianity arrived in Nigeria dressed up in European garb. It was immediately associated with civilization in the sense of being well dressed in European fashion, dexterity in European etiquette and manners, and proficiency (or dabbling) in the use of English language with a corresponding disdain for their own culture, or disdain crystallized into inability to use their own language properly.[1]

Sermon delivery continues to enjoy the first position among the methods of communicating the gospel to the Igbo till today. In most churches of Igboland, sermons take the same format by indigenous preachers as by foreign missionary preachers. The only major difference is language. Many Igbo preachers now use the Igbo language; they have no need for interpreters. Many people go to the church every Sunday morning or attend week-day Christian gatherings and never participate in anything except to listen. The choir sings and the preacher preaches and at the end, people walk up to the altar to "give their lives to Jesus" and then go home. These people do not ask questions because questions are not allowed in church. They go home with their concerns and doubts still lingering. It is possible that a few preachers employ some dialogical elements in their sermons once in a while, especially in their use of rhetorical questions. This is not adequate. Dialogical preaching requires long hours of preparation. A good number of preachers "feel that preaching in dialogue requires skills which they lack: a lively imagination, the dramatic sense, an ability to write crisp dialogue, acting know-how."[2] This is one of the major reasons why many preachers object to dialogical preaching. Other objections are:

1. Dialogue preaching takes extensive preparation.
2. The congregation needs to be prepared for listening.
3. Feedback from the congregation is very important but hard to secure.
4. It is difficult to maintain unity within the sermon.
5. Achieving a satisfactory resolution of the issue is also difficult.[3]

William D. Thompson and Gordon C. Burnett recognize the fact that it is natural for preachers to hesitate about a radical departure from their normal way of preaching—monologue. So they suggest that "an effective preacher need not choose one of the more highly dramatic motifs of dialogue preaching. He can use the skills he has in a format which differs slightly from his usual way of working."[4]

Thompson and Burnett are also aware that dialogical preaching may cause the following reactions from the congregation: some people may tend to look at this method as play-acting, looking at the message as unreal, a mere show, contrived or phony. Others, especially the "traditionalists," may be startled by its novelty, "causing them to be caught up in the method rather than to relate to the message."[5] This method of preaching may leave out a good segment of the audience.

> People are startled by having a fellow parishioner stand up during the sermon introduction to voice his disagreement with the pastor. Persons who are slow to accept change may not easily adapt to the idea of hearing two voices from the pulpit. Worshippers whose need is to hear a word from the living God may indeed feel frozen out of a chancel debate on a question which does not seem to merit being asked.[6]

Other objectors to this method contend that "the sermon which involves the congregation in direct verbal dialogue as in intrinsic part of the sermonic presentation poses some difficult problems.[7] They observe that

> Clergymen who have used this method warn about three primary dangers: (1) initiating the discussion, especially in a large congregation, is very difficult; (2) some persons tend to dominate any discussion, and will dominate it even in the sanctuary; (3) the minister may pose as an answer-box and cut off honest dialogue with the people.[8]

Thompson and Bennett respond to these objections by stating that "the objections raised to dialogue preaching have a great deal more to do with the sensitivity of the persons handling it than with any inherent defects in the method."[9] According to Thompson and Bennett, any preacher "who is highly skilled in discussion leadership will be able to surmount these barriers."[10] They therefore suggest six advantages of dialogical preaching over monological preaching:

1. Dialogical preaching raises higher the congregation's level of interest.
2. Dialogical preaching involves people in the communication of ideas.
3. It sharpens issues.
4. It forces listeners to consider fresh ideas.
5. It deals with the real life questions which people struggle with.
6. It brings out the latest methods in the communication of the gospel.[11]

Monological preaching has its place in Christian worship. We are not in any way suggesting its abandonment in the mature Igbo Christian congregation. However, we observe that for non-Christian audiences and also for new Christian converts, monological preaching may be an inadequate method to effectively communicate the gospel or/and lead new converts towards deeper levels of commitment to Christ, and to His church. We join Thompson and Bennett to state that

Monological preaching has dominated the church's communicative effort for centuries; it has done its work well.[12] As an exclusive method, however, it tends to limit, sometimes even distort, the Christian message. Its content may communicate the gospel accurately and movingly, but its method cannot help but emphasize the authority of God, the revelatory nature of His Word, and the passivity of man. Dialogue preaching, by its very nature, communicates the "other side of God." It says that God is in encounter with his people, that he is listening as well as talking. In addition, it involves and demands a personal participation on the part of each individual. It makes people react and respond to the divine Word and to each other, actively and creatively, enabling them to move toward those relationships of love which are man's highest response to the love of the Lord.

The person who listens creatively to a chancel dialogue or who participates vocally in a congregational dialogue may learn some unique insights about the Christian faith; he may find that some of those dry-as-dust theological terms actually have a relation to his own experience at home, in the office or shop, at school or at city hall; he may discover through dialogue a moment of spiritual ecstasy or sheer joy in the engagement of meaningful ideas. Whatever happens, he will find himself responding in some way to the Word and will of God. The nature of that response is up to him and the Holy Spirit; the inevitability of his responding is assured by the force of the dialogue form, which God may well have meant for such a time as this.[13]

Crusades

Banners bearing "Jesus Christ the same Yesterday, Today and Forever" are common sights in almost every community in Igboland. These banners indicate crusade arrangements by churches and other Christian groups. Crusades have become the major avenue for outreach programs. Those who conduct crusades spend large amounts of money and many hours preparing for crusades. They spend money for radio and/or television announcements, and for the printing of handbills and posters. In some cases, crusade organizers hire musical groups and dramatic players and pay them much money. Other items which attract significant amounts of monetary spending include: transportation, housing and feeding.

Crusade planners spend weeks, months and in some cases years planning for crusades. The sole goal of these efforts is the salvation of the individual sinner. In recent times, it appears that the Deeper Life Bible Church, Nigeria, is ahead of all other Christian groups in the organization and the conducting of crusades all over Nigeria. In Igboland, Deeper Life crusades come up almost every week in different communities. The Deeper Life Bible Church is truly aggressive in their attempt to reach many souls for Christ. This aggressiveness may stem from their first aim, "To lead sinners to Christ." The other two aims of this organization are: "To help nourish and sustain all believers in the total counsel of God and sound truth of the Gospel and to resuscitate unity and perfect love in the church."[14] The Assemblies of God, the Baptists, the Evangelical Churches of West Africa and also Anglicans, Presbyterians, Methodists and Catholics organize some kind of crusades to reach souls for Christ. Almost every Christian group in Igboland uses crusades for conversion of souls and in some cases, for membership drives.

Crusades have been over-done in Igboland. Crusade results have become very scanty. Many who still attend crusades do so to support their churches or Christian groups. Crusade messages seem to be the same everywhere, every time, and many people appear to be bored easily. The attendance of non-Christians to crusade grounds seems to have dropped significantly. Crusade sermons do not seem to actively involve the listeners. As a result, many people appear to have lost interest in crusades. Many of those who go appear to go in order to receive divine, physical or emotional healing, and to find solutions to some of their physical, emotional and psychological problems. In many cases crusade organizers promise prospective attendants these things.

This is one of the reasons why the National Evangelism Christian Outreach (NECO), a Nigerian inter-denominational Christian organization, which is committed to "the Commission, the Vision and the Mission" of our Lord and Savior Jesus Christ stated:

> One of the greatest challenges facing today's Church is the dilemma of reaching with the gospel today's teeming billions of unbelievers. If the church fails in this awesome duty the world would perish in its sins, but God says the watchman, the Church, is held accountable. Thus, Evangelism is the Number One Commission of the regenerate church.

> Our present methods of evangelism—mainly staying inside churches and on crusade grounds, waiting for sinners who often do not show up—is grossly inadequate. In order to fulfill the Great Commission for our time, we must do what Christ did: send evangelists to the roads, to the homes of people, to their markets, and meet the sinners in their natural locations; witness to them there, and bring the new converts to the church for grooming.[15]

Bill Glass, in his article, "Developing a Citywide Crusade," said:

> The entire attitude of any citywide evangelistic team from the preacher to all those involved, should say with a powerful voice, "I believe that Christ can change you. Yes I love you. Yes, you are worth any difficulty I have to go through to reach you. Yes, I care enough to pay attention to your hurts. Yes, I will listen to you attentively. Yes, I understand your loneliness. Yes, I know that there is still hope for you."[16]

While we respect the views of Glass on crusades, and while we are aware of the positive feelings of many evangelists and pastors world-wide for crusades, we recognize some tension between crusades and dialogical evangelism in Igboland. It appears that crusades suggest a militant method of gospel communication. If this is true, the crusade, as a method of gospel communication to Igbo audiences, is a misfit. Crusades run contrary to the dialogical method of communication. Therefore its use in any Igbo community is irrelevant and non-productive. Therefore, it should be dropped.

Drama

Harold Ehrensperger, in *Religious Drama: Ends and Means*, quotes Marvin Halverson:

> Drama is an art form which has evocative and communicative power which causes one to confront the human situation—and one's self. This is true of Greek tragedy and contemporary skeptical drama. Christian drama, however, points beyond the depths of tragedy to that fulfillment of life which is seen in Jesus, the Christ. Christian drama, like corporate worship, derives its content as well as its structure from the drama of the biblical story, and particularly, the Incarnation, ministry, Passion, death and resurrection of Jesus Christ. Such drama makes men experience not only pity, fear, and catharsis, but also guilt, judgment, and the forgiveness of God which brings the "peace that passeth understanding."[17]

Ehrensperger highlights some definitions for religious drama which were formulated during the 1959 Religious Drama Workshop at Boston University. They include:

> Religious drama is action involving man and God for the purpose of aiding him in his search for maturity.

> Religious drama is the enactment through staged action and dialogue of human situations that convey men's concepts about ultimate reality; and the transcendence of that enactment into a relationship that involves the participants (actors and audience) with the concepts presented.

> A religious drama is any drama which allows man to discover or deepen his own relationship to the Ultimate, or God.

> Religious drama is a peculiar attempt to communicate through involvement of writer, actors, and audience by means of psychological, physical and mental action, man's endeavor to respond with his whole being to that which is most real and most important.[18]

Fred Eastman and Louis Wilson contend that the use of drama in the church is not for money-making. It is not "a new wrinkle in religious education, nor simply as a means of making Bible stories interesting to children."[19] Rather they use it as a means to interpret human existential struggles from the perspective of religion. They state churches are using religious (Christian) drama

> in a deliberate attempt to develop strength, beauty, and power in the imaginative and creative life of the players and the audiences. . . . If a play sends an audience away exalted in spirit, with a deeper sense of fellowship with God and man, it has been religious. But if it does not have that effect it is not religious although all its characters are biblical and its story taken from the Bible itself.[20]

Herein lies the challenge for the Christian church in Igboland regarding its use of drama as a means of communicating the gospel message to its Igbo watchers and listeners.

Many dramatic presentations in Igbo communities and churches lack cultural identity. Many actors act Jewish, Greek, Roman, European or American depending on the type of drama. They sometimes hesitate to use local props in an attempt to maintain "authenticity." Sometimes, non-Christians do not appear to understand the meanings of the symbols and concepts these Christian dramas portray because they do not have common frames of reference with the symbols and concepts. In many cases, the actors are more concerned about how correctly they play their roles than how well their audience understands the message of the drama for them.

Bible objects which bear foreign names to Igbo listeners appear at intervals during Christian plays. This situation makes it more difficult for the audience to understand the play, much more relate to its message. Drama as a method of gospel communication to Igbo audiences is still inadequate unless something is done to enhance its use. In most cases, the interpretation of dramatic presentations is left for the audience. This is the point at which we suggest dialogue for better understanding and consequent commitment to the Christian faith.

At the close of every Christian drama, we suggest that some kind of discussion should take place between actors or drama organizers and the audience. Through questions and answers, meanings of unclear symbols and concepts will be given. Faith and theology are closely related; symbols play important roles in the doing of theology. "The task of theology is to chart and clarify the meaning and content of Christian faith. This task has many sides."[21] Therefore it is important for theology to study the

symbolic language, its potentials and also its functions for effective communication. Commenting on the effectiveness of dramatic dialogue
J. L. Styan said:

> If dialogue carefully follows the way we speak in life, as it is likely to do in realistic
> play, the first step towards understanding how it departs from actuality can be
> awkward. It is helpful to cease to submit to the pretense for the moment. An
> apparent reproduction of ordinary conversation will be, in good drama, a con-
> struction of words set up to do many jobs that are not immediately obvious.[22]

However, for the benefit of the audience, our view is that nothing should
be left hanging. Realistic dialogue between the actors and the audience
should be done in every Christian drama.

> Drama in the church must not be used to dress up an occasion merely to give it
> prominence or popularity. Drama should be a tool of the ministry of the people in
> the church who feel that their interests, capacities, and abilities can best be used
> through this particular medium . . . In the presentation of the formal play the
> whole process can be an educational experience, and in the church it should also
> be a religious experience. This can only happen when we recognize that the
> uniqueness of drama in the church arises out of what the activity does, both to
> the actors and the production crew as well as to the congregation that comes to
> participate.[23]

Group Bible Study

Group Bible Study is an important part of most churches and Christian
ministries in Igboland. These Christian groups organize Bible study sessions for almost every age group in their membership. Bible study sessions are conducted primarily for those who have had initial contact with
Christianity and have identified with one Christian group or the other.
Occasionally, non-Christians who have accepted invitation from "Christians," attend. The Bible appears to be the primary textbook which most
groups use for their study. However, different groups use different supplementary materials—commentaries, guidebooks, catechism books and other
aids. In some cases, the use of these supplementary materials outweighs
the use of the Bible. Many of these supplements and aids are parochial in
content. They tend to teach the Bible dogmatically, instead of Biblically. A
few of them explain Biblical facts the way they are in the Bible.

Igbo Christians love Bible study sessions because most of these sessions afford them the opportunity to dialogue with one another. They ask
questions, answer questions and make contributions. Bible study groups
range from a group of three persons to about one thousand or more.

A typical Bible study session is characterized by the singing of familiar Igbo and English choruses, clapping of hands and the use of local musical instruments in some places, personal testimony times, exposition of the Scripture and the giving of invitation for the acceptance of Jesus Christ. Also, there is the expectation of miracles at Bible study sessions during crusades. Frances Lawjua Bolton writes about her experience at the Nnewi Crusade:

1st May 1971
Divine healing from Exodus 14:13–16 preached by brother Stephen. People flocked to the altar call (sic) for deliverance prayers. I must say that it was at Nnewi that the greatest number of miraculous healings was recorded. Complete deaf hears, hunch back disappears etc. Chinwe Ofodum wonderfully healed etc.[24]

The importance of Bible study sessions to the health of Igbo Christianity cannot be over-emphasized. However, the language of communication and the interpretation of Scripture appear to be two major areas of concern. The Igbo language is the vernacular to Igbo people. We believe that the use of Igbo as the primary language of teaching the Bible to Igbo people will be the best thing to do and will also lead to a better and deeper understanding of the Bible and its teachings. To the contrary, many of those who teach Igbo audiences use the English language and, in some cases, teach through interpreters. This situation may seem puzzling, especially when one considers that most of these teachers are Igbo. However, in Igboland, there is a kind of higher social status which goes with the use of the English language as the language of communication. This may explain the reason for this practice. Also, there are dialectical differences in the Igbo language. As a result, those who do not speak the Onwu orthography (official Igbo language orthography) may find it easier to use the English language in communicating with those Igbo who speak different dialects of the Igbo language.

The second area of concern is the interpretation of the Bible itself. Many of those who teach the Bible in these Bible study sessions have little or no theological training. We believe that the Holy Spirit is the interpreter of God's word in people's minds and hearts. We believe also that Jesus Christ who is the model teacher, taught His disciples what to teach before He sent them out to teach other people. Jesus Himself spent many hours alone, apparently receiving instructions from his Father and preparing for His teaching encounters with His audiences. He was knowledgeable in the Jewish law. He knew what the Scriptures said about every life issue and the religious leaders of His day recognized that ability in

Him. Annie Ward Byrd, writing about "Christian Knowledge and Conviction," with respect to the Bible and the great realities of the Christian faith, suggests that Bible teachers should help their students to

1. Develop a growing love for the Bible.
2. Accept the Bible as a way by which God speaks to them and as the final authority in all matters of faith and conduct.
3. Understand something of the origin of the Bible and God's use of man in preparing and preserving it.
4. To grow in understanding and mastery of biblical content, including customs, geography, history, and the great realities of Christian faith.
5. To acquire a growing comprehension of the meaning of the Christian faith and of how these Bible truths apply to personal daily living and to community and world problems.[25]

Byrd's suggestions call for better teacher preparation because "the blind cannot lead the blind." It is also important that Igbo Bible teachers acknowledge the fact that

> God's personal self-disclosure in the Bible was given in terms of the hearers' own culture .... The biblical writers made critical use of whatever cultural material was available to them for the expression of their message. For example, the Old Testament refers several times to the Babylonian sea monster named "Leviathan," while the form of God's "covenant" with his people resembles the ancient Hittite Suzerain's "treaty" with his vassals. The writers also made incidental use of the conceptual imagery of the "three-tiered" universe, though they did not thereby affirm a pre-Copernican cosmology. We do something similar when we talk about the sun "rising" and "setting."

> Similarly, New Testament language and thought-forms are steeped in both Jewish and Hellenistic cultures, and Paul seems to have drawn from the vocabulary of Greek philosophy. But the process by which the biblical authors borrowed words and images from their cultural milieu, and used them creatively, was controlled by the Holy Spirit so that they purged them of false or evil implications and thus transformed them into vehicles of truth and goodness.[26]

Igbo Bible teachers should endeavor to understand Biblical concepts and symbols as they were originally and culturally conditioned and then draw suitable comparisons between their Igbo counterparts. If this is done, and with the leadership of the Holy Spirit, Igbo audiences will gain a deeper meaning of Biblical affirmations and respond to them appropriately and with deeper commitment to the Christian faith. It will help for a greater level of audience participation and consequent understanding and commitment if Bible teachers do not teach the Bible dogmatically. They should allow the Bible to speak for itself. Too much theologizing may distort Biblical messages. The teacher should be objective with the content of the Bible, engage the audience in mutual dialogue, and allow the Holy Spirit of God to do the work of conviction and conversion of souls. William H. Stephen observes:

> Adults must carry the learning process to its conclusion if a lesson is to be effective. A teacher may allow considerable discussion and plan for group responses, but if he sums up the lesson in a way that tells members the decision to make, he aborts the learning experience. The teacher is a colearner. Therefore, he is entitled to express an opinion, even to introduce biblical information into the discussion for evaluation. Ultimately though, adults must make their own decisions.[27]

Our opinion is that dialogue is that method for Igbo audiences.

Christian Literature

Christian literature, books, magazines, periodicals, pamphlets, and tracts are important media of evangelism in Igboland. Churches and ministries use these media to reach the literate members of the various Igbo communities. Big denominations, especially the Roman Catholics and the Anglicans, own their own printing presses. In Owerri, there is the Asumpta Press (Catholic) and Diocese of Owerri Printing Press (Anglican). These printing presses, which also serve as these denominations' publishing companies, put out a good amount of Christian literature every year as funds become available to them. They publish materials both in Igbo and English. However, it appears that their English publications outnumber their Igbo ones, perhaps because the average Igbo prefers reading materials written in English to those written in Igbo. A good illustration of this fact is the situation with the Baptists of Igboland. There is no Baptist Press in Igboland, but there is one in Ibadan, the Western part of Nigeria—Baptist Press Ibadan, which prints church literature for the churches of the Nigerian Baptist Convention. For many years, the Nigerian Baptist Convention, through its publication department has tried to get Igbo Baptists to develop interest in Igbo church literature. That interest is yet to be developed.

Christian literature, as a means of evangelization, knows no bounds, especially in the eastern part of Nigeria where it suffers no censorship. Books, pamphlets, and tracts are distributed to people almost every day in their homes, at church, at bus stations and inside mass transit buses. Most Igbo love to receive Christian literature. Crusade organizers, revivalists and other Christian program organizers take advantage of this evangelistic opening. Literature distribution appears to be a common practice by evangelists all over the world.

> For years it has been standard practice at Billy Graham crusades and those of other evangelists to encourage inquirers to establish their Christian life by regularly reading God's Word. The counseling process includes a booklet called *Living in Christ*. It contains specific Scriptures about what it means to become a Christian. Further, the gospel of John is distributed to those making decisions for Christ.[28]

Hilary C. Achunike points out the fact that during the sixties, a good number of American evangelists intensified their evangelistic efforts in Nigeria through the use of Christian literature, in addition to the use of radio and television, using the English language in the three media.

> However, the impact of these evangelistic activities was not felt in higher institutions in Igboland. Rather, the religious lives of some Igbo were influenced by the Sudan Interior Mission[29] magazine, *The African Challenge* before the sixties. Indeed their activities were intensified in the sixties, especially through their magazine, *The African Challenge*. Howard Jones, an associate evangelist of Billy Graham in America, authored "The Hour of Freedom Evangelistic Ministry" in the sixties and through Eternal Love Winning Africa's (ELWA) radio[30] . . . he reached out to countries in West Africa. The influence of this ministry touched Igboland.[31]

In the 1960s and early 1970s, Barraka Printing Press published an enormous number of tracts both in English and Igbo. Most of the literature was given free of charge to Christians and non-Christians. The few that were sold, went at very affordable prices to churches and other Christian organizations for use during crusades, revivals and personal evangelistic outreaches. The Scripture Gift Mission, London, England, sent large amounts of Christian literature to the Igbo during this same period. Though this organization still sends Christian literature to Igbo Christians, the amount it sends has declined considerably. We do not know the reason for this reduction, but it appears that cost of production and postage may be responsible. The organization has always sent its literature free of charge to Nigerians.

Christian literature societies exist in almost every country where Christianity has taken root. But how do they perform generally?

Certain characteristics are common to these Christian Literature Societies. They have had a comparatively long history and have accumulated substantial capital funds . . . They own and occupy valuable buildings. Their working capital is, however, insufficient for the prompt publication of many of the manuscripts that have been approved for publication . . . Only a few missionaries and Christians of several countries have the literary scholarship and administrative ability to supply expert guidance to such ventures. . . . The evident need is for open-mindedness, originality and freedom in the publication of Christian literature. Missionaries, no matter what their qualifications of character, experience and scholarship, are seriously handicapped because of the foreignness in their attempts to supply this need. No satisfactory explanation has come to our attention as to why the control of these societies by missionaries to the exclusion of nationals should be perpetuated. We are convinced that the Christian movement in the several countries is being retarded by such a policy.[32]

These factors appear to hamper genuine evangelistic work in the mission fields. In the places where management and control have been turned over to the nationals, for example, the case of the Catholics and Anglicans in Igboland, the question of correct publication materials comes up from time to time. Some Western missionaries and mission organizations feel hesitant to accept Christian literature written and published by Africans. The impression one gets is that a Christian book, article, tract and so on has to be proof-read by someone from Europe or America and possibly published by a European or an American company in order to gain approval and acceptability.

This situation poses a big challenge to indigenization. African theologians understand the spiritual condition of their fellow Africans better than Euro-American theologians. These African writers "know where the shoe pinches," and they know how best to address the African spiritual condition, so as to lead them to the ultimate Savior, Jesus Christ. The fear by the West that Africans are not capable of "correct" theological creativity is unfounded.

There is no Christian theologian in Africa who denies the fact that the Bible is a primary and basic source for any Christian theology. . . . The theologians who assembled at Immanuel college at Ibadan in 1966 set for themselves "the task of finding an answer to the delicate question of whether there is any correlation between the biblical concept of God and the African concept of God". . . . The anticipated outcome would be a Christian theology because the raw materials of tradition are reinterpreted in the light of the gospel, making the latter of relevance to the African people.

Given that the Bible is a primary source for African theology, theologians need to employ a special hermeneutic to produce a theology that speaks to the African people. We are cautioned that "such Biblical theology will have to reflect the African situation and understanding."[33]

The African mind is different from the Western mind. These two different minds conceive many things differently and assign different meanings to them. Since meaning is related to understanding, it is important that familiar concepts and symbols be used in the writings which are targeted to Africans. This is the reason why Gwinyai H. Muzorewa suggests that

> African Christians need to develop a theology that is evangelistic and practical. Consequently, it would be futile for them to spend too much time on abstract truths and theological speculations, without attempting to develop a practical theology that the African believer can live by. African theologians must reinterpret the gospel because the way in which it was taught by most missionaries and some conservative Westernized Africans no longer speak [sic] effectively to the African.[34]

Certainly, Christian literature is a good means of communicating the gospel to non-Christians. However, its effectiveness is yet to be proved. In Igboland, a few factors raise questions as to the effectiveness of Christian literature for evangelistic purposes:

1. Illiteracy: Though there is no agreement between Igbo scholars about the actual population of the literate versus the illiterate ("literates" in this context includes everyone who has at least elementary school education in a formal school setting), there is a general consensus that the illiterate Igbo may be two-thirds or more of the total population. If this is true, it stands to reason that most of the literary materials which Christian churches and organizations distribute, fall into illiterate hands, and are consequently never read.
2. Christian literature which is written in English outnumbers that written in Igbo. The implication of this for those Igbo who can only read in Igbo and not in English is obvious. The number of potential readers becomes narrower.
3. Most of these who write in English are Westerners. They use Western concepts, symbols and illustrations, many of which are foreign to the educated Igbo who can read in English. These readers may read the materials, but the probability of their not understanding what they read is high.
4. Some of the indigenous writers of Christian literature simply copy the writing styles of their Western counterparts and thereby fail to communicate to their fellow Igbo.

5. Some publishing companies and printing presses do more of re-printing of foreign literature than produce indigenous works. Also, there is less of creativity and originality in much indigenous Christian literature. Many writers tend to translate and modify foreign works, without actually bringing out the messages in a clear and culturally understandable manner.

To remedy these situations, we will again suggest dialogue. We suggest that those who write Christian literature should in most cases write dialogically. The materials should be interactive in style and format. We also suggest that all those who distribute Christian literature should read the materials before they give them out. They should also arrange situations or forums where discussions of the content of their literature will take place. This kind of arrangement will help to clarify concerns which the readers may have. In our opinion, literature may not be the best means to reach the illiterate Igbo for Christ. If Christian witnesses must use literature, they must make sure that they read the materials to those illiterates whom they are evangelizing. They should also interpret and explain the content of the materials and be willing to answer questions from their prospective converts.

Having said all this about the context and content of gospel communication to the Igbo, let us now go to the next chapter and examine briefly five basic Biblical teachings, comparing and contrasting them with their meanings and relevance to Igbo religion and therefore propose points of contact for authentic Igbo Christianity. These basic teachings are: God, Christ, humanity, cosmogony, and life after death.

Notes

1   Bolaji Idowu, *Towards an Indigenous Church* (London: Oxford University Press, 1965), 5.

2   William D. Thompson and Gordon C. Bennett, *Dialogue Preaching: The Shared Sermon* (Valley Forge, Pa: Judson Press, 1969), 66.

3   Ibid., 66–67.

4   Ibid., 66.

5   Ibid., 67.

6   Ibid.

7   Ibid.

8   Ibid., 67–68.

9   Ibid., 68.

10   Ibid.

11   Ibid., 68–70.

12   Monological preaching may have done well in some other parts of the world, but in Igboland, it has left some marks of inadequacy, considering the lack of in-depth permeation of Christianity.

13   Thompson and Bennett, *Dialogue Preaching*, 72.

14   Matthew Akintunde Ojo, "New Trends in Nigerian Christianity: A Case Study of the Scripture Union" (M.A. Thesis, University of Ife, Nigeria, 1981), 128–129.

15   National Evangelism Christian Outreach (NECO), *The Commission, the Vision and the Mission* (Port-Harcourt, Nigeria: n. p., 1991; reprint, n. p., 1992), 20.

16   Bill Glass, "Developing a Citywide Crusade," in *NACIE 94 Equipping for Evangelism* (Minneapolis: World Wide Publications, 1996), 547–548.

17   Harold Ehrensperger, *Religious Drama: Ends and Means* (Nashville: Abingdon Press, 1962), 70.

18   Ibid., 69.

19   Fred Eastman and Louis Wilson, *Drama in the Church: A Manual of Religious Drama Production* (New York: Samuel French, 1933), 18.

20   Ibid.

21   Gustav Aulen, trans. Sydney Linton, *The Drama of the Symbols: A Book on Images of God and the Problems They Raise* (Philadelphia: Fortress Press, 1970), 90.

22   J. L. Styan, *The Elements of Drama* (Cambridge: Cambridge University Press, 1960), 12.

23   Ehrensperger, *Religious Drama: Ends and Means,* 99 and 101.

24   Frances Lawjua Bolton, *And We Beheld His Glory: A Personal Account of the Revival in Eastern Nigeria in 1970/71* (Harlow, Essex: Christ the King Publishing, 1992), 119.

25   Annie Ward Byrd, *Better Bible Teaching for Intermediates* (Nashville: Convention Press, 1959), 6.

26   John Stott and Robert T. Coote, *Gospel and Culture* (Pasadena, Calif: William Carey Library, 1979), 435.

27   Wallace H. Carrier, compiler, *Teaching Adults in Sunday School* (Nashville: Convention Press, 1976), 42–43.

28   Bill Jefferson, "Evangelism and Scripture Distribution," in *NACIE 94 Equipping for Evangelism,* 776.

29   The Sudan Interior Mission (SIM) is an American-based Christian organization which worked in Nigeria for many years and established churches and educational institutions. It also operated Barraka Printing Press in Kaduna for the publication of Christian literature. This foreign organization has since left Nigeria, but the churches and institutions it established are alive and active. Barraka Printing Press has ceased to exist. The denomination's new name is Evangelical Churches of West Africa. Both churches and institutions are totally managed by Nigerians.

30   ELWA radio station was set up in 1945 and owned by the SIM. The station was based in Monrovia, Liberia. This station has been taken over by the Liberian military government as a result of the civil war in Liberia.

31   Hilary C. Achunike, *Dreams of Heaven: A Modern Response to Christianity in Northwestern Igboland, 1970-1990* (Enugu, Nigeria: Snaap Printing & Publishing, 1995), 55.

32   William Ernest Hocking, *Re-Thinking Missions: A Laymen's Inquiry After One Hundred Years* (New York: Harper & Brothers, 1932), 187.

33   Gwinyai H. Muzorewa, *The Origins and Development of African Theology* (Maryknoll, N.Y.: Orbis Books, 1985), 92.

34   Ibid., 93.

Chapter 9

The Bible versus Igbo Religion

God

Genesis 1:1 states: "In the beginning God created the heavens and the earth." . Here, we find the first mention of the word, "God." In this same book, Genesis, we are told that God created heaven and earth. He created everything including humanity. But who is this God? Samuel Butler, in a series of articles published in *The Examiner* in May, June and July, 1879, said:

> As to what God is, beyond the fact that He is the Spirit and the Life which creates, governs and upholds all living things, I can say nothing. I cannot pretend that I can show more than others have done in what the Spirit and the Life consists, which governs all living things and animates them. I cannot show the connection between consciousness and the will, and the organ, much less can I tear away the veil from the face of God, so as to show wherein will and consciousness consist. No philosopher, whether Christian or Rationalist, has attempted this without discomfiture; but I can, I hope, do two things: Firstly, I can demonstrate, perhaps more clearly than modern science is prepared to admit, that there does exist a single Being or Animator of all living things—a single spirit, whom we cannot think of under any meaner name than God; and Secondly, I can show something more of the personal or bodily expression, mask, and mouthpiece of this Living Spirit . . .[1]

Butler contends that both God's existence and His attributes cannot be disproved because humanity reflects the likeness of God. God possesses all the essential human qualities in addition to His exclusive divine qualities. He created and sustains all living things. In God, there is "Trinity in Unity" and also "Infinity in Unity." There is also "a Unity in an Infinity."[2] He states that God is

> eternal in time past, for so much time at least that our minds can come no nearer to eternity than this, eternal for the future as long as the universe shall exist; ever changing, yet the same yesterday, and today and forever.[3]

The doctrine of God has been an on-going issue in the affairs of humanity since creation. Adam and Eve asked God who He was. In Plato's *Republic*, there is a dialogue between Socrates and Adeimantus about the stories of gods, Uranus and Cronos and his sons regarding their "truth." The dialogue continues:

Adeimantus: . . . if anyone says, "which stories are these?" what will our answer be?

Socrates: Why Adeimantus, you and I are not poets, (379) but, at present builders of a society. The builders will say what the fictions have to do, but they are not forced to make up the stories themselves.

Adeimantus: You are right. But of the gods what is to be said?

Socrates: In general, may we say this? It is right I take it, in all ways to give God the qualities he truly has.

Adeimantus: Yes.

Socrates: Then is not God certainly good, truly good, and always to be pictured so?

Adeimantus: Well, but nothing which is good does damage or ill, does it?

Adeimantus: No.

Socrates: Then that which is good is not the cause of all things, but only of things which are as it is right for them to be. So that which is good is not responsible for the coming into being of evil.

Adeimantus: Right.

Socrates: If that be so, then God, in as much as he is good, is not the cause of all things, as the common belief goes. No, from him comes only a small part of the events of man's existence, the greater part does not come from him. For our evils are far greater in number than our goods. And though the good things come from no other than God, the causes of the ill things are in something other, not in him.[4]

Commenting on this dialogue between Adeimantus and Socrates, Gerald Bray in *The Doctrine of God* said:

We are still a long way from a theology rooted in divine self-disclosure, but it is important to note that Plato believed that God's greatest attribute (as he saw it) could be defined as a statement of fact, without recourse to myth in any form. In other words, belief in a good God is not a myth; it is the hard core of truth around which the myths were to be constructed. It is this basic substance of truth, not the poetic expression of it, which constitutes the subject matter of *Christian* theology, and distinguishes it from Platonic or modern mythological interpretations.[5]

Mircea Eliade observes that Africans believe in the existence of God. In his analysis of this belief which is based on his concept of the "sky god," Eliade observes that Africans and most "primitive" peoples believe that the "sky god" is the same as the Supreme Being. He goes further to observe that Africans rarely worship the Supreme Being because their conception of him is that he is too distant from them:

> . . . the Great God of Heaven, the Supreme Being, Creator omnipotent, plays a quite insignificant part in the religious life of the tribe. He is too distant or too good to need worship properly so called, and they invoke him only in cases of extreme need.[6]

Eliade substantiates his observation by citing examples of selected African communities from his studies which gave that impression of the supreme Being. These communities according to him, recognize the autonomy, majesty and primacy of this Being; but because of His distant nature, humans do not seem to care much about Him. Rather they tend to look for help from the lesser divinities who reside on earth with them. For these Africans, and others, the local deities and the ancestors appear to be more active and accessible, hence humans turn to them with their daily concerns. This situation, according to Eliade, leaves room for a forgotten Supreme Being.

> Men only remember the sky and the Supreme divinity when they are directly threatened by a danger from the sky; at other times, their piety is called upon by the needs of everyday, and their practices and devotion are directed towards the forces that control those needs.[7]

Eliade then infers that both the "primitive" peoples and the "civilized" peoples quickly forget the "supreme sky beings" when they do not need them. When humans face hardships, they "look more towards earth than towards heaven."[8] They discover the importance of heaven only when they are "threatened with death from that direction."[9]

Without undermining Eliade's research and assertions, we doubt the validity of his conclusions. Reacting to Eliade's assertions, Justin S. Ukpong in his article, "The Problem of God and Sacrifice in African Traditional Religion," says that "Eliade's interpretations of these facts . . . leaves much to be desired."[10] However, Ukpong commends Eliade for bringing out certain basic facts about African religions. Eliade's analysis makes it clear that the "Supreme Being is not a figment of the imagination; he is not an abstraction." Rather "he is capable of maintaining a personal relationship with man and actually maintaining such a relationship, and that he is worshipped, though not frequently. From this analysis then, one basic aspect of God's personality (in African thought) stands out clearly—that he is distant yet near to man."[11] This is the reason why in Igboland God is often referred to as *Nwoke no n'elu-igwe ogodo ya na-awu n'ala*, meaning "the man who stays in the sky but his loin-cloth keeps flowing down the earth."

Ukpong asserts that

> The Eliadean interpretation does not seem to know or take seriously the fact that Africans generally look on the lesser divinities as creatures of God appointed by Him to administer certain affairs in the world—a situation which puts God in absolute control, and therefore negates any idea of "substitution" and "victory" on the part of the lesser gods. That God is distant is undeniable, but that he was pushed away by the lesser gods is unacceptable. Neither is the fact of God's distance (transcendence) the basis of the scant worship given to him for if it were so, to be logical, he would not be worshipped at all, since he would be too transcendent for man's reach.[12]

The debate about God, His existence and nature is inexhaustible in the arena of scholarship. We will not exhaust the subject in this work. However, we state that from what the Bible says about God, God is a being. He is a divine being, but He has both divine and moral attributes similar to what humans have because humans are made in the image of God. The second important thing about God is that He is knowable. Through His self-disclosure, humans can enter into a relationship with him. It is also important to state that God is eternal. He has no beginning and no end. He is the creator of the universe including humans. The Psalmist says this about God:

> In the beginning you laid the foundations of the earth, and the heavens are the works of your hands. They will perish, but you will remain; they will wear out like a garment. Like clothing you will change them and they will be discarded. But you remain the same, and your years will never end.[13]

Igbo religion shares similar beliefs about God, His nature and attributes. The Igbo call God, *Chukwu* (Supreme Being) and *Chineke* (the God who Creates) These two names, among numerous other descriptive names, are very significant in the Igbo conception of God.

In very precise language when the Igbo describe Chukwu's eternal self-existence, they say that he is "Chigbo." This is, as if to say: He is the chi that is made by no other chi; the unmade chi, the chi-that-exists-of his own and beyond whom there is none, for he is the totality of being.[14]

Jesus Christ

Matthew 1:21 and 23 bear the information about Jesus Christ[15] the Messiah or the Anointed One of God. Earlier in Isaiah 9:1-7, his birth was predicted and his functions outlined.[16] In this passage, Jesus Christ is called Mighty God. In John 14:9-10a, Jesus defines His identity Himself. He said to Philip, one of His disciples:

Don't you know me, Philip, even after I have been among you such a long time? Anyone who has seen me has seen the Father. How can you say, "Show us the Father?" Don't you believe that I am in the Father, and that the Father is in me?[17]

Chinua Achebe mentions an incident during an evangelistic preaching in the Igbo village of Mbanta in which one of the non-Christian listeners confronted the missionary's interpreter with the following question:

You told us with your own mouth that there was only one god. Now you talk about his son. He must have a wife, then. The crowd agreed.[18]

Adherents of Igbo religion believe in God, the Supreme Being, but they do not have any conception of Jesus being one with God. It appears that while the place of *Chukwu* or *Chineke* is pronounced and His functions defined, there is no place for Jesus in Igbo religion. Consequently, He does not have any roles. There are divinities or deities. These are created by *Chineke* and they serve as messengers of *Chukwu*. In Igbo religious thought, none of the deities can be equated to the Jesus Christ of the Bible. Jesus Christ cannot also be thought of as an ancestor in Igbo religion. This means that for the Igbo worshipper, Jesus is a stranger both to God and to Igbo religion. Therefore, the challenge facing the Christian evangelization in Igboland is how to make Jesus Christ part of Igbo life and religion and elevate Him to the same position as *Chukwu*.

W. Norman Pittenger mentions the four affirmations of Christendom concerning the identity of Jesus Christ. He observes that these affirmations are essential to the life of the Christian church, and must be understood as one seeks to understand the "basic ground of its being."[19] These four affirmations are:

1. Jesus is truly human.
2. Christ is truly divine.
3. Jesus Christ is one person.
4. Jesus Christ is intimately related to the more general action, presence and revelation of God in his world and supremely in human history.[20]

In Igbo religion, there is no defined place for Christ, therefore Christological formulations are difficult. However a number of African theologians have made various suggestions regarding the integration of Christ in African religious life. Henry Johannes Mugabe mentions an article in which John Mbiti stated that Christology does not exist in African concepts. Mugabe also mentions Aylward Shorter as stating that the church in Africa has failed to "produce a convincing African Christology."[21] One wonders why Shorter speaks of "African Christology" when in reality there is no such thing. Christocentric theologies are different from Afro-centric theological formulations because while the former emphasize the centrality of Christ in Christianity, the latter emphasize the importance and relevance of African thought and concern in Christianity. While it may seem like these two positions are poles apart and while we do not suggest a syncretistic amalgamation of the two, our opinion is that both are necessary for authentic African Christianity.

The Bible states that Christ is the Savior of the world. That world includes Africa. Therefore, for Christ to fulfill His salvific role for Africans, He must be introduced to the Africans in such a way that they will not be suspicious of Him. He must be introduced to the Africans the way He is, with all His divine and human characteristics still intact. His incarnational nature, which is different from the African concept of re-incarnation, should be emphasized, and the mystery of His incarnation retained. For the African, re-incarnation is a process whereby those who die and are buried, the "living-dead," are reborn on earth as humans, while incarnation refers to the divine manifestation in the human Jesus. In incarnation, God is with humanity in Jesus Christ. This is a divine mystery and it is different from the Igbo concept of re-incarnation. The Christian witness should not be afraid of doing this because Africans can relate to mystery in a way that will help them understand the true identity of Christ.

For this reason, we feel that the Christological formulations which suggest models for the African Christ are inadequate and sometimes misleading. These models include Christ as king, Christ as elder brother,

Christ as healer, Christ as ancestor, and Christ as warrior and liberator. Some apparent dangers for authentic Christian faith in Africa exist with these models. In many instances, there are African communities where people have suffered oppression, suppression, injustice, and all kinds of deprivation from the hands of their fellow Africans who assumed those positions in society. Many Africans will be hesitant to give their allegiance and loyalty to a Christ who assumes any of those positions. Christ is a unique personality. The uniqueness of His personality should be preserved even in the process of cross-cultural communication of the gospel.

It does not matter which term a person uses to describe authentic African Christianity—indigenization, contextualization, adaptation or inculturation. What matters is that Christ be relevant to the African peoples in such a way that Christ does not lose His divine identity nor His human identity. Fon Wilfred Tatah Wirsiy observes that indigenization and inculturation have created some problems for the church in Africa because while Protestant churches have generally favored indigenization, Catholic churches have favored inculturation. He states:

> The history of African Christology is rooted in the ideas of indigenization, inculturation and contextualization. Though the first two have given birth to the discussion on contextualization in the African church, they have also created problems for the church. The indigenization principle produced the "three-self program" in the mission fields. . . . Inculturation is the preoccupation to produce a church that fits within a given culture. The desire to consider the cultural context and not produce a misfit for a given society, therefore, predominated the inculturation agenda. The Protestant Churches have generally favored the indigenization approach while inculturation has been the Roman Catholic watchword in Africa. In the modern day, most Protestant evangelicals have substituted the concept of indigenization with that of contextualization. The Roman Catholic theologians still favor inculturation.[22]

If the goal of both indigenization and inculturation is to produce an authentic African Christianity, we do not see where the problem is. The issue is not which group has what approach. The issue is not Protestant versus Roman Catholic methodologies and how different they are. The real issue is how well any of these approaches can work to produce an authentic African Christianity. We have chosen inculturation as the most effective approach to achieving this goal, considering the fact that inculturation brings Christianity home to Africans without compromising Biblical affirmations. An authentic Igbo Christianity requires this approach to evangelism.

Humanity

In Genesis 1:26 and 27 we find these words:

> Then God said, "Let us make man in our image, in our likeness, and let them rule
> over the fish of the sea and the birds of the air, over the livestock, over all the
> earth, and over all the creatures that move along the ground. So God created
> man in his own image, in the image of God he created them.[23]

Also Psalm 8 states:

> . . . what is man that you are mindful of him, the son of man that you care for
> him? You made him a little lower than the heavenly beings and crowned him with
> glory and honor. You made him ruler over the works of your hands; you put
> everything under his feet . . .[24]

According to the Genesis account, humans are the creation of God. They
did not evolve from an ape or from any other living organism. They came
into being as a result of the creative act of God. At creation, God commis-
sioned humans to be in charge of other created beings and things. The
Bible also makes it clear that humans are created in the image of God,
their creator. This image of God which humans possess is the principal
distinguishing feature between them and other created beings.

> . . . in Christian thought, man is seen from the stand-point of God, "rather
> than from the uniqueness of his faculties or his relation to nature." He is made in
> the "image of God" (Imago Dei). . . . Man is like God because he possesses
> such powers and qualities which are the attributes of God. . . . Man can
> plan and can make decisions, although in a relative degree. Man can make deci-
> sion because he is free. He is free because God, his creator, is free. . . .[25]

It has always been the desire of God for humans, whom He made in His
image, to remain in communication with Him. So He shows love to
humans and expects them to love Him back through the warmth of
fellowship.

The Igbo, like most African communities, view humans as creations of
God. However, the aspect of the "image of God" in humans, is absent in
Igbo anthropological religious thoughts.

> Man in African Religion is seen primarily as a creature of God. This is borne out
> by myths, proverbs, names and folktales found all over Africa. The way in which
> it is said man has [sic] been created may vary in some societies, but it is commonly
> held that God created man. Man is endowed with intelligence. This puts him far
> above other creatures in the physical world . . .[26]

Emefie Ikenga Metuh recognizes humans as God's creation, according to Igbo belief system. He discusses four vivifying principles which link humans with other life forces in the universe. These are: *Obi* (breath or heart); *Chi* (personal destiny); *Eke* (ancestral guardians); and *Mmuo* or *Onyinyo* (spirit or shadows).[27]

Africans also believe in the dual dimension of human existence. Humans exist as single individuals as well as a corporate group belonging to various communities. Each individual is endowed with specific gifts and destiny. However, no individual exists exclusively for himself or for herself. Each person is expected to contribute positively to the community's well-being, utilizing his or her God-given gifts and abilities.

> Man is linked to the universe of forces by an ontological principle from inside man himself. Through his life-force ("obi" in Igbo) he can influence and be influenced by other forces outside himself. This life-force can be strengthened, weakened and may die. Man is integrated into his family, clan and other social groups through another potent principle—the ancestral life-force. Through this, the life-force of the family flows in him. Man's individuality is assumed by his personal destiny. This destiny received from the creator is uniquely his, and each person has to work out its content by himself. He may count on the help of his ancestors and the deities, but he has also to contend with the snares of the countervailing forces, like witches, sorcerers and evil spirits. How he steers his course successfully or unsuccessfully through this spiritual economy will determine his status in the after-life.[28]

For the Igbo, humans are the most important creation of God. The Igbo believe in the sacredness of human life, but they also believe that *mmadu abughi chi* (man is not God).

> . . . human beings are the centre of creation. They are the main actors in the drama of existence and life. Their actions evoke reactions from the gods and have deep implications for the lower beings and forces, who may have to be manipulated to satisfy the needs of the human beings. In the drama of life man is the actor while the pure spirits are the moderators and the lower forces and beings are the agents (and hence victims as well). Viewed from another angle, if life's drama is a game of chess, man is the chess player, the disembodied spirits of the rank of deities and ancestors are the referees while the animals, birds and other animate and inanimate beings (in fact, including the abstract forces) are the pawns.[29]

Cosmogony

Genesis 1:1 says: "In the beginning God created the heavens and the earth."[30] The writer of Psalm 24:1 and 2 stated: "The earth is the Lord's and everything in it, the world, and all who live in it; for he founded it upon the seas and established it upon the waters."[31] The Bible strongly affirms that the universe was created by God. The Bible also affirms that God, who created, is also in control of the forces of nature. God is not a passive creator; He is an active creator. Discussing "The Problem of Origins," Howard A. Snyder makes reference to two major worldviews, the "Divine Design" theory and the "Big Bang" theory. According to Snyder, some people say that both creationism and the Big Bang theory are weak. These people say that humans do not need any answer for the origin of the universe because such an answer is not necessary.

> Many have argued that faith in God is simply a human projection (or retrojection) from our cause and effect experiences in daily life. In order to explain the universe, we imagine an Ultimate Cause who is simply a sort of super human being, a cosmic super human. We make God in our own image. How does it help to say that God caused the universe to exist when we can't answer the question of why God exists?[32]

Those who hold this view ask whether or not God answers the question of causation or merely pushes it back. To these people, the "Divine Design" worldview gives two main answers. First, it argues that it appears that more people find satisfaction and plausibility in the belief that "a God of will, purpose, and power" created all things than those who think that the universe caused itself. However,

> The question of the origin of God is unanswerable. But it seems more plausible to believe in a divine being, a divine personality who exists in a dimension of reality where time, space, origin and causality have no meaning or are transcended in some kind of higher meaning (or higher dimensions) than to believe the universe caused itself.[33]

The credibility of this viewpoint lends itself to the assertion that "the ultimate reality is personal, not impersonal; purposive, not random or deterministic; conscious, not unthinking and unfeeling."[34]

Secondly, "Divine Design" worldview regards God as an eternal spiritual being who possesses consciousness and will. The implication of this belief is that God's sphere of existence surpasses those of time and space. Therefore, "we are, perhaps dealing in a realm of multidimensionality that goes far beyond the four dimensions we normally sense."[35]

The Igbo cosmogony allows room for belief in a Creator-God, *Chineke*. The Igbo cosmological concept presupposes two basic beliefs, the unity of all created things and an ordered relationship among them.[36] This belief suggests the existence of a planner and a creator. The Supreme Being is that person. He is a person because He relates to His creatures, especially humans. He does this sometimes directly and at other times through His intermediaries (deities). According to the Igbo, the Supreme Being designed the universe and everything in it well. His purpose was for order, peaceful interaction between beings in the two realms of the universe, *eluigwe* (the sky) and *elu-uwa* (the earth). Unfortunately, things on earth have turned out differently because *madu bu njo ala* (man is the corrupter of the land or earth).[37]

An important thing to note is that Igbo cosmogony operates within the realm of myth and folklore. There are diverse versions of the Igbo creation story because of the diversity of Igbo autonomous communities; but there are certain basic cosmological beliefs which these communities share. For example, throughout Igboland the belief that God created the universe is never questioned. The Igbo believe that God is in charge of the created order. They also believe that He is capable of punishing any individual or any community which goes against His laws.

Life After Death

Many passages of the Bible speak about life after death. The resurrection of Jesus Christ from death presupposes the resurrection of Christians who will die before the second coming of Christ. Jesus made the following statement to Martha, whose brother, Lazarus had died:

> I am the resurrection and the life. He who believes in me will live, even though he dies, and whoever lives and believes in me will never die . . . [38]

In another place, Paul confirms the resurrection of Christ and its positive implication for Christians:

> But if it is preached that Christ has been raised from the dead, how can some of you say that there is no resurrection of the dead? If there is no resurrection of the dead, then not even Christ has been raised. And if Christ has not been raised, our preaching is useless and so is your faith. More than that, we are then found to be false witnesses about God, for we have testified about God that he raised Christ from the dead. But he did not raise him if in fact the dead are not raised. For if the dead are not raised, then Christ has not been raised either. And if Christ has not been raised, your faith is futile; you are still in your sins. Then those also who have fallen asleep in Christ are lost. If only for this life we have hope in Christ, we are to be pitied more than all men. But Christ has indeed been raised from the dead, the first fruits of those who have fallen asleep.[39]

What does the Bible say about where the resurrected will spend eternity and what conditions they will be in? Jesus and Paul answer:

> Do not let your hearts be troubled. Trust in God; trust also in me. In my Father's house are many rooms; if it were not so, I would have told you. I am going there to prepare a place for you. And if I go and prepare a place for you, I will come back and take you to be where I am. . . . [40]

> But someone may ask, "How are the dead raised? With what kind of body will they come?" How foolish! What you sow does not come to life unless it dies. . . . There are . . . heavenly bodies and there are earthly bodies, but the splendor of the heavenly bodies is one kind, and the splendor of the earthly bodies is another. . . . So will it be with the resurrection of the dead. The body that is sown is perishable, it is raised imperishable; it is sown in dishonor, it is raised in glory; it is sown in weakness, it is raised in power; it is sown in a natural body, it is raised in a spiritual body. . . . When the perishable has been clothed with the imperishable, and the mortal with immortality, then the saying that is written will come true: "Death has been swallowed up in victory." "Where, O death, is your victory? Where, O death, is your sting?" The sting of death is sin, and the power of sin is the law. But thanks be to God! He gives us the victory through our Lord Jesus Christ. [41]

In the Bible, Jesus is a life-giver. He gives life here on earth and life in the after life. Jesus Christ is the essence of mission enterprise. Jesus said, "The thief comes only to steal and kill and destroy; I have come that they may have life, and have it to the full." [42] The phrase, "to the full" may refer to both the quality and length of life, the everlastingness of life with Christ, even in the hereafter. In their Biblical affirmations for evangelism, the North American Conference for Itinerant Evangelists during their 1994 conference, which was organized by the Billy Graham Evangelistic Association, stated:

> Jesus Christ is coming again. Each person will stand before Him in Judgment. Those whose names are in the lamb's Book of Life shall dwell eternally in God's presence as His redeemed, resurrected people. Those who reject Jesus Christ shall spend eternity separated from God in the place the Bible calls hell. [43]

Life after death is a basic Igbo belief. Those who die go to *Ala mmuo*, (the spirit world). There are good and bad spirits. Whether or not a person becomes a good spirit in *ala mmuo* depends on his or her moral status here on earth. Good moral behavior on earth will transfer to the world beyond here. Death does not mean the end of existence. It is the end of one segment of life and the beginning of another. "Many Igbo funeral songs describe death as *ila ulo*, going home or *ila ala Mmuo*, going home to the spirit-land." [44] A good example of a funeral song is:

Uwa dika ahia; onye zurucha, ya alaa (the earth is like a market place, once a person is through with his or her purchases, he or she will go). Though death involves the loss of loved ones and it is painful to be bereaved, the Igbo do not necessarily regard it as a bad occurrence. "Death is not a disaster, it is rather 'going home.'"[45]

Though death is perceived as "going home," not everyone who dies actually gets home. Emefie Ikenga Metuh observes that the nature of a person's death determines whether or not that individual reaches home. Metuh points out three main types of death in Igbo conceptual thought: *Onwu Ekwensu* (violent death or literally, devil's death), *Onwu ojoo* (bad death), and *Onwu chi* (natural or good death).[46]

Onwu Ekensu is the kind of violent death which is caused by accidents. It becomes more violent and traumatic when it involves a young person. Bad medical conditions, such as heart-attack and stroke, could cause this kind of death. But because the average Igbo does not believe in *Onwu nkiti* (ordinary death), the cause of this death may be attributed to either the actions of mischievous disembodied spirits or to poison by their enemies. Rarely do the Igbo regard this kind of death as *akara aka* (destiny). When this kind of death occurs,

> It is believed that the person has not run the full course of his life nor accomplished the task for which the Creator sent him to the world. He has not achieved his destiny... He is therefore believed to have been snatched away from life by evil forces. Whatever the actual cause of death, he becomes a purposeless, wandering evil spirit in the spirit-world.[47]

Onwu Ojoo is related to a person's moral conduct while he or she was living on earth. Different communities have different market days which are sacred. Nobody is expected to die on a sacred market day. When a person dies on such a day, which happens occasionally, such a person is said to have died a bad death. Other bad deaths include suicides, death by lightening, leprosy, cholera, smallpox and dropsy.[48] Sin on the part of the individuals is said to be responsible for such deaths.

> Such people are not mourned or buried in their homes but thrown into bad bush, *Ajo ohia*. There is no formal announcement of the death and people go about their normal businesses. . . . Those guilty of very grievous crimes such as suicide, or notorious robbers, witches, sorcerers etc. become . . . wandering evil spirits, at once and are banished to . . . desolate, unhappy place between the living and the spirit-world.[49]

Metuh notes that for those who died as a result of the breaking of minor taboos, such as dying on the sacred market day or as a result of dropsy, their living relatives may upgrade their status by offering "elaborate and expensive purification rites"[50] on their behalf. These will then receive full funeral rites and in about one year of their death, will become ancestors. The third kind of death Metuh mentions is *Onwu Chi*.

> *Onwu Chi* is death that follows a ripe old age. However, by itself it is not enough to gain a person's entrance to and (sic) ancestral status in the spirit-land. He would also have to have a surviving son or relative to give him the fitting rites and feed him, *inye ya nri*, during the daily ancestral cult at the Ndichi (Elders) shrine. Elders who have no surviving male issue may not get to *Ala Mmuo*.[51]

The Igbo believe that *Chukwu* is actively involved with humans not only here on earth, but hereafter. He created, he sustains and keeps those who relate to Him well. "There is a general belief that when men have run their course on earth, they return to their master, the Supreme Being, *Chukwu*, and live with him in the spirit world."[52] It appears that this belief contradicts the concept of reincarnation. Adherents of Igbo religion are yet to come up with an explanation for this contradiction.

Notes

1   Samuel Butler, *God: Known and Unknown* (Girard, Kans: Haldeman-Julius Co., n.d.), 9–10.

2   Ibid., 11.

3   Ibid.

4   I. A. Richards, *The Republic of Plato: A New Version Founded on Basic English* (New York: W.W. Norton and Co., 1942), 55–56.

5   Gerald Bray, *The Doctrine of God* (Leicester, U.K.: Inter-Varsity Press, 1993), 22–23.

6   Mircea Eliade, *Patterns in Comparative Religion*, trans. Rosemary Sheed (London: Sheed and Ward, 1958; reprint, New York: New American Library, 1974), 47.

7   Ibid., 50.

8   Ibid.

9   Ibid.

10 Justin S. Ukpong, "The Problem of God and Sacrifice in African Traditional Religion," *Journal of Religion in Africa 14* (1983): 191.

11 Ibid., 190.

12 Ibid., 191.

13 Psalm 102:25–27.

14 Cosmas Okechukwu Obiego, *African Image of the Ultimate Reality: An Analysis of Igbo Ideas of Life and Death in Relation to Chukwu-God* (Frankfurt am Main: Peter Lang, 1984), 77.

15 Matthew 1:21,23, "She will give birth to a son, and you are to give him the name Jesus because he will save his people from their sins. . . . The Virgin will be with child and will give birth to a son, and they will call him 'Immanuel'—which means, 'God with us.' "

16 See Isaiah 9:1–7.

17 John 14:9–10a.

18 Achebe, *Things Fall Apart*, 103.

19 W. Norman Pittenger, *The Word Incarnate: A Study of the Doctrine of the Person of Christ* (New York: Harper & Brothers, 1959), 11.

20   Ibid., 11–19.

21   Henry Johannes Mugabe, "Christology in an African Context," *Review and Expositor* 88 (1991): 343.

22   Fon Wilfred Tatah Wirsiy, "The Influence of African Traditional Religions on Biblical Christology: An Evaluation of Emerging Christologies in Sub-Sahara Africa" (Ph.D. diss. Westminister Theological Seminary, 1995), 66–67.

23   Genesis 1:26–27.

24   Psalm 8:4–6.

25   J. A. Omoyajowo, "The Christian View of Man," *Orita* 6, no. 2 (December 1972): 120–121.

26   Amba Oduyoye, ed., *The State of Christian Theology in Nigeria* (Ibadan, Nigeria: Daystar Press, 1986), 89–90.

27   Emefie Ikenga Metuh, *God and Man in African Religion: A Case Study of the Igbo of Nigeria* (London: Geoffrey Chapman, 1981), 87–90.

28   Ibid., 92.

29   T. Uzodinma Nwala, *Igbo Philosophy* (Lagos, Nigeria: Lantern Books, 1985), 41–42.

30   Genesis 1:1.

31   Psalm 24:1 and 2.

32   Howard A. Snyder, *Earth Currents: The Struggle for the World's Soul* (Nashville: Abingdon Press, 1995), 199.

33   Ibid.

34   Ibid.

35   Ibid., 200.

36   Nwala, *Igbo Philosophy*, 54.

37   Ibid., 29–30.

38   John 11:25, 26.

39   1 Corinthians 15:12–20.

40   John 14:1–3.

41   1 Corinthians 15:35–57.

42   John 10:10.

43   Lewis A. Drummond, ed., *Biblical Affirmations for Evangelism: NACIE 94, North American Conference for Itinerant Evangelists* (Minneapolis: World Wide Publications, 1966), 208.

44   Metuh, *God and Man in African Religion*, 138.

45   Ibid., 139.

46   Ibid., 140.

47   Ibid.

48   In most Igbo communities today, people no longer regard these events of death as bad. They now know that there are medical or natural conditions which are beyond the individual's power.

49   Ibid., 141–142.

50   Ibid., 142.

51   Ibid.

52   Ibid., 152.

Conclusion

The key to establishing effective points of contact with adherents of Igbo religion and with those Igbo church-goers for whom Christianity is yet to become authentic is a genuine interest in the Igbo culture and institutions by the Christian witness. The Christian witness, whether foreign or indigenous, must understand the Igbo language and culture, its concepts, symbols, proverbs and idioms. Effective communication requires such understanding.

> Culture is closely bound up with language, and is expressed in proverbs, myths, folk tales, and various art forms, which become part of the mental furniture of all members of the group. It governs actions undertaken in community—acts of worship or of general welfare; laws and administration such as clubs and societies, associations for an immense variety of common purposes.[1]

In addition to a genuine interest, which gives expression in actual understanding of the Igbo culture, the witness should respect the people's traditional forms and institutions. This respect is expected to create room and a cordial atmosphere for dialogue. We are aware of Donald McGavran's "people movement" strategy. While this strategy may work in isolated Igbo communities, it may not in most. We are also aware that McGavran does not regard his "people movement" plan as "a mass movement." According to McGavran,

> The term "mass movement" should not be used. It gives an incorrect idea of what happens. A people seldom move *en masse* into a new faith. What happens is that here a group of fifty and there a group of eighty and yonder one of six, after much instruction and weighing of the issues, decide as groups to accept the Christian Faith. The process goes on year after year as new groups make up their minds to follow Christ. Thus churches arise without the social dislocation of the village. This is not mass movement . . .

A "people movement" to Christ affords opportunity for systematic instruction and community worship from the very beginning. There is in it a large amount of personal decision. We see more and more clearly that the "people movement" to Christ provides both more and better Christians than the "one by one against the current of the people" method does.[2]

In spite of the popularity and consequent acceptability of this strategy by many modern missiologists and evangelists, we see some holes in its workability in Igboland. McGavran denies the use of the term, "mass movement" for his plan, stating that "there is a large amount of personal decision" involved. It appears that to substitute the word "people" for "mass" is a matter of semantics, not substance. It is also not clear in this plan how the individual actually makes his or her decision for Christ, since this individual is still expected to conform to the group's social norm. Again, we do not know what this individual should do when his or her decisions for Christ conflict with those of some members of the group who may not be as serious with their new faith as this individual. McGavran also failed to address the issues of coercion, intimidation, material considerations and "group think" in the process of decision-making.

There may be some African communities where McGavran's "people movement" will work, but its effectiveness and workability in most Igbo communities is a matter for debate. Every Igbo community is autonomous. The individual comes before the community, in spite of the sense of community which exists among the Igbo. The socio-political structures of most Igbo communities may resist this type of religious "movement." Though the concept of collective bargaining is strong in many Igbo communities, the Igbo act individually concerning commitment to foreign religions. Hence they can say, *obi bu akpa; onye obula nya nke ya* (the heart is a bag; everyone is carrying his or her own).

Most Igbo will examine for themselves individually the options which they have been presented with, weigh the options and make their decisions. These decisions are normally based on their personal convictions, not on their communities' pressures or approval. In order to come to the point of genuine commitment to Christ, which is based on personal conviction, the average Igbo will like to be given the opportunity to talk things over with the presenter of the gospel message. Once this dialogical door is opened, the prospect for conviction and conversion is enhanced.

Theological relevance is the third area of concern for the Christian witness. The carrier of the Good News should distinguish between Biblical affirmations and theological presuppositions. Bruce J. Nicholls notes that

The failure of missionary communicators to recognize the degree of cultural conditioning of their own theology has been devastating to many Third World churches, creating a kind of Western theological imperialism and stifling the efforts of national Christians to theologize within their own culture. Unfortunately the imposition of Western theological systems is often perpetuated by the national theologians themselves. I remember the dismay I felt when a leader of one of the "indigenous" churches in Japan expressed his enthusiasm for translating a three-volume American systematic textbook into Japanese without any apparent desire to evaluate critically the highly culturalized system itself.

Every attempt to make theology relevant to people in a given cultural context will of necessity be culturally conditioned, for theology that communicates is always missiological.[3]

E. A. Asamoa feels that it will not help the cause of Christianity in Africa for Christian leaders, whether missionary or indigenous, to continue to look down on the African ways of life and to regard African beliefs as bearing no significance.

Anybody who knows African Christians intimately will know that no amount of denial on the part of the church will expel belief in supernatural powers from the minds of the African people. What often happens as a result of such denunciation is that a state of conflict is created in the mind of the Christian, and he becomes a hypocrite who in official church circles pretends to give the impression that he does not believe in these things, while in his own private life he resorts to practices which are the results of such beliefs.[4]

Though Asamoa's observation may not be true for every African Christian, he makes a valid point here regarding what is Biblical and what is "Christian." Church leaders should make it clear to members of Two-Thirds World churches when they are speaking Biblically and when they are speaking culturally. The Good News is about Jesus Christ and the reality of His life, death and resurrection. It is not about the texture, color or substance of the cross or His tomb. It is not about whether or not the cross was gold or wood; white or black, ten feet high or twenty feet high. It is about what Christ did on the cross for humankind. It is about the redemption of humankind through the cross event and the resurrection event. This good news is about telling sinners, including the Igbo, in the way they can understand, that because Jesus lives, they also will live qualitatively, meaningfully and purposefully now and eternally after now, if they make Jesus their friend. With the use of Igbo concepts, symbols and metaphors, the Christian witness must stay focused on Jesus as he or she, through the empowerment and direction of the Holy Spirit, makes in-roads into people's minds and hearts.

The fourth point of contact is the awareness that Igbo religion shares similar beliefs with the Bible in subjects such as God, humanity, cosmogony and life after death. Using the method of participant observation, without compromising Biblical standards, the Christian witness in Igboland can construct conceptual bridges which will lead the Igbo to a clearer and better understanding of his or her relationship to the Supreme Being, who is in-charge of life and death. Given the belief that life does not end here on earth, every Igbo desires a good life in the hereafter. It is the responsibility of the Christian witness to introduce Christ, not as a deity, an ancestor, king, elder brother, warrior or first son models, but as a distinct individual who is unique in His personality and compares with nobody else, except God.

Using the concepts of sacrifice and atonement and their symbolic expressions, which Igbo worshippers understand, the uniqueness of Christ's sacrifice and atonement for the salvation of humankind should be explained to the Igbo in a dialogical form. The Holy Spirit should then be trusted to work in hearts of Igbo men and women and lead them to convictions and conversion and to consequent authentic appropriation of Christianity.

A good tool to use for the construction of these bridges is story-telling. The Igbo love stories. The Bible is full of story events. From Genesis to Revelation stories of God's encounter with human personalities abound. There are also stories of human interaction which involves individuals, groups of individuals and communities. Biblical stories could be told like moonlight stories to individuals and groups of individuals in Igboland. For effective story-telling, the story-teller must be willing to engage his or her listeners in dialogical interaction. Story-telling is a vital part of Igbo socio-religious life.

James O. Stallings makes the following significant statement about story-telling:

> A community cannot avoid telling its own story. Self-understanding, beliefs, and attitudes are passed on through the telling of stories. Stories come in many forms: songs, tales, legends, jokes, and even gossip. Story is how we live.[5]

Jesus was a good story-teller. The Jewish culture was a story-telling one. The Igbo can relate very well to the Christian faith, which grew out of a story-telling community because the Igbo live and function in the context of story. The communicator of the gospel message to the Igbo should take advantage of this medium. Joseph P. Russell advises the church:

We who are the church need to be aware of our role as storyteller for the faithful. The liturgist, musician, church-school teacher, dramatist, and craftsman are all storytellers in the ancient and time-honored sense of that title. We shape people's ideas, values, and world view by means of that ancient art of story sharing. Seeing our role in this light will point up for us the immense importance of our task in the church.[6]

It is important to restate that dialogue, as an inculturation model for the re-evangelization of Igboland, will yield good results for authentic Christianity. The Igbo are truly religious; they are religious to the core. But it appears that many Igbo church-goers have not passed the level of religiosity into the level of personal commitment to Jesus Christ. Many factors may be responsible for this apparent situation as we have discussed; but our contention is that lack of true involvement in and understanding of the demands of Christianity, coupled with the foreignness of Christian concepts, symbols and metaphors, may be the principal reason for this situation. Hence we suggest dialogical interactions between preachers and teachers of Christianity and the Igbo. The Igbo flourish in dialogues. The depth of their commitment to Christ will to a great extent depend on the depth and width of their religious "room" for participation, and whether or not this "room" is located in their culture and becomes part of their social milieu.

Authentic Igbo Christianity is a product of dialogical evangelism. Evangelism which takes Igbo history, culture and institutions into consideration and mediates the gospel message through them, using Igbo concepts, symbols and metaphors, is likely to have a deep and lasting impact on the Igbo. The Igbo are a peculiar African nation. Unlike most of their African counterparts, they have a high sense of individualism and function as autonomous persons, both socially and politically. On the other hand, like almost all African communities, there is no clear division between religious and secular life. Life is a unity. The sustenance of this unity involves the interactions which take place between *Chukwu*, the deities, the ancestors and the living humans on a moment by moment basis. *Chukwu* is always active and no social, political economic or religious happening eludes His notice or attention. He is in the center of humankind's existence. The Igbo are intelligent, enterprising and inquisitive. These qualities reflect in their total life endeavors. They take pride in the things they can do for themselves and in the decisions that direct their lives. The implications of this fact of "Igboness" for authentic Christianity cannot be over-emphasized.

For Christianity to become authentically Igbo, there must be a re-examination of the early methods of Christian evangelization in Igboland. From the current nature of Christianity in Igboland, it appears that something went wrong somewhere. It could be that most of the early missionaries failed to understand the peculiarity of the Igbo among all other African communities. It could also be that these missionaries destroyed the base of Igbo philosophical operation and replaced it with their Western thought-pattern. Unlike the West, the Igbo and most other African peoples do not think in a vacuum. They do not rationalize from the abstract. Instead, they rationalize from the known to the unknown. Therefore, it appears that the early missionaries did not provide adequate and culturally understandable philosophical and even theological concepts, symbols and metaphors for the new convert from Igbo religion to Christianity. As a result of the confusion in the difference between Igbo culture and Christianity, and between Western culture and Christianity, the average Igbo Christian seems to live in two worlds, if not three worlds—the Igbo world, the Christian world and the Western world. We see this situation as the primary reason for inauthentic Igbo Christianity.

In his article, "The Christian Church and African Heritage," E. A. Asamoa quotes part of a report which a former missionary to Africa presented to the International Missionary Council (I.M.C.) meeting at Willingen:

> Most Christians [i.e. African Christians], it is suggested, live on two unreconciled
> levels. They are members of a church, associated all too often in their mind with
> benefits and discipline rather than with loyalties and fellowship. As such they
> subscribe to a statement of faith. But below the system of conscious beliefs are
> deeply embedded traditions and customs implying quite a different interpretation
> of the universe and the world of spirit from the Christian interpretation. In the
> crisis of life—birth, marriage, death—the "customary" matters more than the
> Christian; the church is at those great moments an alien thing. This is true even
> of those younger people who have forgotten or have never known clearly what
> their forefathers believed; there is some inheritance in their minds, some fear of
> vague unknown forces of evil, some residual belief in magic, which makes them
> easy converts to some new fetish with a big following, even if they are well-
> educated Christians.[7]

There is an on-going struggle in the minds of most Igbo Christians regarding how best to resolve the issues connected with their "cosmetic Christianity." The Igbo love Christianity. Most of them desire to become genuine Christians. They also want to function actively in their various communities and take part in the social, political, economic and religious life of their communities. But they fear to offend the church because the church seems to put Christianity and Igbo culture in two separate worlds. The impression one gets from this separation, which is a perpetuation of the initial attitude of most missionaries to Igboland, is that one cannot be a Christian and still be Igbo.

This book has been written to highlight the current nature of Christianity in Igboland and to counter the impression that one cannot be a Christian and function culturally, and then suggest that Christianity must be authentically Igbo before it can have any meaning for the Igbo people. It is also our contention that there is a difference between authentic Igbo Christianity and syncretism. Authentic Igbo Christianity is one which recognizes the uniqueness of Jesus Christ regarding His birth, life and ministry and subscribes to His headship of the Christian church, but employs Igbo concepts, symbols and metaphors to express worship and loyalty to Christ. In doing this, we suggest that the Bible should be the guide for the formulations of liturgical and theological statements or affirmations. If Biblical principles are maintained in the process, the fear of syncretistic practices by the Igbo churches and Christians will subside. Dialogue between preachers, teachers, evangelists and their church members or audiences is the principal road to attaining this status. Re-evangelization of Igboland demands dialogical interactions. Dialogue can also serve as "bridge-building" between Igbo religion and Christianity so that the few Igbo who are still outside the church can be convinced to come in. In going this dialogical route, the church in Igboland should be aware of the principles of effective dialogue, which among other things regards the listener as an equal and respects his or her views. This is the essence of inculturation.

Notes

1 Stott and Coote, *Gospel and Culture*, 435.

2 Donald McGavran, "New Methods for a New Age in Missions," *The International Review of Missions* 44 (1955): 398.

3 Bruce J. Nicholls, *Contextualization: A Theology of Gospel and Culture* (Downers Grove, Ill: InterVarsity Press, 1979), 25.

4 E. A. Asamoa, "The Christian Church and African Heritage," *The International Review of Missions* 44 (1955): 297.

5 James O. Stallings, *Telling the Story: Evangelism in Black Churches* (Valley Forge, Pa: Judson Press, 1988), 91–92.

6 Joseph P. Russell, *Sharing Our Biblical Story* (Minneapolis: Winston Press, 1979), 5–6.

7 E. A. Asamoa, "The Christian Church and African Heritage," *International Review of Missions.* 44 (1955), 293.

Appendix I

Survey of the Practice of Christianity in Igboland

Personal Data

Directions: Please check the applicable space(s).

1. Sex
   a. ( ) Male
   b. ( ) Female

2. Age Range
   a. ( ) 20 and under   b. ( ) 21–30
   b. ( ) 31–40   d. ( ) 41—50
   c. ( ) over 50

3. I Am
   a. ( ) A professing Christian
   b. ( ) Non-Christian
   c. Denominational affiliation (   )
   d. What year did you become a Christian? (   )

4. How did you become a Christian?
   a. ( ) Conversion experience
   b. ( ) Infant baptism
   c. ( ) Birth into a Christian family
   d. ( ) Other (please specify) _____

5. What is your position in the church?
   a. ( ) _____ clergy (please give title, e.g. Bishop, Reverend, Apostle, Captain, etc.)

b. ( ) Layperson (Please give church office held or currently holding) (   )

6. Level of formal education
    a. ( ) None
    b. ( ) Did not finish elementary school
    c. ( ) Elementary school
    d. ( ) Secondary school
    e. ( ) Vocational School
    f. ( ) Post secondary institution (specify) _____
    g. ( ) Postgraduate programme (specify, e.g. MA, Ph.D. etc.)
        (   )

7. Job status
    a. ( ) Professional (doctor, lawyer, accountant, etc.)
    b. ( ) Civil servant
    c. ( ) Government political appointee
    d. ( ) Business person (mention type of business)
        _____
    e. ( ) Other (specify) (   )

Inventory of the Practice of Christianity in Igboland

Directions: Please respond to each of the following statements by indicating what your opinion is. Do you strongly agree (SA), mildly agree (A), mildly disagree (D), strongly disagree (SD), do not know (DK) or undecided (U)? Please circle the one that most closely corresponds with what you believe. There are no wrong answers. Pleas answer according to your own opinion.

SA	A	D	SD	DK	U
strongly agree	mildly agree	mildly disagree	strongly disagree	do not know	undecided

8. The Igbo are better Christians than Christians of other parts of Nigeria.   SA A D SD DK U

9. A majority of Igbo people love to attend church.
                                             SA A D SD DK U

10. Igbo church-goers understand what it means to be a Christian.

     SA   A   D   SA   DK   U

11. For the Igbo, the church is simply a symbol of civilization and mo-
     dernity.   SA   A   D   SA   DK   U

12. The line between Christianity and traditional religion is not clearly
     drawn in Igbo Christianity.   SA   A   D   SA   DK   U

13. Most Igbo churches congregate to meet social needs.

     SA   A   D   SA   DK   U

14. Pioneer Euro-American missionaries had some difficulty understand-
     ing the Igbo culture.   SA   A   D   SA   DK   U

15. Igbo people think that being a Christian is synonymous with being
     civilized and being modern.   SA   A   D   SA   DK   U

16. Today, indigenous church groups are growing in Igboland.

     SA   A   D   SA   DK   U

17. Igbo customs and traditions are inferior to Western customs and
     traditions.   SA   A   D   SA   DK   U

18. Integrating any part of Igbo culture into the church will negatively
     affect the essence of the Christian faith.

     SA   A   D   SA   DK   U

19. For the local Igbo mission or indigenous church to succeed, it must
     affiliate itself with a foreign missionary body or organization.

     SA   A   D   SA   DK   U

20. Non-Igbo preachers do a better job explaining the meaning of Chris-
     tianity to Igbo hearers than their indigenous counterparts.

     SA   A   D   SD   DK   U

21. The Igbo Christian church cannot actualize its mission to Igbo people
     without foreign financial support.   SA   A   D   SD   DK   U

22. To maintain status, the local Igbo church or denomination must
     have a foreign (Western) leader.   SA   A   D   SD   DK   U

23. To maintain status, the local Igbo church or denomination must have a foreign (Western) headquarters. SA A D SD DK U

24. Igbo culture must be taken into consideration in the planning and conducting of worship services.   SA A D SD DK U

25. In preaching to the Igbo, preachers should use more local examples and illustrations.   SA A D SD DK U

26. The Igbo church must re-examine the benefit, meaning and relevance of some age-long church rituals to the spiritual health of the average Igbo worshipper.   SA A D SD DK U

Appendix II

The Igbo-Speaking Peoples

Main Divisions	Location by Administrative Divisions (1935–40)	Approximate number of active adult males
I. Northern or Onitsha Ibo		
(a) Western or Nri-Awka	Onitsha, Awka (ON)	115,400
(b) Eastern or Elugu	Nsukka, Udi, Awgu (ON),) Okigwi (OW	213,000
(c) Onitsha Town	Onitsha (ON)	7,000
	Total	335,400
II. Southern or Owerri Ibo		
(a) Isu-Ama	Okigwi, Orlu, Owerri (OW)	167,600
(b) Oratta-Ikwerri	Owerri (OW), Ahoada (R)	55,000
(c) Ohuhu-Ngwa	Aba, Bende (OW)	62,300
(d) Isu-Item	Bende, Okigwi (OW)	19,500
	Total	304,400
III. Western Ibo		
(a) Northern Ika	Ogwashi Uku, Agbor (B)	33,000
(b) Southern Ika or Kwale	Kwale (W)	19,500
(c) Riverain	Ogwashi Uku (B), Onitsha (ON), Owerri (OW), Ahoada (R)	46,600
	Total	99,100

IV. Eastern or Cross River Ibo
    (a) Ada (Edda)   Afikpo (OG)   20,300
    (b) Abam-Ohaffia   Bende, Okigwi (OW)   14,800
    (c) Aro   Aro (C)   <u> 1,800</u>

                                                  Total   36,900

V. North-Eastern Ibo
    (Ogu-Uku)   Abakaliki, Afikpo (OG)   <u>91,900</u>

                                                  Total   91,900

Approximate total of active adult males for all divisions   867,700

Demography

Official estimates of total population are:

	1921	1931
Total for Nigeria	3,930,085	3,184,585
Northern Nigeria only	2,666	11,796

It should be noted that these figures are unreliable, particularly those for 1931, when, for administrative reasons, no attempt was made to take a complete census.

Density of Population

Official provincial estimates per square mile were: Onitsha (1921) 306, (1931) 224; Owerri (1921) 268, (1931) 154. But much higher local densities have been estimated for parts of these provinces, e.g. estimates of 600–1,000 persons per square mile over much of *Okigwi* Division. Present data are not adequate to determine closely the areas that are densely populated, and such areas are often flanked or intersected by others of much lower density.

Note: Provincial names are abbreviated as follows: Owerri (OW), Onitsha (ON), Benin (B), Ogoja (G), Warri (W), Rivers (R).

Bibliography

Books

Achebe, Chinua. *Things Fall Apart.* London: Heinemann Educational Books, 1958.

———— *No Longer At Ease.* London: Heinemann Educational Books, 1960.

———— *Arrow of God.* London: Heinemann Educational Books, 1964.

Achunike, Hilary C. *Dreams of Heaven: A Modern Response To Christianity In North Western Igboland, 1970–1990.* Enugu: Snaap Printing and Publishing Co., 1995.

Ahumibe, Chukwuma, and Austin Orisakwe. *The Anglican Enterprise in Egbu.* Owerri, Nigeria: Upthrust Design and Print, 1996.

Amadi, L. E. *Igbo Heritage.* Owerri: Imo Onyeukwu Press, 1987.

Animalu, Alexander O. E. *1990 Ahiajoku Lecture.* Owerri: Government Press, 1990.

Animo Baptist Conference. "Proceedings of the First Animo Baptist Conference Held at First Baptist Church, Uwani, Enugu." Enugu, Nigeria: Animo Baptist Conference, 11–14 December 1978.

Atanda, J. A. *Baptist Churches in Nigeria: 1850–1950: Accounts of Their Foundation and Growth.* Ibadan, Nigeria: University Press, 1988.

Aulen, Gust. *The Drama of the Symbols: A Book on Images of God and the Problems They Raise.* Trans. Sydney Linton. Philadelphia: Fortress Press, 1970.

Awolalu, J. Omosade. *Yoruba Beliefs and Sacrificial Rites*. London: Longman Group, 1979.

Ayandele, E. A. *The Missionary Impact on Modern Nigeria, 1842–1914: A Political and Social Analysis*. London: Longmans, 1966.

Basden, George T. *Niger Ibos*. London: Seeley, Service & Co., n.d.

Bolton, Frances Lawju. *And We Beheld His Glory: A Personal Account of the Revival in Eastern Nigeria in 1970/71*. Harlow, Essex: Christ the King Publishing, 1992.

Bray, Gerald. *The Doctrine of God*. Leicester, U. K.: Inter-Varsity Press, 1993.

Busia, K. A. *Christianity and African Culture*. Accra, Ghana: Christian Council of the Gold Coast, 1955.

Butler, Samuel. *God: Known and Unknown*. Girard, Kans.: Haldeman-Julius Co., n.d.

Byrd, Annie Ward. *Better Bible Teaching for Intermediates*. Nashville: Convention Press, 1959.

Carnochan, J., and Belonwu Iwuchukwu. *An Igbo Revision Course*. London: Oxford University Press, 1963; reprint, 1976.

Carrier, Wallace H., compiler. *Teaching Adults in Sunday School*. Nashville: Convention Press, 1976.

Catholic Church of Nigeria. "Owerri Diocese" In *1995 Catholic Diary and Church Directory*. Lagos: Catholic Press, 1995.

Chiromba, Frederick E. *Evangelicalization and Inculturation*. Gweru, Zimbabwe: Mambo Press, 1989.

Collins, Travis. *The Baptist Mission of Nigeria, 1950–1993: A History of the Southern Baptist Convention Missionary Work in Nigeria*. Ibadan, Nigeria: Associated Bookmakers Nigeria, 1993.

Costa, Ruy O., ed. *One Faith, Many Cultures: Inculturation, Indigenization, and Contextualization*. Maryknoll, N.Y.: Orbis Books, 1988.

Costas, Orlando E. *The Church and Its Mission: A Shattering Critique From the Third World*. Wheaton, Ill.: Tyndale House Publishers, 1974.

de Gruchy, John W., and Charles Villa-Vicencio, eds. *Doing Theology in Context: South African Perspective.* Maryknoll, N.Y.: Orbis Books, 1994.

Dialogue and Proclamation. Rome: Pontifical Council for Interreligious Dialogue and Congregation for the Evangelization of Peoples, 20 June 1991.

Diocese of Owerri. "Diocesan Bible College" In *Synod Report.* Owerri: The Church of Nigeria [Anglican Communion], Diocese of Owerri, 1984.

Drummond, Lewis A., ed. *Biblical Affirmations for Evangelism: NACIE 94.* Minneapolis: World Wide Publications, 1996.

Eastman, Fred, and Louis Wilson. *Drama in the Church: A Manual of Religious Drama Production.* New York: Samuel French, 1933.

Ehrensperger, Harold. *Religious Drama: Ends and Means.* Nashville: Abingdon Press, 1962.

Ehrenstrom, Nills, and Gunter Gassmann. *Confessions in Dialogue: A Survey of Bilateral Conversations Among World Confessional Families 1959–1974.* Geneva: World Council of Churches, 1975.

Ekechi, F. K. *Missionary Enterprise and Rivalry in Igboland, 1957–1914.* London: Frank Cass and Co., 1972.

Eliade, Mircea. *Patterns in Comparative Religion.* Trans. Rosemary Sheed. London: Sheed and Ward, 1958; reprint, New York: New American Library, 1974.

Ezeala, J. O. L. *Can the Igboman Be a Christian in View of the Osu Caste System.* Orlu, Nigeria: B. I. Nnaji and Sons Press, n.d.

Fafunwa, Babs A. *History of Education in Nigeria.* London: George Allen and Unwin, 1974.

Forde, Daryll, and G. I. Jones. *The Igbo and Ibibio-Speaking Peoples of South-Eastern Nigeria.* London: Oxford University Press, 1950.

Galloway, Alland. *Faith in a Changing Culture: Keer Lectures Delivered at Glasgow University, 1966.* Longon: George Allen & Unwin, 1967.

General Secretary of the Assemblies of God. *Assemblies of God, Nigeria, Current Facts, 1994*. Enugu, Nigeria: Assemblies of God, Nigeria, 1994.

Gibellin, Rosino, ed. *Paths of African Theology*. Maryknoll, N.Y.: Orbis Books, 1994.

Glass, Bill. "Developing a Citywide Crusade." In *NACIE 94 Equipping for Evangelism*. Minneapolis: World Wide Publications, 1996.

Golomb, Jacob. *In Search of Authenticity: From Kierkegaard to Camus*. London: Routledge, 1995.

Grimley, John B., and Gordon E. Robinson. *Church Growth in Central and Southern Nigeria*. Grand Rapids: William B. Eerdmans Publishing Company, 1966.

Haviland, William A. *Cultural Anthropology*. 5th ed. New York: Holt, Rinehart and Winston, 1987.

Hocking, William Ernest. Re-Thinking Missions: A Laymen's Inquiry After One Hundred Years. New York: Harper & Brothers, 1962.

Idowu, E. Bolaji. *Olodumare: God in Yoruba Belief*. London: Longmans, 1962.

——— *Towards an Indigenous Church*. London: Oxford University Press, 1965.

———*African Traditional Religion: A Definition*. London: SCM, 1973.

Ilogu, Edmund. *Christianity and Igbo Culture*. Leiden: E. J. Brill, 1974.

Imasogie, Osadolor. *African Traditional Religion*. Ibadan: University Press, 1982.

The International Who's Who: 1995–96. 59th ed. London: Europa Publications, 1995.

Isichei, Elizabeth. *A History of the Igbo People*. New York: St. Martin's Press, 1976.

Jathanna, Constantine D., ed. *Dialogue in Community: Essays in Honour of Stanley J. Samartha*. Balmatta, India: The Karnataka Theological Research Institute, 1982.

Jefferson, Bill. "Evangelism and Scripture Distribution." In *NACIE 94 Equipping for Evangelism*. Minneapolis: World Wide Publications, 1996

Kalu, Ogbu U. *The Nigerian Story: Christianity in West Africa*. Ibadan: Daystar Press, 1978.

Kato, Byang H. *Theological Pitfalls in Africa*. Kisumu, Kenya: Evangel Publishing House, 1975.

———— *African Cultural Revolution and the Christian Faith*. Jos, Nigeria: Challenge Publications, 1976.

Knitter, Paul F. *No Other Name? A Critical Survey of Christian Attitudes Toward the World Religions*. Maryknoll, N.Y.: Orbis Books, 1985.

Kraft, Charles H., and Tom N. Wisley, eds. *Readings in Dynamic Indigeneity* Pasadena, Calif.: William Carey Library, 1979.

Liddell, Henry George. *Greek-English Lexicon*. Abridged from *Liddell and Scott's Greek-English Lexicon*. Oxford: Clarendon Press, 1980.

Lochhead, David. *The Dialogical Imperative: A Christian Reflection on Interfaith Encounter*. Maryknoll, N.Y.: Orbis Books, 1988.

Mbiti, John S. *African Religions and Philosophy*. London: Heinemann, 1969.

Meorloo, Joost A. M. *Conversation and Communication: A Psychological Inquiry Into Language and Human Relations*. Now York: International Universities Press, 1952.

Metuh, Emefie Ikenga. *God and Man in African Religion: A Case Study of the Igbo of Nigeria*. : London. Geoffrey Chapman, 1981.

Mortemm C. David. *Communication: The Study of Human Interaction*. New York: McGraw-Hill Book Company, 1972.

Muzorewa, Gwinyei Henry. *The Origins and Development of African Theology*. Maryknoll, N.Y.: Orbis Books, 1985.

———— *An African Theology of Mission*. Lewiston, N.Y. Edwin Mellen Press, 1990.

National Evangelsim Christian Outreach (NECO). *The Commission, the Vision and the Mssion.* Port-Harcourt, Nigeria: n.p., 1991; reprint, n.p., 1992.

Nicholls, Bruce J. *Contextualization: A Theology of Gospel and Culture.* Downers Grove, Ill.: InterVarsity Press, 1979.

Nigerian Baptist Convention. "Animo Conference." In *1995 Directory of the Nigerian Baptist Convention,* 29th ed. Ibadan, Nigeria: Baptist Press, 1995.

Nwabueze, Ben O. *1985 Ahiajoku Lecture.* Owerri: Government Press, 1985.

Nwala, T. Uzodinma. *Igbo Philosophy.* Ikeja, Lagos: Lantern Books, 1985.

Nwankiti, Benjamin. *The Growth and Development of the Church in Nigeria.* Owerri: Ihem Davis Press, 1996.

Obiego, Cosmas Okechukwu. *Affican Image of the Ultimate Reality: An Analysis of Igbo Ideas of Life and Death in Relation to Chukwu-God.* Frankfurt am Main: Peter Lang, 1994.

Oduyoye, Amba, ed. *The State of Christian Theology in Nigeria.* Ibadan, Nigena: Daystar Press, 1986.

Office of the Secretary to the State Government Imo State of Nigeria. "Report of the Judicial Commission of Inquiry into the Disturbances of 24–25 September 1996." In *Imo State of Nigeria Government White Paper.* Owerri, Nigeria: Office of the Secretary to the State Government, 19 February 1997.

Ogbajie, Chukwu. *The Impact of Christianity on the Igbo Religion and Culture.* Umuahia, Nigeria: Ark Publishers, 1995.

Oji, Oji U., A. U. Okorie, M. E. Okogo, I. N. Kalu, Udu Ukpai Okoro, and Agwu Ikwecheghe. *Presbyterian Evangelism in Imo State.* Owerri: Presbyterian Church of Nigeria, Owerri Parish, 1996.

Okigbo, Bede N. *1980 Ahiajoku Lecture.* Owerri :Government Press, 1980.

Okigbo, Pius N. C. *1986 Ahiajoku Lecture.* Owerri: Government Press, 1986.

Okoro, Mark Chijioke. *1989 Ahiajoku Lecture.* Owerri: Government Press, 1989.

Okorocha, Cyril C. *The Meaning of Religious Conversion in Africa: The Case of the Igbo of Nigeria.* Aldershot, England: Grower Publishing Company, 1987.

Onu, Charles OK. *Christianity and Igbo Rites of Passage: The Prospects of Inculturation.* Frankfurt am Main: PeterLang, 1992.

Onwubiko, Oliver A. *African Thought, Religion, and Culture.* Enugu, Nigeria: SNAAP Press, 1992.

———— *Theory and Practice of Inculturation: An African Perspective.* Enugu, Nigeria: SNAAP Press, 1992.

Parrinder, Geoffrey. *African Traditional Religion.* 3d ed. London: Sheldon Press, 1974.

Pittenger, W. Norman. *The Word Incarnate: A Study of the Doctrine of the Person of Christ.* New York: Harper & Brothers, 1959.

Richards, I. A. *The Republic of Plato: A New Version on Basic English.* New York: W. W. Norton and Co., 1942.

Russell, Joseph P. *Sharing Our Biblical Story.* Minneapolis: Winston Press, 1979.

Santoni, Ronald E. *Bad Faith, Good Faith, and A uthenticity in Sartre's Early Philosophy.* Philadelphia: Temple University Press, 1995.

Schineller, Peter, S. J. *A Hanbook Inculturation.* New York: Paulist Press, 1990.

Sheard, Robert B. *Interreligious Dialogue in the Catholic Church Since Vatican II: A Historical and Theological Study.* Lewiston, N.Y.: Edwin Mellen Press, 1987.

Shorter, Aylward. *Toward a Theology of Inculturation.* Maryknoll, N.Y.: Orbis Books, 1988.

Smith, Donald K. *Creating Understanding. A Handbook for Christian Communication Across Cultural Landscapes.* Grand Rapids: Zondervan Pubhshing House, 1992.

Snyder, Howard A. *Earth Currents: The Struggle for the World's Soul.* Nashville: Abingdon Press, 1995.

Stallings, James O. *Telling the Story: Evangelism in Black Churches.* Valley Forge, Pa.: Judson Press, 1988.

Stott, John, and Robert T. Coote, eds. *Gospel and Culture: The Papers of a Consulatation on the Gospel and Culture, Convened by the Lausanne Committee's Theology and Education Group.* Pasadena, Calif.: William Carey Library, 1979.

Styan, J. L. *The Elements of Drama.* Cambridge: Cambridge University Press, 1960.

Swearer, Donald K. *Dialogue: The Key to Unalerstanding Other Religions.* Philadelphia: Westminister Press, 1977.

Taylor, John B. "Inter-Faith Dialogue." In *Christianity and Change.* Norman Autton. London: S.P.C.K., 1971.

Thompson, William D., and Gordon C. Bennett. *Dialogue Preaching.- The Shared Sermon.* Valley Forge, Pa.: Judson Press, 1969.

Ukpong, Justin S. *African Theologies Now: A Profile.* Eldoret, Kenya: Gaba Publications, 1984.

1992 Diary of Imo State. Owerri: Government Press, 1992.

Articles

Asamoa, E. A. "The Christian Church and African Heritage." *The International Review of Missions* 44 (1955): 292–301.

Baker, Samuel. "The Races of the Mde Basin." In *Transactions of Ethnological Society of London* (1891): 423–424.

Banjo, Ajao. "New Wuie Burst the Old Wineskin during Aba '94 Evangelism Explosion." *The Nigerian Baptist* (June 1994): 17.

Barrett, David B. *Annual statistical Table on Global Mission. International Bulletin of Missionary Research* (Januiuy 1993): 22.

"Crisis in the House of God." *Sunday Sketch* [Nigerian Weekly Newspaper], 20 October 1996, 8–9.

/Kalu, Ogbu U. "Color and Conversion: The White Mssionary Factor in the Christianization of Igboland." *Missiology: An International Review* no. 1 (Januwy 1990): 68.

McGavran, Donald. "New Methods for a New Age in Missions." *The International Review of Missions* 44 (1955): 398.

Mugabe, Henry Johannes. "Christology in an African Context." *Review and Expositor* 88 (1991):343.

Nwala, Uzodimma. "Sonie Reflections on British Conquest of Igbo Traditional Oracles 1900–1924." *Nigeria Magazine* (1982): 31.

Ojo, Matthews A. "The Charismatic Movement in Nigeria Today." *International Bulletin of Missionary Research* (July, 1995): 114–118.

Omoyajowo, J. Akin. "The Cherubim and Seraphim Movement—A Study in Interaction." *Orita* 4, no. 2 (December 1970): 127.

————— "The Christian View of Man." *Orita* 5, no. 2 (December 1972): 120–121.

Osadolar Imasogie. "A Christian Attitude to Cultural Revival. " *Ogbomoso Journal of Theology* 7 (December 1992) 6–7.

Osuagwu, Chidi G. "Erima—Concept of the Organic Community in Obowu." *ANU: A Journal of Igbo Culture,* no. 5 (February 1989): 52–53.

Outreach Newsletter 1. (February 1979): 5.

"Owerri District Triennial Report." General Council, Assemblies of God, Nigeria Owerri District, (23–27, May 1994): 103.

Plumbline: Journal of the Pilgrims Ministry 1, no. 921 (1992): 45.

"Report of the Judicial Commission of Inquiry into the Disturbances of 25–25 September 1996." *Imo State of Nigeria, Government White Paper* (19 February 1997), 15–18.

Salmnone Frank A., and Mchael C. Mbabuike. "The Plight of the Indigenous Catholic Priest in Afiica: An Igbo Example." *Missiology* 23, no. 2 (April 1995): 166–167.

Swidler, Leonard. "The Dialogue Decalogue: Ground Rules for Interreligious Dialogue." *Journal of Ecumenical Studies* 20 (Winter 1986): 1.

"Trouble in Bro. Peter's Church." *Beaton* [Nigerian Monthly Newspaper], August 1994, 5.

Turner, Harold W. "Pentecostal Movements in Nigeria." *Orita* vol. 4, no. 2 (1970): 39–47.

Ukpong Justin S. "The Problem of God and Sacrifice in African Traditional Religion." *Journal of Religion in Africa* 14 (1983): 191.

Uya, Kúúbra-Afiakóyó, editor-in-chief. "120 Mnutes With Archbishop Anthony Obinna," *Catholic Post.* Owerri: National Association of Catholic Corpers, Imo State (1995): 6–14.

Unpublished Materials

Arulampalam, Sriganda E. M. "Toward an Exclusivistic Model of Dialogue in a Religiously Pluralistic World." Ph.D. diss., The Southern Baptist Theological Seminary, 1994.

Babalola, Festus Kunleola. "The Role of Nigerian Higher Education Institutions in Preparation of Christian Religious Studies Teachers." Ed.D. diss., The Southern Baptist Theological Seminary, 1993.

Iroezi, Chukwunia Jude. "Igbo World View and the Communication of the Gospel." D. Miss. project, Fuller Theological Seminary School of World Mission, 1982.

Nedosa, Uchechukwu Anastasia. "Reasons for non-participation m basic literacy programs and educationally relevant profiles of illitterate adults in rural areas of Imo State of Nigeria." Ph.D. diss., University of Pittsburgh, 1984.

Nwagbo, Nkeiruka M. "Missionaries and Educational Development in Owerri L G A Before the Government Take Over of Schools from the Missionaries." B.A. thesis, School of Education, Alvan Ikoku College of Education, Owerri in Affiliation with the University of Nigeria, Nsukka, Nigeria, 1989.

Ogbonaya, Anthonia Chinyere. "Chinua Achebe and the Igbo World View (Nigeria)." Ph.D. diss., The University of Wisconsin, 1984.

Ojo, Matthew Akintunde. "New Trends in Nigerian Christianity: A Case Study of the Scripture Union." M.A. Thesis, University of Ife, Nigeria, 1981.

Wirsiy, Fon Wilfred Tatah. "The Influence of African Traditional Religions on Biblical Christology: An Evaluation of Emerging Christologies in Sub-Sahara Africa." Ph-D. diss., Westminster Theological Seminary, 1995.

Interviews

Aghaizu, Alphonsus, Msgr, Senior Priest, St. Paul's Catholic Church, Owerri. Interview by author, 11 January 1996, Owerri, Nigeria.. Tape recording.

Akagha, Kevin C., Editor, *The Leader* (Catholic Newspaper in Owerri). Interview by author, 11 January 1996, Owerri, Nigeria. Tape recording.

Amaramiro, Alex, Provincial Secretary, Eternal Order of Cherubim and Seraphim, Owerri. Interview by 10 January 1996, Owerri, Nigeria. Tape recording.

Chiagoro, Cyprain Ogazi, Juju Priest in Ulakwo, Owerri. Interview by author, 9 January 1996, Owerri, Nigeria. Tape recording.

Durham, J. B., Retired Southern Baptist Missionary to Nigeria. Interview by author, 19 April 1997, Lithonia, GA. Telephone.

Ebo, D. J. I. Anglican Archdeacon of Owerri Archdeeaconry. Interview by author, 9 Januwy 1996, Owerri Nigeria. Tape recording.

Gbazie, Steve. President, Cornerstone Theological Seminary, Owerri. Interview by author, 11 January 1996, Owerri, Nigeria. Tape recording.

Locke, Russel L. and Veda L., Retired Southern Baptist Missionaries to Nigeria. Interview by author, 19 April 1997, Springfield, MO. Telephone.

Logan Wayne, Retired Southern Baptist Medical Missionary to Nigeria. Interview by author, 19 April 1997, Minneola, TX. Telephone.

Nwaosu, I. B. President, Basil Nwaosu Evangelistic Aswdation, Owerri, Imo State, Veteran Baptist Pastor. Interview by author, 10 March 1997, Owerri, Nigeria. Tape recording.

Obijuru, Christian, Deacon, First Baptist Church, Owerri. Interview by author, 17 January 1996, Owerri, Nigeria. Tape recording.

Ogbah, Mchael O., District Superintendent, Assemblies of God Nigeria, Owerri District. Interview by author, 17 January 1996, Nekeda, Nigeria. Tape recording.

Onwukwe, Daniel, Senior Lecturer, Alvan Ikoku College of Education, Owerri. Interview by author, 14 March 1997, Owerri, Nigeria. Tape recording.

Onyeagocha, O. A., Community Leader, Obinze Autonomous Community, Owerri-

Interview by author, 10 March 1997, Obinze, Migetia. Tape recording.

Oparaechekwe, Nnanna, His Royal leghness, Eze Ebubedike 2 of Uakwo, Owerri. hiterview by auflwr, 16 January 1996, Ulakwo, Nigeria. Tape recording.

Onh, Vincent, Area Secretary, Scripture Union of Nigeria, Owerri Zone. Interview by author, 23 January 1996, Oweni, Nigeria. Tape recording.

Osueke, Charles O., General Superintendent, Assemblies of God Nigeria. Interview by author, 15 Jamiary 1996, Enugu, Nigeria. Tape recording.

Osuji, Eric, His Royal Highness, Duruojinnaka I of Umudim, Ikeduru, Owerri. Interview by author, 17 January 1996, Umudim, Nigeria. Tape recording.

Uwadi, R. O., Diocesan Bishop, Methodist Church of Nigeria, Owerri Diocese. Interview by author, 9 January 1996, Owerri, Nigeria. Tape recording.

Index

collective bargaining, in Igbo culture, 1, 34
commercialization, problem of, 2, 78, 79–82, 85. *See also* materialism
communication
concept of, 143–144
elements of, 144–146
role of, 141–142
community
in African culture, 141, 189
in Igbo culture, 2, 34, 135–136
condoms, in Pentecostal church, 79
Confessions, 155
"contextuality," 119
contexualization, concept of, 119–120
conversation, as communication, 141–142
conversions
evangelical efforts, 95–96
superficiality of, 2
Cornerstone Theological Seminary, 100
"cosmetic Christianity," 204
cosmogony
Christian view of, 189–190, 202
Igbo, 190–191, 202
Costas, Orlando E., 77
Council of Elders, Igboland, 135
covenant-making (*igba ndu*) ritual, 40
cowries, traditional religion, 5
Craft, William de, 61
creation myths, in Igbo traditional religion, 33–34
Crowther, Ajayi, 20, 51–52
Crusades, evangelism method, 78, 93, 163, 166–168, 171
cultural contextualization, 119
cultural imposition, consequences of Western, 2
culture, definition of, 13

D

Dahunsi, Emmanuel Ajayi, 60
Daily Guide, 68
death
rites of passage, 38
traditional Igbo beliefs, 6, 193–194

"Decade of Evangelism," 94
"Decade of Harvest," 93
Deeper Life Bible Church, 67
evangelism program, 93–94, 163–164
deities, in Igbo traditional religion, 31, 32–33
democracy, in Igbo culture, 1, 8, 21–22
Dennis Memorial Grammar School, 98
Dennis, Thomas John, 52, 53–54
denominationalism, problem of, 77
dental care, Baptist mission, 60, 100
destiny, in Igbo traditional religion, 31
"Detarium Senegalense tree," Ofo stick, 26
Devadutt, V. E., 114
dialogical evangelism, 148, 152–153, 203
dialogical inculturation, 156, 205
dialogical preaching
advantages of, 165
objections to, 164–165
dialogue
commandments of, 139–140
definition of, 136–137
Igbo culture, 7–8, 135, 136, 137–138
inculturation model, 1, 7, 8, 101, 203
meaningful, 138–139
Platonic tradition, 148–150
Roman Catholic view of, 148–149
dibia afa (diviner), 27, 29
Dibia Afa Society, 29
dibia, medicine man/woman, ix, 5, 25, 28
Diocese of Owerri Printing Press, 173
divination
elements of, 28
Igbo traditional religion, 21, 25
process, 28–29
divine healing, 85
"Divine Design," 190
diviners, in Igbo traditional religion, 24, 27–29, 31
Doctrine of God, The, 182
dogmatic contextualization, 120